The GODDESS RE-AWAKENING

QUEST BOOKS
are published by
The Theosophical Society in America,
Wheaton, Illinois 60189-0270,
a branch of a world organization
dedicated to the promotion of the unity of
humanity and the encouragement of the study of
religion, philosophy, and science, to the end that
we may better understand ourselves and our place in
the universe. The Society stands for complete
freedom of individual search and belief.
In the Classics Series well-known
theosophical works are made
available in popular editions.
For more information
write or call.
1-708-668-1571

The GODDESS RE-AWAKENING

THE FEMININE PRINCIPLE TODAY

COMPILED BY
SHIRLEY NICHOLSON

*This publication is made possible with
the assistance of the Kern Foundation*

The Theosophical Publishing House
Wheaton, Ill. U.S.A.
Madras, India / London, England

The Theosophical Publishing House
306 West Geneva Road
Wheaton, IL 60187

A publication of the Theosophical Publishing House, a department of the Theosophical Society in America.

Library of Congress Cataloging in Publication Data

The goddess reawakening : the feminine principle today / compiled by
  Shirley Nicholson. -- 1st ed.
     p.   cm. -- (A Quest book)
  Includes bibliographies.
  ISBN 0-8356-0642-2 :
  1. Goddesses. 2. Femininity of God. 3. Women and religion.
4. Theosophy. I. Nicholson, Shirley.
BL325.F4G63   1989   88-40488
291.2'11--dc19   CIP

Printed in the United States of America

Cover design by Anne Kilgore

Contents

Contributing Authors

Kathleen Alexander-Berghorn holds an M.A. in Art History from Northwestern University. She is a freelance writer and dealer in folk art of India and South Asia, living in Framingham, Massachusetts. Her articles on the archetypal feminine in art and mythology have been published in *Lady-Unique-Inclination-of-the-Night*, *Woman of Power*, and *SageWoman*. Her area of special interest is in the imagery of the feminine as expressed in the visual arts, mythology, and religion.

Roberto Assagioli, M.D., 1888-1974, was a psychiatrist who devoted himself to writing and training. A pioneer of psycho-analysis in Italy, he spent his professional life elaborating a comprehensive psychology that he called "Psychosynthesis." He wrote more than three hundred papers and several books, including *Psychosynthesis* and *The Act of Will*. Psychosynthesis is still widely practiced, and there are training centers in its approach both in this country and abroad.

Beatrice Bruteau, Ph.D., received her doctorate in philosophy from Fordham University. Her academic background includes mathematics and physics; her religious background, Vedanta and Catholicism. Having written books on Sri Aurobindo *(Worthy is the World)*, Teilhard de Chardin *(Evolution Toward Divinity)*, and theory of knowledge *(The Psychic Grid)*, she has in recent years been developing a systematic spirituality of transformed consciousness. Her essays have appeared in *Cross Currents*, *Contemplative Review*, *New Blackfriars*, *Cistercian Studies*, and *Anima*. Some of them have been collected in *Neo-Feminism and Communion Consciousness.* A set of conferences for contemplatives has just been completed, tentatively titled *Peepholes on an Infinite Universe.* She lives in Pfafftown, North Carolina, where she and her husband, James Somerville, have founded Schola Contemplationis as a center in which to continue research and teaching. The center publishes a quarterly newsletter, *The Roll,* in which her most recent work regularly appears.

Gina Cerminara, Ph.D., ?-1984, earned three degrees at the University of Wisconsin—in modern languages, education, and psychology. She was also a graduate of the Wisconsin Conservatory of Music in piano and voice. After obtaining her Ph.D., she spent two years researching the files of Edgar Cayce, which led to the publication of *Many Mansions,* the first of her several books which include *The World Within; Many Lives, Many Loves;* and *Insights for the Age of Aquarius.*

Riane Eisler, J.D., did her graduate work at the U.C.L.A. School of Law. An international peace activist, she has taught at the University of California and Immaculate Heart College at Los Angeles. A peace researcher and educator known internationally, she pioneered important legislation to help women and children and has appeared on television and radio and spoken at many conferences both in the United States and abroad. She is cofounder of the Center for Partnership Studies (P.O. Box 51936, Pacific Grove, CA 93950). Among books she has authored are *The Chalice and the Blade, The Equal Rights Handbook,* and *Dissolution.*

Joan Chamberlain Engelsman, Ph.D., received her doctorate in Historical Theology at Drew University, Madison, New Jersey. Her areas of special study include Patristics and symbolic motifs in theology. Her dissertation explored the feminine dimension of the divine. She participated in a study of women in suburbia funded by the Auburn Foundation, and she has published a number of book reviews dealing with women in church and society.

Judith Gleason, Ph.D., received her doctorate in comparative literature from Columbia University. For the last twenty years she has conducted research on African religion in Brazil, Haiti, Nigeria, Mali, and Lagos. She has published books and articles on African mythology and literature. Among her books are *Agotine: Her Legend; Orisha: The Gods of Yorubaland; Recitation of Ifa, Oracle of the Yoruba; Leaf and Bone;* and most recently *Oya: In Praise of the Goddess.*

Elizabeth Dodson Gray is an environmentalist, futurist, and feminist theologian. Currently codirector of the Bolton Institute for a Sustainable Future in Wellesley, Massachusetts, she also coordinates the Theological Opportunities program at Harvard Divinity School. Her works include *Green Paradise Lost* (1979), *Patriarchy as a Conceptual Trap* (1982), and she is editor of *Sacred Dimensions of Women's Experience* (1988). She is coauthor of *Growth and Its Implications for the Future* (1974), a book originally prepared as staff work for Congressional hearings. She holds the graduate professional degree in theology, the B.Div. from Yale Divinity School.

Geoffrey Hodson (1887-1983) was author of over forty books, many of which are based on his clairvoyant investigations, often done in collaboration with specialists such as physicians and physicists. Also a student of world mythology, he lectured in many countries for the Theosophical Society. Among his works are *Clairvoyant Investigations, Concealed Wisdom in World Mythologies, The Hidden Wisdom in the Holy Bible,* and *The Miracle of Birth.*

Stephan A. Hoeller, Ph.D., is associate professor of Comparative Religions at the graduate school of the College of Oriental Studies in Los Angeles. He is also a member of the lecturing faculty of the Philosophical Research Society and executive director of Sophia

Gnostic Center in Los Angeles, an institution devoted to Gnostic and Kabalistic studies. Dr. Hoeller has lectured and written in the areas of religion, philosophy, and parapsychology and is author of *The Gnostic Jung* and *The Royal Road; A Manual of Kabalistic Meditations on the Tarot,* as well as contributor to numerous periodicals. He has a book in progress on a Jungian interpretation of the Nag Hamadi Library and the Dead Sea Scrolls.

Patricia Hunt-Perry, Ph.D., is professor of Social Thought at Ramapo College of New Jersey. She received her Ph.D. from Syracuse University. She serves on the governing council of the International Society of Political Psychology and the advisory board of International City, an organization that promotes peace through culture. Author of numerous articles on religion and politics, she was host-commentator for the PBS series *Prospects for Humanity* and produced twenty-five programs for WBAI (New York City) on religious and social topics. She has a book in progress on the relationship between personal change and social and political change.

Jenette Jones, Ph.D., is a family counselor for Hennepin County (Minnesota) Court Services. A trainee in the Inter-Regional Society of Jungian Analysts, she has taught courses on the relationship between Jungian psychology and anthropology.

Mary Ann Mattoon, Ph.D., is a Jungian analyst in private practice in Minneapolis. A graduate of the C. G. Jung Institute of Zurich, she is the author of two books, *Understanding Dreams* and *Jungian Psychology in Perspective.*

Char McKee is Editor of *Woman of Power* magazine. Among her interests are feminist futurism, generating affirmation for women who are visionaries and social activists, and building community among women of many nations, cultures, races, sexual preferences, and spiritual traditions. She lives in Somerville, Massachusetts, with her family.

Shirley Nicholson is Senior Editor, in charge of the publishing program of the Theosophical Publishing House, Wheaton, Illinois. She is author of *Ancient Wisdom—Modern Insight* and a children's book on cycles, *Nature's Merry-Go-Round*, as well as compiler of an anthology, *Shamanism*.

Rabbi Léah (a.k.a. Lee) Novick is a teacher of the female path in Judaism. She leads workshops that facilitate the experience of the "Shechinah" through meditation, music, and storytelling and has presented this work throughout the United States as well as in Canada, Europe, and Israel. Her research on female spiritual leaders within the Jewish tradition over the centuries forms the basis of a new liturgy which she has been performing in the San Francisco Bay area. Prior to her ordination at the age of fifty-five, she was a public policy maker serving in the Carter administration and in the California state government of Jerry Brown.

Eleanor Olson, 1905-1982, Curator Emeritus of the Oriental Collections of the Newark Museum, Newark, New Jersey, made a special study of Buddhist, and especially Tibetan Buddhist art and religion. She is the author of a five-volume catalogue of the Newark Museum's famous Tibetan collection and a catalogue of *Tantric Buddhist Art* published by the China Institute in America, New York. She also contributed many articles to museum and art journals.

Elizabeth Petroff, Ph.D., is professor of Comparative Literature at the University of Massachusetts at Amherst, where she teaches courses on Women and Men in Mythology, Spiritual Autobiography, and Medieval Women Writers, as well as more traditional courses. She is author of *The Consolation of the Blessed: Women Saints in Medieval Tuscany* (1978) and *Medieval Women's Visionary Literature* (1986). She has a book in progress on the images of desire in the writings of medieval women.

Dane Rudhyar, 1895-1986, is known for his work as a composer, painter, poet, author, philosopher, lecturer, and astrologer. He has long been recognized as an influential figure in esoteric and New Age circles. Among his literary contributions are over fifteen hundred articles in various journals, and a list of books too long to enumerate. Included among them are *Astrology of Transformation, Rhythm of Wholeness,* and *Occult Preparations for a New Age.*

Claude Servan-Schreiber was a distinguished French writer and journalist. She wrote in France for *Le Monde, L'Express,* and *Le Nouvel Observateur,* and in the United States for *Ms.* and the *New York Times.* She was especially interested in women's progress in society and had a book published in France—*La fin des immigrés.*

June Singer, Ph.D., is a Jungian analyst practicing in Palo Alto, California. She is author of *Boundaries of the Soul: The Practice of Jung's Psychology; Androgyny;* and *The Unholy Bible: Blake, Jung and the Collective Unconscious;* and coauthor of *The Singer-Loomis Inventory of Personality,* a new test based on Jung's theory of psychological types. She is a founding member of the C. G. Jung Institute of Chicago and of the Inter-Regional Society of Jungian Analysts and is a member of the C.G. Jung Institute of San Francisco.

James M. Somerville, Ph.D., received his doctorate in philosophy from Fordham University. He later became Chairman of the Department of Philosophy at Fordham and was instrumental in the founding of *International Philosophical Quarterly,* a review now in its twenty-eighth year. He has written extensively on the thought of the late French philosopher Maurice Blondel, and his scholarly articles have appeared in publications such as *Thought, Cross Currents, Continuum,* and in various encyclopedias. Professor Emeritus from Xavier University in Cincinnati, he is currently

Editor of *The Roll*, a quarterly publication which features contributions by people interested in contemplation and global spirituality.

Merlin Stone is the author of *When God Was a Woman* and *Ancient Mirrors of Womanhood*, director of the Canadian Broadcasting Corp. radio series *Return of the Goddess*, and author of "Goddess Worship in the Ancient Near East," which appears in the new Macmillan *Encyclopedia of Religion*. Since 1962 she has studied many archaeological records of Goddess reverence, visiting excavation sites and museums of the Near and Middle East, such as Beirut, Byblos, Delphi, Eleusis, and Knossos. An art historian, she was formerly on the faculties of the State University of New York in Buffalo and the University of California in Berkeley extension. She holds the MFA in art history and has also worked as a sculptor, having been awarded various architectural commissions.

Nancy C. Zak, Ph.D., is of Inuit descent. She earned her doctorate in Comparative Literature from the University of California, Berkeley. She has written on sacred women figures from native North America and female figures in medieval romance. She has taught at the University of California, Berkeley, the Institute of American Indian Arts in Santa Fe, New Mexico, and at the University of New Mexico.

Acknowledgments

Thanks to the following authors and publishers for permission to reprint their material:

Judith Gleason, "Oya, Black Goddess of Africa" is from *Oya: In Praise of the Goddess* by Judith Gleason, ©1987. Reprinted by arrangement with Shambhala Publications, Inc., 300 Massachusetts Ave., Boston, MA 02115.

Kathleen Alexander-Berghorn, "Isis: The Goddess as Healer" appeared in *Woman of Power*, Winter, 1987.

Selena Fox, "Isis Healing Meditation," ©1986, was first published in the Spring, 1986, issue of *Circle Network News*, Circle, Box 219, Mt. Horeb, WI 53572.

Geoffrey Hodson, "The World Mother" is a shortened version of "The Influence and Work of the World Mother" that appeared in *The Spiritual Significance of Motherhood*, a pamphlet published by the New Zealand Section of the Theosophical Society, 10 Belvedere St., Epsom, Auckland, S.E.3. It has been lightly edited to conform with current usage.

Roberto Assagioli and Claude Servan-Schreiber, "A Higher View of the Man-Woman Problem" first appeared in *Synthesis; The Realization of the Self*, no. 1.

Gina Cerminara, "Sex-Based Superiority Complexes" is printed by permission of the Edgar Cayce Foundation, 67th and Atlantic, Virginia Beach, VA 23451.

Mary Ann Mattoon and Jennette Jones, "Is the Animus Obsolete?" appeared in *Quadrant*, vol. 20, no. 1, and is printed by permission of the C. G. Jung Foundation, New York.

James M. Somerville, "Maria Avatara" appeared in *Anima*, 15/2, Spring 1989, and is reprinted by permission of the publisher.

Patricia Hunt-Perry, "The Wisewoman in the Western Tradition" appeared in *Chrysalis: Journal of the Swedenborg Foundation* (I:2), Summer, 1986, and is reprinted by permission of the publisher.

Char McKee, "Feminism: A Vision of Love" appeared in *Woman of Power*, Summer, 1985.

Nancy Zak, "Sacred and Legendary Women in North America" appeared in a somewhat different version in *Wildfire* (P.O. Box 9167, Spokane, WA 99209-9167), 1, no. 1, Winter Solstice, 1984, and 2, nos. 1 and 2, September, 1986. In her article in this anthology she quotes with permission from *The Sacred Pipe: Black Elk's Account of the Seven Rites of the Oglala Sioux*, recorded and edited by Joseph Epes Brown. Copyright ©1953 by the University of Oklahoma Press; from *Black Elk Speaks* by John G. Neihardt (Flaming Rainbow), copyright John C. Neihardt Trust, published by the University of Nebraska Press; and from *This Song Remembers* by Jane B. Katz. Copyright ©1980 by Jane B. Katz. Reprinted by permission of Houghton Mifflin Company.

Elizabeth Dodson Gray, "Nature as an Act of Imagination" appeared in *Woman of Power*, Spring, 1980. In this article the author quotes from a poem, "In Praise of Diversity," from *The Love Letters of Phyllis McGinley* by Phyllis McGinley. Copyright 1953 by Phyllis McGinley. Copyright renewed ©1981 by Julie Elizabeth Hayden and Phyllis Hayden Blake. All rights reserved. Reprinted by permission of Viking Penguin, Inc.

The following articles appeared in *The American Theosophist*, Special Issue, "The Feminine Principle," Spring, 1976: Beatrice Bruteau, "The Unknown Goddess"; Stephan A. Hoeller, "Sophia, the Gnostic Archetype of Feminine Soul-Wisdom"; Joan Chamberlain Engelsman, "Rediscovering the Feminine Principle"; Shirley Nicholson, "The Way of the Uncarved Block"; Eleanor Olson, "The Buddhist Female Deities"; Dane Rudhyar, "Toward the Companionate Man-Woman Relationship."

Introduction

MERLIN STONE

There is no question in my mind that the Goddess is reawakening. And as she rises, we learn more and more about what it is to be women. We have reclaimed role models of woman as wise, courageous, creative at the highest levels, as healers and physicians, as architects and builders, as the inventors of written language and so much more. The ancient images of the Goddess have allowed us to reconstruct core concepts of the feminine principle that would not have been possible without knowing of them.

Over this last decade more and more women have been discovering the Goddess as she had been known and worshipped in many ancient cultures around the world. This interest has grown primarily from within the women's movement, as women began to question what kept us from being who we really wanted to be and from doing what we really wanted to do. Among many other issues raised by the women's movement, women began to consider and challenge the role that mainstream religions played in keeping women in helper or subordinate roles. In hindsight, rediscovering ancient Goddess reverence could almost have been predicted.

From the initial challenging of biblical decrees of divinely ordained secondary status for women, the interest in the Goddess began to branch out. Over the last years the thirst for more and more details about ancient Goddess worship

1

began to be satisfied by a continually mounting number of articles and books on the subject, as well as by a heightened interest in reading long-ignored ancient texts. Simultaneously, it has led a large number of women and some men to create and take part in rituals and holidays celebrating the Goddess in contemporary life. The varieties of the forms and contents of these celebrations reflect the extremely rich racial and ethnic diversity of the ancient Goddess images that are being reclaimed.

Along with the scholarly studies and the direct experiences of contemporary Goddess celebrations, other branches and flowers have grown from this reclamation of deity as female. These include the exploration of the theological and philosophical underpinnings of both ancient and current Goddess reverence, as viewed from various perspectives. These considerations have led to the expression of a vast range of ideas and thoughts on what Goddess worship might be about. As with all other studies of Goddess reverence, the diversity of insights, commentary and conclusions is almost staggering.

When I first began seriously researching and writing *When God Was A Woman,* in the late sixties, just at the start of the second half of my life, my goal was to show how narrow and binding our society's images of women were. We were still functioning on biblical concepts and decrees. All throughout the Old and New Testaments were statements that women should defer to the wishes of men because Eve fed an apple to Adam. The idea that the male should rule over the female was deeply embedded in even the most atheistic minds. Over the centuries, this attitude had been so completely absorbed into the general social outlook that most people assumed such a gender stratification was simply the natural gender pattern.

Since collecting ancient prayers and legends associated with Isis, Ishtar, Inanna, Demeter, Cybele, Cerridwen and many other Goddess figures had been a sort of hobby of mine all throughout the fifties. I knew that the traits attributed to female figures in ancient cultures were quite different from this so-called natural gender pattern. When I entered the women's movement, which was just beginning in the late sixties, I began to realize that other women knew little or nothing about these ancient Goddess figures. It was then that I decided that it was vital for us to reclaim this rich heritage and that I would put what I had collected on various Goddess figures over the years into a book. If nothing else, it would show that images of women in ancient periods were quite different from those on which we had been raised.

Not quite satisifed with the quantity of material I had found and collected until that time, I began to research more intensively. There was so much information hidden away in archaeological log books and translations of ancient texts that it was difficult to decide when I had enough for the book that was to be my contribution to the women's movement. It would also be an invitation to other women to join me in exploring our Goddess heritage, since from my research, it was clear to me that I could only cover the tip of the iceberg and give an overall sense of ancient Goddess worship. All I really wanted to say was that the secondary roles of women were neither natural nor divinely ordained. ''Come look at the way it used to be, in the real beginning of time. A lot of people used to envision a Goddess creating the entire world and all life on it!'' As it turned out, I had gathered so much material in my years of research at the Ashmolean Library in Oxford and from my travels to the museums and excavation sites of the Near and Middle East that it proved to be more than enough for two books, thus the publication of *Ancient Mirrors of Womanhood—Our Goddess and Heroine Heritage,* following my first. And still I have envelopes stuffed with notes that I include in various articles or that lie there patiently waiting to be used.

Since I finished *When God Was a Woman* in 1975, which included that invitation to other women to continue the research and help to make this knowledge of the past better known in the present, I have been joyously astonished at the multitude of research and writings about the Goddess that has appeared. Numerous in-depth studies of specific Goddess figures have been done. There is a wealth of information written from a contemporary point of view now available, and the number of books and articles published each year about some aspect of Goddess reverence has grown geometrically rather than diminished over these past thirteen years. And none is redundant. Each author has added new material and viewed it and used it in some new and innovative way. The reclaimed information has been incorporated into writings on ecology, healing, sociology, history, psychology, philosophy, theology, the visual arts, and general global concerns. The Goddess has also found her way into paintings, sculpture, films, poetry, novels, drama, dance, and song. I had the pleasure of meeting and interviewing many of the women doing this work when I directed the CBC (Canadian Broadcasting Corporation) radio series, *The Return of the Goddess,* in 1985. It seemed to me that an entirely new culture had been born, and was quickly growing.

The twenty articles included in this anthology have been brought together with the goal of examining what emphasis on a divine feminine principle or Goddess might mean to and for us today. There has been a real effort on the part of editor Shirley Nicholson, who collected the articles for this anthology, to include a rich diversity of materials and attitudes. Each author has approached the material included from a unique perspective. Some authors appear to agree with each other, while some contradict others. Most of the authors are women, but there are several articles by men. Some of the articles deal with specific historically known Goddess images, while others are more concerned with what we are learning from Goddess reverence or emphasis on the feminine principle as a whole.

As consciousness of the Goddess awakens, we find ourselves wondering if it is not actually the Goddess who is awakening—and if we are simply being called upon to witness and testify to her increasing presence in our lives. Many women feel that they have been magnetically, almost magically, drawn into their awareness of her. If this is so, are there specific reasons that she has been awakening at this particular time? This question leads us to ask what this return or awakening of the Goddess, the reclamation of a sacred female or feminine principle in the universe, might mean for us today.

There are numerous papers, articles, and books that incorporate the concept of a universal feminine principle. They have posed a variety of theories and have been written from diverse points of view, yet they seldom if ever question the validity of the characteristics long assigned to the category of "feminine." At the same time, most feminist writers of the last two decades have simply avoided the concept of a feminine principle and proceeded to define womanhood as it has been observed and experienced by the individual authors.

The Goddess Reawakening: The Feminine Principle Today is a collection of articles that have been brought together to open a serious consideration of this concept of a universal feminine principle, and if it exists what it might be. Much like a large panel discussion, this anthology does not intend to provide final or definitive answers. But as long as the concept of a feminine principle continues to be used as an underlying premise in theories of psychology, philosophy, and spirituality, affecting the thinking of so many people, we feel that this concept requires long-overdue examination. Hopefully, this anthology will begin this important process and lead to a more careful consideration and analysis of an idea that has gained such a stronghold in Western thought.

For the last three millennia the mainstream religions of the world have stressed the masculine principle. Despite the many differences between Judaism, Christianity and Islam, each regards their highest or sole divinity as male. Buddhism, though not actually professing belief in a divinity, has placed the male figure of the Buddha, Siddartha Gautama, in the most exalted position of sanctity. Despite the power attributed to Goddess figures such as Shakti or Devi, Hinduism is for the most part a religion of patriarchs and patriarchal attitudes. The holy figures of Mary in Christianity, Kwan Yin in Buddhism, and other sacred female images are paid honor today, but it is clear they are not regarded as primary powers in the universe.

But these religions are relative newcomers to the world scene. Goddess reverence is traced back to the early Neolithic periods of some ten thousand years ago, some would say even to the Venus statues of the Paleolithic periods of some thirty thousand years ago. In discussing the awakening of the Goddess, or our awakening to Her existence, this anthology not only explores many aspects and questions related to this reclamation of the Goddess but will raise many more questions that are well worth considering.

What happens when the female or feminine principle is regarded as the subject of a sort of affirmative action on a universal level and perceived as being in equally balanced status with the male principle today? What happens if this feminine principle is experienced with an intensified sanctity that supersedes the male principle? Does this simply mean referring to God as a woman? Is that what we mean when we use the term ''Goddess''? And just what is this female or feminine principle? Can we describe or define it? In responding to these last questions, readers may notice their reactions to the differences implied by the words ''female'' and ''feminine.'' Can these two words be used interchangeably?

The word ''feminine,'' especially in these days of consciously defining our identity as women, has been regarded almost as the antithesis of the images we strive toward. It is a word that summons up numerous visual images and terms that are rife with stereotypical or even negative implications. Words come to mind such as helpless, fragile, gentle, modest, petite, graceful, tender, soft, selfless, delicate, quiet, timid, weak, docile, dependent, patient, nonintrusive, soft-spoken, girlish or childlike, receptive and needing protection. We think of sheer, gauzy fabrics, not heavy woolen tweeds. We envision the Muse that inspires the male writer or musician, not the woman author or composer herself. We think of opinions spoken in a quiet, somewhat hesitant, half-questioning voice or even of silence, not the self-confident voice of one who knows. There are images of ribbons and lace, petticoats and flowers. The woman envisioned is somewhat ethereal, moving with a light graceful motion, not quite grounded by gravity. We sense a fragility. The word "feminine" seems to fit the nymphs of the forest in the ballet *Les Sylphides,* not the large woman singing a Valkyrie aria in a Wagnerian opera.

What is most astonishing in our contemplation of the word "feminine" is the irony of knowing that it stems from the Latin *femina,* simply meaning "female," while at the same time we sense that a woman sweating and crying out with the labor of childbirth, her ninth month belly swollen with an infant, would not be described as feminine. At the moment of childbirth, an act solely associated with women, a woman is very obviously female, but what author would think to describe her as feminine?

It is clear that although "feminine" simply means "characteristic of females," it has been loaded with implications to suggest a very specific image of what female is or should be. Considering the various traits associated with the word "feminine," we cannot help but notice that these traits may have more to do with what others, perhaps male lovers and husbands, and yes, many parents, might prefer that we were. It is difficult not to notice that the attributes ascribed to femininity are those that would make life a lot easier, more pleasant, and perhaps ego-inflating for others, than for the so-called feminine woman.

Just as women have been reclaiming the words "female" and "woman," even changing the spelling of the latter to "womyn" or "womon," we can reach out to a word that now seems distorted almost beyond repair. We can and perhaps must reclaim the word "feminine" as simply meaning "characteristic of a female." Thus, in discussing the Goddess, or the concept of a divine principle in the universe that is specifically associated with the female gender, we may refer to the female principle or the feminine principle interchangeably.

We can then ask the question of how Goddess, as representative of the feminine principle, might differ from God as representative of the masculine principle. We quickly notice that the word "masculine" has also become almost a caricature, rather than simply describing what is characteristic of males. We are face to face with Western societies' insistence upon creating or exaggerating dualities. With experiential knowledge of the vast spectrum of what females can be and what males can be, we see that the terms "feminine" and "masculine" have been used to create a duality far beyond what actually exists—and not necessarily in the most positive directions for women or for men.

Upon considering the real differences, we face the questions of what is biologically determined, what is socially determined, and even what may be divinely ordained. Beyond the actual physical differences, all other traits associated with gender have provided grist for widespread discussion and examination. One study observed that mothers of infant girls most often carry them facing inward toward the mother with an arm around the back, while mothers of infant boys carry them facing outward with an arm around the waist. Are the mothers conditioning the boys to pay more attention to the outside world than do the girls? Or are the mothers responding to the seeming wishes of the infants expressed by crying or silence?

So many of the characteristics associated with feminine and masculine relate to this idea of facing inward or outward, living a rich inner and personal life or being more interested and able to function in the external world. Again we confront the implicit duality and the suggestion that women and men can't have both in full measure. Along with the duality, we can also see that certain traits are viewed as more worthy, more valuable than others. Women are said to be more passive and conciliatory, men more aggressive and competitive. Another set of dualities, that of rational behavior (supposedly an attribute of men) as opposed to emotional behavior (supposedly an attribute of women), not only suggests that women cannot think and behave with logic and rationality, but that men's emotions do not really affect their behavior.

Thus we find that associated with what we call the male principle are traits or aspects such as aggression, competitiveness, rational thought and behavior, wisdom, practicality, objectivity, protectiveness, heroism, goal orientation, courage, risk-taking, linear thinking, creativity at the highest levels and the ability to plan and organize on a grand scale, i.e., less concern with so-called petty details.

From this dualistic perspective, women as a group are regarded as more passive, compassionate, nurturing, intuitive, cooperative, emotional, subjective, impractical, conciliatory, dependent, relationship oriented, sympathetic, empathetic, creative only in so-called lower levels, i.e., crafts, home decorating, and capable of sensing natural cycles and flow. Aside from any questions about the truth of these dualities, we can see that certain traits are valued above others, depending upon one's point of view. Despite lack of reality in the traits and the mass of evidence contradicting many of these stereotypes, both female and male, our society's projection of worth or value on to each of these traits is heavily weighted on the side of the male.

Gina Cerminara's article in this anthology, ''Sex Based Superiority Complexes: A New Perspective,'' offers a very interesting point of view about what is intrinsically feminine or masculine, as she explores gender dualities in the context of karma and reincarnation. From this unique perspective, she points out the values assigned to each gender, and explains why she feels this sharply drawn duality may be much less real than supposed.

The less we accept an exaggerated duality of gender traits, with its accompanying value system, the more we may ask how and why these stereotypes have become so ubiquitous in our society. Who drew these images and why are they drawn as they are? Some of the interesting materials, perhaps the origins of the gender duality, can be found in early historic texts. One of these is the *Skanda Purana* of India. Here we read of Shiva telling Kali that the reason she is a woman, not a man, is that she has not gained enough good karma because she has not practiced asceticism long enough. The concept of stored karma from lifetime to lifetime, in conjunction with the caste system, included the idea that being male was superior to being female, implied gender was a result of previous karma. This also applied to caste levels, which were closely identified with racial identity. (The caste system was known as *varna,* literally meaning "color.") This too is clearly value laden in the *Skanda Purana,* as Shiva tells Kali that her black skin is also the result of not having accrued enough karmic credits.

Another pertinent early example of gender duality is the classic conflict between the Greek Goddess Gaia (Earth) and the Sun God Apollo. Both Aeschylus and Euripedes wrote of Gaia's shrine in Delphi passing to Apollo. Aeschylus says it was a present; Euripedes writes that it was taken by Apollo through violence. What makes this conflict between Gaia and Apollo so interesting is that Gaia was associated with the darkness and mysteries of earth and caverns. She was associated with mystical revelations of the future and wild physical and psychic abandon in the rituals celebrated in her honor. Apollo, as the sun, was regarded as the god of light and rationality. Apollo's taking of the shrine of Gaia at Delphi symbolized the conquest of so-called rational and abstract thinking over the knowledge gained through the emotions, intuition and mystical revelation. [Philosopher Friedrich Nietzsche drew upon this schism between Apollonian stiff and formal rationality versus the wild intuitive abandon of Dionysus, a boyish, somewhat effeminate deity associated with Gaia at the Delphi shrine. Although Nietzsche came down on the side of what he referred to as the Dionysian, Gaia seems to have been completely ignored.]

At Delphi, as at so many other ancient oracular sites, the person who received and expressed revelations of the future was a woman, often an elderly woman. This image of the wise old woman is a powerful one, so powerful that stereotypes of her have been twisted and transformed into ugly fear-inspiring figures most often known as witches, crones and hags. Despite Mary Daly's wonderful work in reclaiming this image as an extremely positive one, our society still retains many negative connotations of the wise old woman. She is the pattern for the older woman who knows and speaks with authority and assertiveness but is instead painted into the false portrait of the foolish or crazy old lady. Once the image is reclaimed, we can see that she is an embodiment and an important symbol of the feminine principle, a woman who understands the hidden powers of the universe, a woman who understands the language of plants and animals, is familiar with the herbs that can cure or ease pain, especially in childbirth, and moreover, can see into the past and into the future.

The term "wise woman" has been applied to many of the witches who were said to have vast stores of occult knowledge and magical powers. Studies of this term and to whom it was applied may offer a glimpse into this powerful image, and answer questions about why it was maligned so ferociously. "The Wisewoman in Western Tradition" by Patricia Hunt-Perry carefully examines and discusses this view of woman, her association with the "hidden arts," and the concept of spiritual journey and compares her to a male counterpart. Hunt-Perry includes some interesting material on the mystical experiences of Flora Courtois and Sojourner Truth.

Once aware of negative stereotyping of specific traits in women and the benefits to some members of society, we should be able to dismiss them as false and forget them. But this is easier said than done. Not only has the conditioned response of never being quite "feminine" enough hung over women's heads in the form of external values and attitudes, but most of us have internalized these images to such a degree that we have absorbed and formed patterns deep within ourselves into which we continually strive to fit. Life becomes like that of Cinderella's sister, our foot (our self-image) never quite fitting into the perfect little glass slipper. Depending upon our individual conditioning, we still respond at some deeply embedded level to descriptions such as strident, hard, shameless hussy, old maid, whore, dyke, self-centered, conceited, nagging, selfish, dominating, emasculating, too ambitious, frigid, overly sensitive, overly emotional, hysterical, foolish, silly, irrational, illogical and more. Each of these words, from a feminist point of view, might be transposed into traits such as definite, assertive, self-assured, independent, comfortable with one's sexuality. Yet "just like a woman" remains an insult rather than a compliment.

"The Sadness of the Successful Woman" by June Singer is an excellent and insightful article on the double-bind contemporary women face as we deal with trying to break the mold that has been cast for us, while at the same time trying to fit into it. She discusses the balance we must attain between our need for relationship and the guilt we feel when we do less than we think we should, alongside our need to fulfill our potential as individuals and the shame that may come from not achieving as much as we expected. This article, addressed primarily to women in the second half of life, not only raises some interesting questions but offers some interesting solutions.

It is most fitting then that a group of articles in this anthology should deal with specific Goddess images and what can be learned from them. Beatrice Bruteau's "The Unknown Goddess" discusses the concept of reunion, of the gathering together into a oneness, of unity, through her study of Demeter and Persephone of Greece. This mother and daughter, whose memory was celebrated in the well-known, yet secret, Eleusinian Mysteries that affected the entire classical world, still have much to teach us today. Bruteau's insights into the possible interpretations of the symbolism in the legend and rituals of Eleusis are perceptive and thought provoking and allow us to follow her inspired exploration of "wholeness" as "the root meaning of femininity." She leads us into a definition of neofeminism based upon this awareness of the whole; synthesis and joining of the separate parts, as the feminine principle.

"Isis: The Goddess as Healer" is the subject of art historian Kathleen Alexander-Berghorn's article on reclaiming the image of woman as healer, knowledgeable about the uses of plants and herbs as medicines to heal the body and keep it healthy. The article is filled with fascinating details about the Egyptian Goddess Isis, perhaps one of the best-known Goddess figures. Among a multitude of other attributes, she was known as the Divine Physician. There is a strong emphasis here on women reclaiming the role of healer, which has been wrested away by centuries of persecution and propaganda.

12

Both Isis and Demeter are the subjects of Joan Chamberlain Engelsman's "Rediscovering the Feminine Principle." She points out the importance of acknowledging Demeter's rage as well as her grief in the legend of Demeter and Persephone, and enters into a thoughtful and insightful discussion of the value-laden duality which attributes rational mind to men and associates women with matter, with earth, with nature, leading to ideas of spirit being higher than matter, the body being the prison or tempter of the soul. It is interesting to compare Engelsman's analysis of the symbolism in the Eleusinian Mysteries to that of Bruteau. Although they arrive at somewhat different interpretations of the symbolic content of the legend of Demeter and Persephone, they reach quite similar conclusions of how these Goddess figures help us to define and identify the feminine principle.

Judith Gleason, author of an entire book about the African Goddess Oya, has contributed "Oya, Black Goddess of Africa." After years of research and study, Gleason describes the worship, attributes, and powers of this Goddess who was so highly honored by the Yoruban people of Africa and then taken to Brazil, the Carribean, and parts of the United States by the people who came to the Western continent as slaves. This worship, which is still practiced today, offers yet another view of the nature of a Goddess which we will want to consider as we form our perception of the feminine principle. Gleason explains that Oya is related to on a very personal and protective level, yet at the same time is universal, somewhat like a unified field of energy. This article reminds us that research into lesser-known Goddess figures is extremely important if we are looking for universal principles, even as we remind ourselves that studying texts of ancient beliefs is quite different from observing beliefs still in practice today.

Eleanor Olson contributes an informed survey of Goddess figures within Buddhist and Hindu beliefs. In "The Buddhist Feminine Deities," she points out that the Goddess or Shakti energy is depicted as a passive principle in Buddhist thought, while she is portrayed as active and dynamic in Hindu theology. The image of the Prajnaparamita as the "perfection of wisdom" may be compared to the Hebrew Chokhmah of the Apocrypha. Tara as the Great Mother Savior and Kuan Yin both provide female images that are the embodiment of compassion, while in Tibet compassion is identified as the male principle. These flip-flops of traits again raise questions about the universality of gender attributes, questions that are vital for us to bear in mind as we consider the true nature of the female principle.

The role of the Shechinah (Shekhina) is described and discussed by Rabbi Leah Novick. This powerful image of female divinity has long existed within certain Jewish texts and has been joyously reclaimed by many Jewish women. "Encountering the Shechinah, the Jewish Goddess" encourages women to see beyond the more obvious patriarchal images within Judaism, to the feminine principle that weaves throughout so many Jewish concepts and rituals. It is certainly interesting that although God is regarded as transcendent in Judaism, it is the Shechinah that comes down to be with the world.

Spider Woman, Badlands Woman, Changing Woman, Clay Lady and other sacred female deities are explored in "Sacred and Legendary Women of Native North America" by Nancy Zak. From the cultures of the Hopi, the Navajo, and the Sioux, Zak covers the attributes of these Goddess figures and their roles in creation, thinking, crafts, protection, and judgment. Spider Woman, who is regarded as the "Creator of Life," is an especially important female figure to consider in our contemporary reconstruction of the feminine principle, while Changing Woman embodies the sense of flow and process of life.

Each of these articles adds deeper insight and a broader perspective to our understanding of just what the feminine principle is, although they may create as many questions as they answer. And these are just a few of the many Goddesses. When we further consider major figures such as Inanna from Sumer, Cerridwen of Wales, Mawu of Dahomey, Frigga of Scandinavia, Nu Kwa of China, Coatlicue of Mexico, Cybele of Turkey and Rome, and hundreds of others, we realize that we have a wealth of images to draw upon as we contemplate just what woman is and can be.

Elizabeth Petroff finds even among some Christian women a hint that the divine is as much Goddess as God. In her article ''The Beguines in Medieval Europe'' she describes groups of third-century women who lived communally but outside the auspices of the Church, supported themselves by their handiwork, nursing, and other such ''feminine'' pursuits, and devoted themselves to God. The passionate mystical writings of some of these women reveal experiences of union with the divine in sensual terms, not uncommon among mystics, with suggestions that in the divine male and female merge.

One of the most important realizations we have as we study this multitude of Goddess images is that they are often quite complex and multifaceted. Unlike the way in which the Goddesses of classical Greece have been portrayed, each representing a specific facet of life (Aphrodite as love, Athena as wisdom, Artemis as protectress of animals, etc.), we see that most contain a combination of many attributes. Very early Greek Goddess figures were equally complex, having been initially identified with Egyptian and Levantine images, but were whittled down to singular aspects over the centuries. It is fascinating to read the archaic inscriptions to Aphrodite as the Great Mother of all people or to Athena as the helper in childbirth.

The fact that ancient Goddess figures were seen as multifaceted is vital to note, as contemporary women struggle to balance lives in which work, children, and mates are all very real aspects of everyday life. I am not suggesting that we should each be superwomen or all things to all people and capable of accomplishing everything. Yet this understanding of multiplicity as being as natural to women as menstrual periods informs us of our choices. We are free to take all, some or none of the above.

Psychologist Carl Gustav Jung, in his efforts to reconcile and deal with the complexities and diverse abilities he observed in women, with his social conditioning which convinced him that certain capacities or abilities were natural

15

only to men, developed the anima/animus theory. This suggests that the qualities a woman possesses that do not seem to be typically "feminine" should be credited to her "animus," a sort of male part of her. Conversely, traits that a man exhibits, such as compassion or nurturing, are attributed to his "anima," the female within him.

Stephan Hoeller, in his article "Sophia, the Gnostic Archetype of Soul-Wisdom," appears to accept Jung's theory, for he discusses the figure of Sophia in a way that cannot help but make us think of Nora in Ibsen's *A Doll's House.* Making use of the Gnostic accounts that stress Sophia's imbalance when she is separated from her consort, we read quite a different perception of the feminine from that found in the other articles of this anthology. Dane Rudhyar's "Toward the Companionate Man-Woman Relationship" also deals with woman in relation to man, including a consideration of Jung's theory. Rudhyar approaches the subject from a perspective different from Hoeller's, and we can sense a man in transition as he makes an honest and genuine effort to gain a feminist consciousness. Still both of these articles are clearly written from points of view that differ quite markedly from those of the women authors.

Contemporary Jungians have had to deal with Jung's theory in light of the burgeoning women's movement. Challenges to this sort of stereotyping have come fast and furiously over the last decade, and they point out the sort of circular reasoning that Jung would probably have attributed to women or to the "anima." Jean Shinoda Bolen, a Jungian psychoanalyst, offers an interesting compromise on this issue. She suggests that the animus be associated with Athena or Artemis, Greek Goddess figures that represented rational thought and adventurous self-determination, i.e. more "masculine" attributes. Mary Ann Mattoon and Jenette Jones present an interesting defense of the anima/animus theory in "Is the Animus Obsolete?" Approaching the subject with some new and innovative observations, the article airs ideas about the use of the theory, keeping some of its positive aspects while not being burdened by what is useless.

From the multitude of possible traits, each of us will choose, or have already chosen, those that seem most comfortable to us as individuals. Rather than having a small proscribed set of characteristics from which to form our identities, we now have a large treasure chest, like the trunk in Grandma's attic filled with old costumes to rummage through. It permits us to try on all sorts of exciting combinations. With the freedom of understanding that there is no right or wrong in terms of gender identity, we begin to realize that we are who we are, and if we are females, our traits are feminine traits. If a woman hammers a nail into the wall or builds a cabin in the woods, it's not her animus that is doing it, it's she. If she has to justify this love of carpentry as feminine, she can always draw on the Goddess Asherah of Canaan, known among her other epithets as the ''Lady of Masonry and Carpentry.''

Claude Servan-Schreiber's article ''A Higher View of the Man-Woman Problem,'' moves toward this attitude for both women and men. According to Roberto Assagioli, whose ideas are at the core of this article, what really matters is each individual's unique potential and growth. Assagioli does, however, still retain a belief in universal feminine and masculine principles within the psyches, and goes on to say that women have both and men have both, and we must learn to harmonize them. The aspects of the feminine principle mentioned are those traits traditionally attributed to women.

Even as our knowledge of the variety of qualities ascribed to woman as divinity, and our consideration of the feminine principle is expanded by knowledge of ancient or even simultaneous cultures, Shirley Nicholson's article, ''The Way of the Uncarved Block,'' approaches the subject from the other side. Along with our considerations that have led us to a deeper questioning of just what the feminine principle is, she asks that we now turn to examine some of the traditional aspects of the principle, being sure not to throw out the baby with the bath water. After all, wouldn't we be pleased to continue being defined by traits such as compassion, nurturance, cooperation, sympathy, empathy, intuition, the capability of sensing natural cycles and flow? Many of these attributes have been and still are traits that we value enormously. The only problem with them is that they can make us very vulnerable. Nicholson's article suggests that it is time that everyone began to reach out to develop these qualities. Referring to the *Tao Teh Ching* and other Taoist writings, she points out that the values held highest in Taoism are these feminine characteristics associated with the Mother of the World and the Great Sympathy in which ego-boundaries blur out into a Oneness. We are not surprised by Ellen Chen's conclusions that early Taoism was actually a remnant or derivation of the worship of the Great Mother in China. The underlying precepts are quite similar to Bruteau's insights about the symbolism of unity inherent in the reverence for Demeter and Isis. Would that all the world accepted and enacted this. "The Tao" literally means "The Way," and Nicholson reminds us that it is a way of peace and harmony. There may be so-called masculine traits that women can adopt, but only at the cost of an even more aggressive world. Now that we have such a vast catalog of traits to choose from, we need to think carefully about which we choose. And in defining the feminine principle, we also think of the Taoist reminder that each thing does best when allowed to act according to its own nature.

Presenting lectures and workshops to women all across the United States and in Europe, I have been fascinated by the continual development of interest in the Goddess and women's spirituality as a movement in and of itself. I have been very fortunate in being able to speak to and with women from so many diverse backgrounds. As I explained above, there is a rich diversity in the many ways women partake of women's spirituality and the way it is incorporated into individual lives. There is a great variety in the Goddess images focused upon and the way rituals enacted individually and in groups, are created and carried out. Judging from the continual changes and additions that have occurred over the last decade, I can see that women's spirituality will continue to develop and grow as each woman's creativity is incorporated within it. Yet, even within this diversity, I can see certain patterns that have emerged.

There has been great care taken not to set up any rigid hierarchy or clergy. It is understood that every woman can have a "direct line" to Goddess. Acts of creativity are understood to contain a sense of sanctity, to be closely aligned with the creativity or creation of Goddess. New songs, new prayers, new chants, new rituals are welcomed and appreciated. Individual differences are encouraged, and creative contributions are regarded as enriching. If there is any "tradition," it is that of embracing and accepting continual growth and development.

One very important aspect of reclaiming a feminine spirituality is that of the vision or concept one has of deity or the divine. Within nearly all expressions of contemporary women's spirituality is the idea of Goddess not as a woman sitting on a throne above the clouds, i.e., transcendent, apart from us, but as immanent, within ourselves. Many would carry this even further and speak of the Goddess as being within all manifestations of life. And more and more women are relating to the idea of divinity not as an anthropomorphic image, or even a divine spark within ourselves, as much as it is the flowing energy in the very processes of life and living. Thus Goddess would not be in a person, or tree, or river, so much as she would be the actual organic process, the flow, the changes, transitions, and transformations that the person, tree, or river go through. This is an idea that encompasses time as well as space, and is perhaps more closely related to Taoism than any other body of spiritual thought.

Goddess figures such as Shakti in India, Changing Woman of the Navajo, and Nu Kwa of China suggest this perception. The work of Ellen Chen on the *Tao Teh Ching* and other Taoist writings as derivations of an ancient worship of the Great Mother, along with the obvious references to Mother or Matrix within the *Tao Teh Ching,* provide materials well worth considering in this context. One cannot help but think of the very familiar term Mother Nature which, for me, is simply a synonym for Goddess.

The widespread celebrations of the solstices and the equinoxes as special days of the Goddess are thought to direct attention to the continual flow of the seasons and year-ly cycles. New or full moon rituals celebrated by many women draw attention to the monthly cycles. This leads many women not only to associate the monthly cycles with our own menstrual cycles, but to the understanding that everything is continually changing, continually in process. Stages such as birth, maturation, decay, and death are all seen as natural parts of life cycles, leading many women to feel that rebirth is equally as natural. One well-known Goddess song contains the lines, ''Wheat and corn, wheat and corn/All that dies shall be reborn.''

This concept of Goddess as life process leads to another aspect of contemporary women's spirituality noticeable among many groups and individuals. This is the sense of the direct connection with all life. Many say that we are not on top of nature, we *are* nature. This sense of unity, much the same as discussed in Bruteau's and Nicholson's articles, continually surfaces in conversations and writings. It helps us to understand that what we might refer to as compassion or nurturing or sympathy is the result of intuitively sensing this direct connection and oneness. This sense of unity with all life leads many women quite naturally to a directly experiential comprehension of why sexism, racism, agism, or any other ''ism'' that creates a sense of ''us and others'' doesn't really make sense. And contemporary writings and gatherings exhibit a consciousness of how false these separations are. It has also led to a strong concern not only for the land and waters but for all other species as deserving of respect, and care not to harm or exploit them.

It is easy to see why many archaeologists and historians referred to ancient cultures that worshipped the Goddess as ''nature cults.'' Although this term was nearly always written to imply a lesser stage of human development, we need today to consider that a sense of all nature as sacred might have helped to prevent so much of the exploitation and destruction of the earth prevalent today. In such a belief system, dumping chemicals in the rivers, into the air, or beneath the soil might be regarded not only as pollution but as blasphemy! A direct outgrowth of contemplating just what women's spirituality and reclamation of the Goddess may mean has led to a true planetary consciousness—and a conscience.

Riane Eisler's article "Reclaiming Our Goddess Heritage" discusses the importance of this continually expanding movement to reclaim the values of ancient Goddess-revering societies. She suggests that by accepting the feminine principle we can arrive at partnership rather than dominator societies. Elizabeth Dodson Gray agrees with several of the other writers in describing women as having a natural affinity with nature in "Nature as an Act of Imagination." Her presentation of the process of projecting, e.g., male symbolic imaginations projected onto women, will draw nods of positive response. She is less pleased with the mythic gender identification of earth as female, as Mother Earth, suggesting that by doing this we are repeating the same old negative stereotyping, and she makes a plea that each life-form and process simply be seen for what it is. It may be worth noting that in ancient Egyptian religion earth was thought of as the God Geb, husband of the starry heavens, which were identified as the Goddess Nut.

Whether or not one regards the planet Earth as Mother Earth, as many Native Americans do, or as Gaia as the Greeks once called Earth and wrote of her as Mother of All, including heaven (Uranus), there is no question that a concern for all life on Earth has become a major concern of women involved in women's spirituality and reclaiming the values of the feminine principle. Susan Griffin's book *Woman and Nature: The Roaring Inside Her*, 1979, first introduced the perception that women have been regarded as being closer to nature than men have, showing how this idea allowed many men to use and abuse women with as little conscience as they felt when they used and abused forests and rivers. This connection between woman and nature has since led to the concept within feminism that as we women challenge our own oppression, we also challenge the abuse of the entire planet, a concept that led to the development of ecofeminism.

As I explained, no one set of beliefs includes all that has been presented and considered. Even theories presented with a great deal of supportive evidence have been contradicted or slightly changed by other theories with other bodies of supportive evidence. We do well to keep in mind that we are in a process of reconstructing a past in which there are great gaps for want of specific information. Any day, an archaeological find may surface, causing us to reevaluate major portions of this work of reconstruction. This was certainly the case after a century of statements by respected archaeologists and historians that written language had never been truly incorporated into the cultures of Canaan before 1500 B.C.E. And then the discovery and excavations of the ancient state of Ebla, located in western Syria, and dated to about 2600 B.C.E. revealed a library as sophisticated as any of that period. We need always to retain a flexibility and a mind open to what might still lie beneath the earth waiting to be discovered. We can only reconstruct with the understanding that we might face certain contradictions in what may be discovered in the future.

But we do have more than enough bricks and mortar to rebuild our inner temples of the Goddess. Prepared to change the position of a window or a door, we need not postpone our work for want of materials. The Goddess has been waking up, and so have we. Our discussions of the meaning of the feminine principle may include certain controversies or disagreements about specific details, but these discussions only serve to enrich and expand our contemplations and perceptions. The way of the Goddess seems to be that of inclusion and adaptability, rather than exclusion and rigidity. We have no need to set up theories that become so rigid we might be tempted to ignore additional ideas and information just to protect the theory. The theory itself is not sacred. It is our ongoing process of building the theory that becomes a sacred act. And perhaps the very fact that we enter into this process together, with compassion, cooperation, nurturance, intuition, respect for intuition, sympathy, and empathy, capable of sensing process and flow, and with love for each other, each of us a part of the unity of the Goddess, will say more about the feminine principle than any specific article or book.

In Char McKee's "Feminism: A Vision of Love" we find a spirited coalescence of many ideas and precepts that have been formulated by two decades of feminist thought. At the same time, it is an exciting leap of faith into a better world based on the feminine principle. McKee explains why these feminist perceptions of reality can lead us into a new age by leading us out of the current patriarchal mode. This article is almost a manifesto for this transfer of perceptions that McKee describes and predicts must happen if the world is to survive.

As we consider not so much entering but creating a new age, one of compassion and caring, one of sensitivity to all living things, one of planetary consciousness and conscience, one of sharing and love, one of understanding the interconnectedness of all of us to everything, we realize that it is the work of all of us together that offers the only possible way for this to happen. It is this realization that helps us to understand that together we are the Goddess, multifaceted and unified, the embodiment of the feminine principle reawakening.

I

The Goddess

1

Reclaiming Our Goddess Heritage: The Feminine Principle in our Past and Future

RIANE EISLER

In most "traditional religions" the supreme or only deity is male. But what we are now learning is that our most ancient traditions are traditions in which both men and women worshipped a Great Mother, a Great Goddess who was the mother of both divine daughters and divine sons.

As we reclaim these ancient traditions, we are also reclaiming the consciousness that women and men can work in equal partnership, that we can honor the feminine in both sexes, that peace is not a utopian dream. We are increasingly aware that both women and men can be more gentle and compassionate, governed by what sociologist Jessie Bernard calls a "female ethos of love/duty."[1] And we are reminded that the earth is indeed our Mother, to be respected and revered, rather than polluted and exploited.

Recent archeological discoveries indicate that war and the "war of the sexes" are neither divinely nor biologically ordained.[2] They also indicate that a better future *is* possible—and is in fact firmly rooted in the haunting drama of what actually happened in our past.[3] But for us to construct such a future requires that the feminine principle—so long denied, degraded, and subordinated in both our belief systems and our lives—be reinstated to its rightful place.

Our Hidden Heritage: Old Clues and New Findings

The conventional view, still taught us in most of our schools and mass media, is that a just and peaceful society is merely a utopia: an impossible dream. We are taught religious dogmas of "original sin" and their secular updates in sociobiological theories about "selfish genes." Not coincidentally, in both cases, these notions are imbedded in stories about how male dominance is either divinely or scientifically ordained.

We are also taught that Western civilization begins with brutally male-dominant and highly warlike societies and that if there was anything before patriarchy in our prehistory it was so primitive as to be unworthy of serious attention. For example, we have been told that European civilization begins with the Indo-European invasions: with a way of structuring society in which women and anything associated with the "feminine" is held in contempt and relegated to a subordinate and subservient position.

Indeed, history as conventionally written has been literally the story of men, of the male half of humanity, with only an occasional line, or at best page, about "their" women. But if we reexamine our past taking into account the *whole* of our history, including the latest findings about our prehistory, drawing from a data base that includes the *whole* of humanity—both its female and male halves—a very different picture emerges.

A good entry point into this new and more hopeful picture of our cultural evolution is through a fresh look at the many familiar legends about an earlier, more harmonious and peaceful age. The Judaeo-Christian Bible tells of a garden where woman and man lived in harmony with each other and with nature—a time before a male god decreed that woman henceforth be subservient to man. The Chinese *Tao Te Ching* describes a time when the yin or feminine principle was not yet ruled by the male principle or yang, a more harmonious time when the wisdom of the mother was still honored and humanity lived in peace. The ancient writings of the Greek poet Hesiod tell of a "golden race" who tilled the soil in "peaceful ease" before a "lesser race" brought in their god of war.

While for many people these stories are merely religious or poetic allegories, there is general agreement among scholars that in many respects they are based on prehistoric events.[4] However, until now, one key component—the allusion to a time when women and men lived in partnership—has generally been viewed as no more than fantasy.

But just as when archeology was still in its infancy and the excavations of Heinrich and Sophia Schleimann helped establish the reality of Homer's Troy, more recent archeological excavations—deriving from what British archeologist James Mellaart calls a veritable archeological revolution[5]—indicate that stories of a time when women were not dominated by men are also based on earlier realities. For example, Mesopotamian and later biblical stories about a garden where woman and man lived in partnership derive in part from folk memories of the first agrarian (or Neolithic) societies, which planted the first gardens on this earth. Similarly, the legend of how the glorious civilization of Atlantis sank into the sea appears to be a garbled recollection of the matrifocal Minoan civilization, a remarkably peaceful and uniquely creative culture now believed to have ended when Crete and some surrounding islands were massively damaged by earthquakes and enormous tidal waves.[6]

These new archeological discoveries, coupled with reinterpretations of older digs using more scientific methods, reveal a long period of peace and prosperity when our social, technological, and cultural evolution moved steadily upward. They show evidence for many thousands of years when all the basic technologies on which civilization is built were developed in societies that were not male dominant, violent, and hierarchic. Most important, they show that while these early cradles of civilization—going back many thousands of years before Sumer—were not utopian societies in the sense of being perfect; they were societies organized along very different lines from ours.

As Mellaart reports from his excavations of Catal Huyuk

(the largest early agrarian or Neolithic site ever found), the characteristic social structure of these first cradles of civilization appears to have been generally equalitarian. He writes how the comparative size of houses, the nature of their contents, and the "funerary gifts" found in graves show that there were no extreme differences among people in status and wealth.[7] Data from Catal Huyuk and other Neolithic sites also indicate that in these societies, where women were priestesses and craftspeople, the female was *not* subordinate to the male.[8] Indeed, in sharp contrast to most present-day religions, the supreme deity was female rather than male: a Goddess rather than God.[9] Finally, dispelling the notion that war is "natural," these societies do not seem to have had wars. There is a general absence of fortifications as well as an absence in their extensive and considerably advanced art of the scenes so ubiquitous in later art: "noble warriors" killing one another in battles, gods and men raping women, "glorious conquerors" dragging back prisoners in chains.[10]

Even more fascinating, and relevant to our time, is that this type of social organization continued well into the Bronze Age, culminating in the "high" civilization of Minoan Crete. Nicolas Platon, the former director of the Acropolis Museum and Superintendent of Antiquities in Crete (an island he excavated for over fifty years), reports how this technologically developed civilization, with its viaducts, paved roads (the first in Europe), and advanced civic amenities, had a generally high standard of living. Even though there were differences in status and wealth and probably a monarchic type of government, there is evidence of a large emphasis on public welfare, which is very unusual in comparison with other "high" civilizations of the time.[11]

Here, as in the earlier Neolithic, the subordination of women does not appear to have been the norm. Cretan art shows women as priestesses, as figures being paid homage, and even as captains of ships. As Platon writes, in Minoan Crete "the important part played by women is discernible in every sphere."[12] And, as in the earlier Neolithic where images of female deities are ubiquitous, Platon reports that in this last-known matrifocal society the "whole of life was pervaded by an ardent faith in the goddess Nature, the source of all creation and harmony."[13]

These archeological findings provide evidence that, contrary to what we have been taught, the original direction of cultural evolution was in this more peaceful and socially and ecologically balanced direction. But the archeological record also shows that, following a period of chaos and almost total cultural disruption, there occurred a fundamental *social shift*.

At this pivotal branching, the cultural evolution of societies that worshipped the life-generating and nurturing powers of the universe—in our time still symbolized by the ancient "feminine" chalice or grail—was interrupted. There now appeared on the prehistoric horizon invaders from the peripheral areas of our globe, from the arid steppes of the north and barren deserts of the south, who ushered in a very different form of social organization. As University of California archeologist Marija Gimbutas writes, these were people who literally worshipped "the lethal power of the blade"[14]—the power to take rather than give life, which is the ultimate power to establish and enforce human rankings.

Human Possibilities: Two Alternatives

It makes sense that the earliest depiction of divine power in human form should have been female rather than male. When our ancestors began to ask the eternal questions (Where do we come from before we are born? Where do we go after we die?), they must have noted that life for them emerges from the body of woman. It would have been only natural for them to image the universe as an all-giving Mother from whose womb all life emerges and where, like the cycles of vegetation, it returns after death to be again reborn.

It also makes sense that societies with this image of the powers that govern the universe should have a very different social structure from societies that worship a divine Father who wields a thunderbolt and/or sword. It further seems logical that, in societies where the powers governing the universe are conceptualized in female form, women would not be seen as subservient, and that "effeminate" qualities such as caring, compassion, and nonviolence would be highly valued. What does not make sense is to conclude that societies where men do not dominate women have to be societies in which women dominate men.

Nonetheless, when the first evidence of these prehistoric societies began to be unearthed in the nineteenth century, the scholars of that day concluded that since they were not patriarchies they must have been matriarchies.[15] Then, when the evidence did not seem to support that conclusion, it again became customary to argue that human society always was—and always will be—dominated by males.

But matriarchy is not the opposite of patriarchy: it is the other side of the coin of a *dominator* model of society. This is a way of structuring human relations where the primary principle of social organization is ranking, beginning with the *ranking* of one half of humanity over the other. The real alternative to a patriarchal or male-dominant society is a very different way of organizing social relations. This is the *partnership* model where, beginning with the most fundamental difference in our species between male and female, diversity is *not* equated with either inferiority or superiority and the primary principle of social organization is *linking* rather than ranking.[16]

Models of society are abstractions. But societies that orient primarily to one or the other of these models have characteristic configurations or patterns. These patterns, however, are discernible only when we look at the whole picture. In other words, the reason these patterns were not generally seen in the past is that scholars were looking at a very incomplete and distorted picture—one that excluded no less than one half of the population: women.

For example, from the conventional perspective focusing only on the activities and experiences of men, Hitler's Germany, Khomeini's Iran, the Japan of the Samurai, and the Aztecs of Meso-America would seem to represent completely different cultures. But once we also look at the situation of women in these societies, we are able to identify the social configuration characteristic of rigidly male-dominated societies. We then see striking commonalities: all these otherwise widely divergent societies are not only rigidly male dominant but also have a generally hierarchic and authoritarian social structure and a high degree of social violence, ranging from wife-beating within the family to aggressive warfare on the larger tribal or national levels.[17]

Conversely, we can also see striking similarities among otherwise extremely diverse societies that are more sexually equalitarian, societies where to be considered "real men" males do not have to be dominant. Characteristically, such societies tend to be not only much more peaceful but also much less hierarchic and authoritarian. This is evidenced by anthropological data (i.e., the BaMbuti and !Kung), by contemporary studies of trends in more sexually equalitarian modern societies (i.e., Scandinavian nations such as Sweden), and by the prehistoric and historic data (detailed in *The Chalice and The Blade,* some of which has been briefly presented in the previous section).[18]

The larger picture that emerges from this gender-holistic perspective also indicates that, contrary to popular misconceptions, the problems of male dominance and male violence are not innate. There were obviously both women and men in the more peaceful and equalitarian societies now being explored by archeology. Moreover, clearly throughout history not all men have been violent. And today many men are rejecting their stereotypical "masculine" roles—for example, the men who are today redefining fathering in the more caring and nurturing way once stereotypically associated only with mothering.

In short, the problem in dominator societies is not men as a sex. It is rather the way male identity must be defined in male-dominant societies where, by definition, "masculinity" is equated with domination and conquest—be it of women, of other men, or of nature.

To maintain a male-dominant society, boys must be systematically socialized for domination, and therefore for violence. Male violence has to be idealized—as we see in so much of our normative literature celebrating violent "heroes" (for example, the biblical King David, the Homeric Ulysses, and modern "he-men" such as Rambo). Indeed, in these societies violent behaviors are systematically taught to males from early childhood through toys like swords, violent video games, GI Joe dolls, and guns, while only girls are systematically socialized for nurturance, compassion, and caring.[19]

What further becomes discernible by looking at human society from this larger perspective is that throughout recorded history there have been times and places in which the partnership thrust has reasserted itself: times when women, and the more "soft" or "feminine" values, were also in the ascendancy.

For instance, although this is rarely noted by most religious scholars, in many of the early Christian communities women and men lived as equals, with women taking the same leadership roles as men. In fact, according to the Gnostic Gospels, Mary Magdalene was one of Jesus' main apostles: a major leader in the early Church—and the only one who dared to stand up to Peter and reproach him for trying to set up the same kind of hierarchic religious structure Jesus had preached against. It is also notable that many of these early Christian communities, which both preached and practiced nonviolence and equality, saw the deity as female and male, in other words, as holy Mother and Father.[20]

The Troubadours and Troubatrixes, who flourished in the courts of Eleanor of Aquitaine and her daughters Alix and Marie, likewise elevated woman and the feminine from their subservient and despised status. In doing this, they asserted that the feminine principle is integral to both women and men, arguing that masculinity should be a gentle thing—as in the term "gentleman." And it was the Troubadours who introduced what the Church called Mariology: the worship of a Divine Mother, in essence a reinstitution of the ancient worship of the Goddess. At first the Church persecuted the Troubadours as heretics. But when they could not eradicate this deeply rooted worship, they coopted it: the Goddess became the Virgin Mary, the one mortal figure in a holy family where only the father and son were now proclaimed divine.

The most visible recent partnership resurgence in the West occurred during the 1960s. This was a time when the second phase of modern feminism gained unprecedented power as the "women's liberation" movement, and many women and men rejected the violence of war and an unjust and oppressive economic and political system. But, once again, the partnership thrust was met with massive dominator resistance. The progressive sixties were followed by regressive years.

As is characteristic of dominator regressions, massive energy and resources were poured into a drive to reverse women's gains such as to again deprive women of reproductive freedom and to block the proposed Equal Rights Amendment to the United States Constitution. At the same time—in keeping with the dominator configuration of rigid male dominance, a high degree of institutionalized violence, and a generally hierarchic and authoritarian social structure—there was a push for increased militarization and opposition to funding for social programs that would create a more equalitarian social structure. Instead, social and economic policies reversed many of the gains of minorities and women, thus again widening, rather than narrowing, the gap between those on the bottom and those on the top.

Those seeking a return to the "good old days" when most men—and all women—still "knew their place" have throughout recorded history correctly seen so-called women's issues as central to their regressive agendas. But, ironically, even to this day many "progressives," from middle to left, view anything relating to women as a secondary matter—to be dealt with, if at all, only after the "more important" issues are addressed.

And so—because during the centuries of recorded (or patriarchal) history, vital matters profoundly affecting the problems, needs, and aspirations of no less than half of humanity have been generally viewed as "unimportant"—or as "just the way things are''—until now the dominator system has violently reasserted its hold.

Evolution at the Crossroads

But now when the lethal power of the blade, amplified a millionfold by megatons of nuclear warheads, threatens to put an end to all human culture, the dominator system is literally taking us to an evolutionary dead-end. Now we are rapidly approaching another potentially decisive branching point in our cultural evolution when we either move on to a partnership future or we may have no future at all.

It is therefore not coincidental that our time, when the mix of high technology and a dominator system of social organization poses a danger to all life on this Earth, should also be the time when we are reclaiming our hidden heritage: the lost knowledge of millennia-long spiritual traditions when the world was ruled not by the blade but by the chalice, the feminine vessel of regeneration and transformation. Nor is it coincidental that we are today regaining what we call our ecological consciousness. For in essence this is a modern counterpart of our ancestors' reverence for the Goddess, a reawakening of our awareness that nature and spirituality are inextricably intertwined.

Neither is it coincidental that the international women's movement is in our time making unprecedented strides, or that—in implicit recognition of the characteristic partnership society configuration—equality, development, and peace are the three interrelated goals of the first United Nations Decade for Women.

Perhaps the most critical fact emerging from the new view of our past and potential future—made possible by the study of society from a perspective that takes into account the whole of humanity, both women and men—is that the modern movements for social and economic justice, as well as the resurgence of a ''new spirituality,'' are neither radical nor new. Rather, such seemingly diverse progressive movements as the ''rights of man,'' utopian and scientific socialist, abolitionist, and feminist movements of the eighteenth and nineteenth centuries and the anticolonial, peace, ecology, black, and women's liberation movements of the twentieth century are part of a resurging thrust toward a social system that is *not* geared toward men's conquest of women, other men, or nature.

Similarly, the mounting interest in ancient mysticism and shamanistic healing is fundamentally a search for the kind of spirituality appropriate for a partnership rather than a dominator way of life. It harks back to ancient traditions developed in societies where women were not dominated by men. For rather than being a peripheral issue, or what in male-dominant systems is the same: a "women's issue," the reinstatement of women and feminine values to a central social and spiritual place is the single most critical issue of our time.

While all the progressive ideological movements are part of an all-encompassing movement for the transformation of a dominator to a partnership system, this transformation cannot occur until the power to give and nurture life rather than the power to dominate and destroy is again honored above all. For only then will we have the temporal and spiritual foundations for a more balanced, just, and peaceful world.

Notes and References

1. J. Bernard, *The Female World,* New York: The Free Press, 1981.
2. R. Eisler, *The Chalice and the Blade: Our History, Our Future.* San Francisco: Harper and Row, 1987. See also M. Gimbutas, *The Goddesses and Gods of Old Europe,* Berkeley: University of California Press, 1982; J. Mellaart, *Catal Huyuk,* New York: McGraw-Hill, 1967; N. Platon, *Crete,* Geneva: Nagel Publishers, 1966. These works (and this article) focus primarily on Western civilization. The reason is that, due to the ethnocentric bias of Western scholarship, most archeological excavations have until now been carried out in the areas of Europe and Asia Minor around the Mediterranean. However, there are indications of similar patterns in other world regions. See, e.g., J. Nash, "The Aztecs and The Ideology of Male Dominance," *Signs* Vol. 4, Winter 1978, pp. 349-362.
3. Ibid.

4. See, e.g., *The Dartmouth Bible*, annotated by R. Chamberlain and H. Herman, with the counsel of an advisory board of biblical scholars, Boston: Houghton Mifflin, 1950; J. M. Robinson, *An Introduction to Early Greek Philosophy*, Boston: Houghton Mifflin, 1968; *The Way of Life, Lao Tzu, Tao Te Ching*, R. B. Blakney, translator and editor, New York: Mentor, 1955.

5. J. Mellaart, *The Neolithic of the Near East*, New York: Charles Scribner's Sons, 1975; J. Mellaart, *Catal Huyuk*, New York: McGraw-Hill, 1967.

6. The first paper to advance the theory that Minoan civilization was destroyed by earthquakes and tidal waves was S. Marinatos, "The Volcanic Destruction of Minoan Crete," *Antiquity*, Vol. 13, 1939, pp. 425-439. Since then it appears more feasible that this is what so weakened Crete as to make possible the takeover by Achaean (Mycenaean) overlords, as there is no evidence that this takeover was through a full-scale armed invasion.

7. See, e.g., J. Mellaart, *The Neolithic of the Near East*, New York: Charles Scribner's Sons, 1975; J. Mellaart, *Catal Huyuk*, New York: McGraw-Hill, 1967; M. Gimbutas, *The Goddesses and Gods of Old Europe*, Berkeley: University of California Press, 1982; M. Gimbutas, "The First Wave of Eurasian Steppe Pastoralists into Copper Age Europe," *The Journal of Indo-European Studies*, Vol. 5, No. 4, Winter 1977; G. Childe, *The Dawn of European Civilization*, New York: Random House, 1964.

8. Ibid.

9. Ibid. See also E. Neumann, *The Great Mother*, Princeton: Princeton University Press, 1955.

10. See, e.g., M. Gimbutas, *The Goddesses and Gods of Old Europe*, Berkeley: University of California Press, 1982; M. Gimbutas, "The First Wave of Eurasian Steppe Pastoralists into Copper Age Europe," *The Journal of Indo-European Studies*, Vol. 5, No. 4, Winter 1977.

11. N. Platon, *Crete*, Geneva: Nagel Publishers, 1966, Chapter, 3.

12. Ibid, p. 161, p. 177.

13. Ibid, p. 148.

14. M. Gimbutas, "The First Wave of Eurasian Steppe Pastoralists into Copper Age Europe," *Journal of Indo-European Studies*, Vol. 5, No. 4, Winter 1977, p. 281.

15. A later proponent of this view is J. Frazer, *The Golden Bough*, New York: Macmillan, 1969.

16. R. Eisler, *The Chalice and the Blade: Our History, Our Future*. San Francisco: Harper and Row, 1987; R. Eisler, "Woman, Man, and The Evolution of Social Structure," paper for presenta-

tion during the Physis: Inhabiting the Earth conference, Florence, Italy, October 28-31, 1986, published in *World Futures*, Vol. 23, Nos. 1-2, April 1987; R. Eisler and D. Loye, "The Failure of Liberalism: A Reassessment of Ideology from a New Feminine-Masculine Perspective," *Political Psychology*, Vol. 4, No. 2, 1983; R. Eisler, "Violence and Male Dominance: The Ticking Time Bomb," *Humanities in Society*, Vol. 7, Nos. 1-2, Winter-Spring, 1984, pp. 3-18; R. Eisler and D. Loye, "Peace and Feminist Thought: New Directions," *World Encyclopedia of Peace*, Laszlo and Yoo, editors, London: Pergamon Press, 1986.

17. Ibid.
18. For some works on the complex interaction between biological and social factors, see, e.g., R. Hinde, *Biological Bases of Human Social Behavior*, New York: McGraw-Hill, 1974; R. C. Lewontin, S. Rose, and L. Kamin, *Not In Our Genes*, New York: Pantheon, 1984: H. Lambert, "Biology and Equality: A Perspective on Sex Differences," *Signs*, Vol. 4, No. 1, Autumn 1978, pp. 97-117; R. Eisler and V. Csanyi, *Human Biology and Social Structure*, work in progress. Two important feminist works on this subject are *Genes and Gender*, edited by E. Tobach and B. Rosoff, Staten Island, New York: Gordian Press, 1978, and *Genes and Gender II*, edited by R. Hubbard and M. Lowe, Staten Island, New York: Gordian Press, 1979.
19. See C. Gilligan, *In A Different Voice*, Cambridge, Mass.: Harvard University Press, 1982: J. B. Miller, *Toward a New Psychology of Women*, Boston: Beacon Press, 1976. These are two important works on the values stereotypically associated with women and femininity, which in male-dominant societies cannot attain social governance.
20. See E. Pagels, *The Gnostic Gospels*, New York: Random House, 1979, for a fascinating account of some of the suppressed Christian gospels and the importance ascribed to the feminine as divine wisdom or Sophia.

2

Sophia: The Gnostic Archetype of Feminine Soul-Wisdom

STEPHAN A. HOELLER

When seeking meaningful archetypal representations of the feminine psyche, we find that the search inevitably leads us into the realm of myth. Without an informed knowledge and understanding of the universal motifs of mythology, the search for meaning and for essential transformation of the human psyche is difficult indeed. Aristotle said that "myths are a compact of wonders," and in comparatively modern times, H. P. Blavatsky has called attention to the fact that myths are the primary agencies by which spiritual realities were communicated from age to age and from generation to generation. Not history, but the ever-recurring events of the life of the human spirit are depicted in the myths of all peoples and faiths, so the occultists of the nineteenth century told us. At a later date, and claiming a higher degree of academic respectability, there appeared the leading figures of modern psychology, particularly the two giant spirits, Freud and Jung. Both of these men took mythology seriously and regarded myths as psychic entities powerfully operative in the world. While Freud was largely concerned with myths as records of the vicissitudes of the sexual and desire natures, Jung came to regard the essential nature of myth as being a source of wisdom and inspiration. His attitude in this regard is well exemplified in his following statement:

I can only stand in deepest awe and admiration before the depths and heights of the soul whose world beyond space hides an immeasurable richness of images, which millions of years of living have stored up and condensed into organic material. My conscious mind is like an eye which perceives the furthermost spaces; but the psychic non-ego is that which fills this space in a sense beyond space. These images are not pale shadows, but powerful and effective conditions of the soul which we can only misunderstand but can never rob of their power by denying them.[1]

One of these images of immeasurable beauty and power, which even the passage of nearly two millennia could not reduce to a shadow, is the awesome and appealing figure of Sophia in the myths of the Gnostics. The Gnostics have been accused by their always numerous detractors of manufacturing consciously contrived allegories, which were to serve the purpose of synthesizing the pagan mysteries and classical philosophy with the newly emerging faith of Christianity. This grossly unfair interpretation of their myths has contributed to the fact that Gnosticism remained a "faith forgotten," as G. R. S. Mead, one of its modern rescuers, called it. It was not until recent times, due largely to the efforts of C. G. Jung, Joseph Campbell, Gilles Quispel, and other enlightened scholars, that the recognition has dawned upon many that the Gnostics were not syncretist religious theoreticians, but practical psychologists of great insight and creative genius. Nowhere is this genius of the Gnostic proto-psychology more evident than in the story of Sophia, the daughter of the most high gods, who falls into the abyss of outer darkness and is redeemed by her own increasing self-knowledge and self-unfoldment.

Sophia is an Aion, a divinely emanated power-entity descending from the primordial pair of invisible and ineffable transcendental beings, referred to by the Valentinian Gnostics as Depth (masculine) and Silence (feminine). From Depth and Silence there came forth thirty emanations or Aions, i.e., patterns of psychic being or archetypes, arranged in pairs, composed of a masculine and a feminine Aion each.

41

The very youngest of these emanated beings, Sophia, a divine woman, becomes separated from her aionic mate, who in most variants of the myth is called Will. Separated from her masculine counterpart, she becomes subject to a condition of imbalance and begins to seek for Gnosis by mistaken or wrongful means. Having lost her twin, she no longer acts according to her nature, and her love for Divinity is perverted into *hubris*, or inordinate, overweening pride, which impels her to seek the understanding of the unfathomable Depth and Silence of the ultimate dual mystery by way of intellectual or philosophical inquiry. She abandons the way of the understanding or knowing heart *(gnosis kardias)* and devotes herself to the arrogant pursuit of knowledge by way of the power of the mind alone. This act of *hubris* causes a crisis, or catastrophy. Sophia falls from the height of her station in the *Pleroma* (fullness) of divine glory and descends into the dark world of confusion and terror.

Thus Sophia leaps forward and outward from the embrace of the divine wholeness and from the arms of her consort. Having failed to comprehend the nature of the primordial pair of Fore-Beginning (Depth) and Thought-Grace (Silence) she becomes convinced of the futility of her ill-conceived effort. Still, her passion for knowledge and her desire for the father-mother, brought forth from her being curious, formless entities, which came to subsist by themselves as living, unholy creatures in the abyss. (One is reminded here of the Klipoth of the *Kabbala*, as well as of the elementaries of H. B. Blavatsky, and last but not least, of the autonomous complexes of modern psychology.) In the Valentinian *Gospel of Truth*, some of these creatures are graphically described:

> It was ignorance concerning the Father which produced Anguish and Terror. Anguish became dense like a fog, so that no one could see. Therefore Error became fortified. It elaborated its own Matter in the Void.[2]

At this point a further curious event occurs. Sophia appears to separate into two personalities, one of which—the higher Sophia—is purified and steadied by the limiting powers of the void and returns to a state of union with her consort, thus restoring the integrity of the Pleromic divine order. (The ubiquitous mythological theme of the "shining twin" of the human personality that remains in heaven, identified by Jungian thought as the Self, also at times as the elder brother of the prodigal son of the Bible, is thus evident here.)

The lower Sophia, however, remains in the outer darkness where, in addition to the aforementioned complexes, she brings forth yet another fatherless abortion, a shapeless and ugly being of hypostatized immaterial substance, significantly described as "strengthless and female fruit" (the possible psychological implication being, that it is conceived without the conscious presence of the masculine component of the feminine psyche, called the *animus*). Gradually, numerous archetypes of light and darkness, powers of spirituality and materiality, come forth and surround Sophia. Among the beneficent forces we find the Christos and the Holy Spirit, both of whom appear to have a role very much like the classical Jungian archetype, for they act as organizing and constellating agencies around which both the forces of the Pleroma and of the Void order themselves according to archetypal patterns. The forces of the Void, made up largely by the externalized emotions of Sophia—namely her grief, fear, bewilderment, ignorance, and her desire to turn or convert to the light—become the roots of the material world with its four elements, which are directly derived from four of the major emotions of Sophia. The Demiurge, the necessary but tyrannical creating and preserving principle of the differentiated and material cosmos, comes into existence, as well as his spiritual counterpart, the Aion Jesus in whom the Pleroma is gathered together, and who is often portrayed as the offspring of the Christos (masculine) and of the Holy Spirit (feminine). Jesus descends into the void, and into the material universe, where he will rescue Sophia and overcome the dictatorial and patriarchal rule of the Demiurge, who holds Sophia in captivity. (Once again numerous mythological motifs from varied sources suggest themselves as useful analogies: Persephone held captive by Pluto in the nether world; Theseus venturing into the labyrinth to rescue the wisdom-maiden from the clutches of the bull-monster of earth; and many more.) Jesus thus becomes the ''perfect fruit of the Pleroma'' who contains all the elements of the supernal Aions, and who is the true *soter* or ''liberating savior,'' not in the sense of saving from sin, but rather after the fashion of all heroes who journey forth to rescue a beautiful damsel in distress.

The task of saving Sophia is accomplished by way of a relationship between Jesus and Sophia, which is frequently symbolized as a sexual and marital union, a true alchemical *hieros gamos* which brings about the purification of Sophia and of the authentic reawakening within her of the memories of the divine bliss of union with the supreme Godhead. Jesus thus becomes her true ''heavenly bridegroom,'' even as he became the spiritual lover of St. Theresa of Avila and of countless other mystics many centuries later. Chained to the tetramorphic prison of the four elements, composed of Earth (terror), Water (fear), Air (grief), and Fire (dissolution and corruption), Sophia awaits the coming of the liberator, who exorcises from her the four blind elemental emotions and thus frees her from the cross of imprisonment. Prior to the coming of Jesus, the spiritual Christos has already begun the redeeming work, when in a mystical manner he appeared to Sophia in a form stretched out on the transcosmic Tau-shaped cross, awakening her to the awareness of her plight and infusing into her the aroused longing for the celestial beloved. (Thus is the personal psyche often prepared for the coming of individuation by prefigurative experiences of dreams, visions, and so forth.) Sophia is therefore psychically prepared for the liberating love affair with the incarnate Jesus, who then takes her unto himself as his consort.

The enigmatic, yet ever-alluringly sublime figure of Mary Magdalene of the New Testament rises at this point to an important position of symbolic significance in the Sophianic romance of liberation. Numerous passages in the Gnostic variants of the gospels reveal this feminine figure as the physical embodiment of Sophia, and her relationship with

Jesus is frankly portrayed as a *hieros gamos* with physical as well as spiritual overtones. We read in the *Gospel of Philip:*

> The Sophia whom they call barren is the mother of the angels. And the consort of Christ is Mary Magdalene. The lord loved Mary Magdalene more than all his disciples, and kissed her on her mouth often...they said to him, why do you love her more than all of us? The saviour answered: Why do I not love you like her?[3]

The significant element in this aspect of the myth for our purposes is that the female hypostasis represented by Sophia can be made free only through a spiritual pairing which will make her whole. The psychological implications of this are of the greatest importance.

Another interesting element in most forms of the myth is the statement that since Sophia, through her waywardness, has broken the bounds of the twelve ruling powers of the zodiac and has put herself at odds with them, it now becomes necessary for her to approach each in turn and apologize to them in what have been called the twelve repentances. She cries out to the twelve powers and overcomes their binding influence by way of elaborately expressed ritual supplications and magical formulae which are addressed to the Light toward which she aspires. The poetic beauty of these repentances may become evident to the reader even from the following brief samples:

> Rescue me, O Light, from this lion-faced Power and from the emanations of divine Arrogance; for it is Thou, O Light, in whose light I have believed, and I have trusted to thy light from the first...it is Thou who shalt save me...Now then, O Light, leave me not in the Chaos...do not abandon me, O Light, for...they have desired my power, saying to one another all at once: 'The Light has forsaken her; seize her, and let us take away all the light in her.'[4]

> Let those who would take my power be turned to the Chaos and put to shame, let them be swiftly turned to the Darkness...let everyone who seeks after the Light rejoice and be glad!...Thou, then, O Light, Thou art my Saviour...hasten and save me out of this Chaos.[5]

> O Light...let Thy light come down on me, for my light in me
> has been taken and I am in misery...for my power is filled
> with darkness, and my light has gone down to the Chaos...to
> the Darkness below...and I have spread out my hands up to
> Thee and cried out...with all the light in me...I hymn Thee
> in the region on high, and again in the Chaos.[6]

In ever-ascending circles she approaches the Light, guided
and aided by archangelic and angelic powers, and strengthened by the force infused into her being by her heavenly
bridegroom, Jesus. Joy now replaces the deep anguish and
sorrow of her earlier experiences and her hymns change
from the keynote of supplication to that of thanksgiving:

> I have been rescued in the Chaos and loosed from the bonds
> of Darkness; I have come to Thee, O Light for Thou hast be-
> come Light on every side of me...and the emanations of the
> Arrogant one which opposed me Thou has hindered with Thy
> Light...Now hast Thou covered me with the Light of Thy
> Stream and hast purified in me all evil matters...I have become
> encouraged by Thy light...and have shone in Thy great power,
> for it is Thou who savest always![7]

> The Light has become Saviour for me and has changed for me
> my darkness into light; He has rent the Chaos that surrounded
> me and girded me with light!...My power, sing to the Light,
> and forget not all the powers of the Light!...All powers that
> are in me, sing to the Name of His Holy Mystery...which has
> filled thee with refined light, and thy beginning shall be re-
> newed as an Invisible of the Height.[8]

Then, after several other attacks upon her by the powers
of darkness, which continue to assault and trouble her right
up to the very threshold of the highest aionic home of the
Light, the dark powers fall away from her side and she
enters her eternal home of boundless light and unsurpassed
joy. Praising and hymning the liberating glory of the Light,
she bursts forth once more into a paen of praise:

> O Light, I shall reveal to Thee how Thou hast saved me, and
> how Thy wonders have taken place in the human race!...Thou
> hast smashed the high gates of Darkness together with the
> mighty bolts of the Chaos...and I have come up through the
> gates of the Chaos![9]

Thus ends the story of faithful Sophia, the suffering and aspiring prototype and archetype of agonizing and ultimately liberated womanhood. From the glorious Light-realm she descended into alienation and chaos, was afflicted by the terrors of servitude and ignorance, but calling to the Light she received strength and sanctification by the way of her union with the saving bridegroom Jesus, and led by His divine hand she resumed her deserted Seat of Wisdom in the realm of the Ineffable Ones. Like all authentic archetypal myths, the story of Sophia possesses a timeless grandeur that renders it suitable and applicable to the concerns of any place and time. The current interest in women's rights and liberation could most profitably address itself to the lessons to be derived from the Sophianic myth. This myth, like others, fixes in graspable forms the universal, archetypal realities which underlie psychic experience. Modern psychology is increasingly recognizing the immense value of mythological imagery and thinking for the purpose of self-knowledge and true spiritual liberation within the psychic life of persons. A contemporary Jungian psychoanalyst of outstanding credentials, Dr. Edward F. Edinger, writes in a recent article:

> A knowledge of mythological images is an essential requirement if the ego is to have a conscious relation to the deeper layers of the psyche, for they provide forms and categories of understanding by which to grasp and consciously realize the nature of the trans-personal powers. The ego that lacks these categories of understanding will be either confined to the shallow level of personalistic meanings, or it will be taken over by the archetypal energies and forces to live them out unconsciously.[10]

An insightful appreciation of mythology could indeed become an important modality of self-understanding, not only on the level of the individual psyche, but within the context of the wider culture itself. Like Athena's fabled mirror which enabled Perseus to face the terrors of Medusa, archetypal myths may enable men and women to face the perilous and painful problems arising out of the changing inner and outer roles of men and women in society.

Viewed psychologically, the mythological heroine, Sophia, might be defined as a personification of the urge to individuation. The story itself follows with some modification the classical pattern of the four stages of the Greek drama, namely *agone*, or "contest"; *pathos*, or "defeat"; *threnos*, or "lamentation"; and *theophania*, or "the divinely accomplished solution and redemption." This fourfold pattern is a manifestation within the dramatic medium of the fourfold image of totality, the celebrated psychological tetramorph. C. G. Jung has found the number four to be representative of the goal of wholeness within the soul, and discovered that four stages are found in all significant processes of psychological development in all psychotherapeutic processes that involve a deep integration of the unconscious. As in the individuation process, some phrases in the Sophianic myth repeat themselves, although their character remains the same.

Of singular importance to the spiritual predicament of women in our times is the message of the initial *agone* or "contest" of our myth, with the addition of the ensuing *pathos*. Why is Sophia cast out from the paradisical state of her aionial bliss? The reason is her separation from her light-twin and spouse, called by the name Will. Differentiation of the feminine ego brings with itself the dropping into unconsciousness of the contrasexual psychic component, or soul-maleness of woman, called in Jungian psychology the *animus*. The *animus* does not become nonexistent, but by becoming unconscious it can exercise its influence upon the feminine psyche from the shadowland of the unconscious, and its influence becomes distorted. The less aware the woman is of her *animus*, the more malefic and dangerous the influence of this obscured twin becomes. (One must remember, of course, that man experiences an analogous situation with his own submerged feminine component, the *anima*.) The separation of Sophia from her twin coincides with her mistaken effort to obtain Gnosis by way of the intellect and will, in lieu of the *gnosis kardias*, the "way of the knowing heart." An unbalanced being is capable only of an unbalanced attempt at individuation, and such unbal-

48

anced efforts are bound to fail. The result is a profound alienation from the light-world of the Self, a falling out of the *Pleroma* of psychic health and truth. The *pathos* has begun.

The Gnostics were profoundly aware of this psychological predicament and gave utterance to it in many places. Thus we read in the *Gospel of Philip:*

> When Eve was in Adam, there was no death; but when she separated from him, death came into being. Again if she go in, and he take her to himself, death will no longer exist.[11]

> If the woman had not separated from the man, she would not die with the man. His separation became the beginning of death. Because of this Christ came, in order that he might remove the separation which was from the beginning, and again unite the two; and that he might give life to those who died in the separation, and unite them.[12]

The death referred to here is not the death of the body, but the death of the spirit which both men and women undergo when they lose conscious contact with their contrasexual selfhood. Similarly, the goal of individuation or spiritual union is described by the Gnostic Jesus in the *Gospel of Thomas:*

> When you make the two one, and when you make the inner as the outer and the outer as the inner and the above as the below, and when you make the male and the female into a single one, so that the male will not be male and the female not be female, when you make eyes in the place of an eye, and a hand in the place of a hand, and a foot in the place of a foot, and an image in the place of an image then shall you enter the Kingdom.[13]

The stage of *threnos*, ''lamentation,'' is represented by the innumerable vicissitudes and trials of Sophia, all characterized by her state of sorrow and vocalised dejection. Alienation and bondage to the powers of this world, the chief of which might be described as the archetypal male chauvinist, the Demiurge (often equated with the male Jewish *pantheos*, ''YHVH''), are some of the characteristic afflictions experienced by Sophia at this stage of the story. Like women today, she laments her state of bondage, and again like many women today she seeks for a way out in various counter-productive efforts of angry and frenzied emotions which instead of liberating her merely tie her to the elemental cross of servitude. Paraphrasing the quoted words of Dr. Edinger, the woman desirous of liberation who lacks these mythological and gnostic categories of understanding will be either confined to the shallow level of personalistic meanings, or she will be taken over by the archetypal energies and forced to live them out unconsciously. In these two possibilities, indeed, lie the principal dangers of the contemporary scene of woman's liberation. Shallow personalistic concerns void of a deeper psychic content of individuation may demand and even receive many of the trappings of freedom, but this freedom, like so many freedoms gained in violent revolutions, could become the seedbed of new and dreadful tyrannies. When neurotic pressures, occasioned by past hurt and grief, lead to an unconscious, forced living out of the archetypal energies of the suppressed man in women, authentic psychic growth becomes impossible. Unless the current drive for the liberation of womankind is to be accompanied by a collective form of psychological insight which recognizes that the outer liberation can at best be a symbolization of the inward emancipation of the spirit, the entire phenomenon of contemporary feminism is doomed to dismal failure. The emancipation of the spirit alluded to here presupposes a *hieros gamos*, an authentic amalgamation of the *anima* and *animus* within the individual and collective psyche of those desirous of liberation, whether they be men or women.

Great indeed were and still are the collective injustices heaped upon women by men in our civilization. Psychologically they may be said to have resulted from the inability of men to relate their conscious selfhood to the hidden feminine Aion within their unconscious. The less men knew (in the true Gnostic sense of Gnosis) their *anima*, the more they feared her, and the more intent they were to ''keep women in their place.'' Outward tyranny is inevitably symbolic of inner rigidity and insecurity, which is occasioned by a lack of individuation or, in Gnostic terminology, of

Gnosis. Again and again throughout history men have confused their feminine self with the woman without, and in their confusion they have alternately feared and loved, repressed and exalted her. They honored her as mistress, wife, and mother, but only very infrequently did they give her full recognition as a being totally in her own right. Conversely, women, instead of assimilating their own interior masculinity in a balanced and spiritually productive manner, tend to struggle against the consciousness of their animus either by cultivating an image of themselves that is exaggeratedly and unreally feminine, or by yielding to animus possession from the unconscious level. This latter phenomenon is gaining victims as the result of some spiritually unenlightened radical liberationist tendencies today. The woman compulsively emulating patterns of thought and activity which appear to her masculine, will at best only succeed in fashioning herself into a sad caricature of the hitherto traditional male figure. She will be as pitiful to behold as her mincingly effeminate counterpart of the anima possessed, biologically male gender. Both of these extremes represent miscarriages of the all-important effort to integrate the component of the self of the opposite polarity into consciousness. The result is Sophia's fall from the Pleroma, alienation, psychic suffering and misery.

In the myths of antiquity we find the story of the Amazons, a tribe of man-hating, martial women who exhibit practically every sign of animus possession known to psychology. It is perhaps significant that in the legend Jason has to evade the danger presented by the Amazons prior to his obtaining the Golden Fleece, for the hostile animus or anima is always a powerful obstacle on the path of the recovery of authentic selfhood. Men who are hostile to women are in truth hostile to their own internal femininity, and women who because of actual or magnified wrongs become hostile to men are thereby putting great obstacles in the way of their true self-actualization. Our civilization may be said to have rejected women because it rejected its own anima. It would be fatal if women would now collectively reject their animus and thus prevent it from reaching consciousness as it should and, indeed, must. Two wrongs do not make a right in the psyche any more than in ordinary life.

The Gnostic myth of Sophia calls our attention most impressively to the predicament in which we find ourselves, and it points with sublime poetic power toward the goal of ultimate wholeness. Sophia is, of course, not merely the feminine soul, but the soul of every person. All of us, men and women alike, are in desperate need of the restoration of our wholeness by way of the slow but steady accomplishment of the union of our outward selfhood with the hidden glory indwelling. Like Sophia we wander over the face of this earth, our glory degraded and prostituted like that of Mary Magdalene, while through the vastness of the aionic regions there descends the ''ever coming One,'' our divine bridegroom, the Logos of the most high God. Thus the *theophania,* the divine resolution of the great drama is ever here, and it always closely resembles the one symbolized in the myth of Sophia. Anima and animus, Eros and Logos, Magdalene-Sophia and Jesus are destined to unite in the bridal chamber of the soul. The Christ in us and the Sophia in us are our twin hopes of glory, seeking each other in holy longing and divine desire. The Gnostics were perhaps the only school of thought in the history of the Western tradition who consciously recognized this fact, and who gave utterance to its existence as an intrapsychic process. The *Gospel of Thomas* puts it well:

> Jesus said: If you bring forth that within yourselves, that which you have will save you. If you do not have that within yourselves, that which you do not have will kill you.[14]

The salvation of man is union with the woman within his soul, while the liberation of woman depends on her effective union with her twin Aion of psychic masculinity. Responding to an apparently male chauvinist Apostle Peter, who wished to exclude Mary Magdalene from the circle of disciples ''because women are not worthy of life,'' Jesus says in the same Gospel:

> See, I shall lead her, so that I will make her male, that she too
> may become a living spirit...For every woman who makes
> herself male will enter the Kingdom.[15]

And, as we might add, so will every male, who by assimilating the internal Holy Sophia into himself, makes himself
female.

It would be a mistake to assume that the Gnostic myths
are without vital relevance in today's world. We may no
longer possess the detailed techniques of the Gnostic disciplines of transformation: their sacraments, their priesthood
(which unlike the Christian, was available to both men and
women), their majestic dramatic rituals, their secret individuation rite of the bridal chamber. Still, the Gnostics themselves reminded us of the perennial availability of the means
of liberation when they made Sophia exclaim:

> The Light is good and just; this is why He will grant me my
> way to be rescued in my transgression...For all the Gnoses
> of the Light are saving means, and there are mysteries for every
> one who seeks after the regions of his inheritance...To every
> one who trusts in the Light He will give the mystery suited
> to him, and his soul shall be in the regions of the Light.[16]

We may be assured that the means of liberation are at hand
and available; indeed, as it has been said about Deity, they
are nearer than breathing and closer than hands and feet.
The true liberation of the man within women and of the
woman within men cannot be shouted into existence by the
conscious will and intellect. Haste makes waste, for it bears
testimony to the unholy pressures of the unenlightened ego,
as symbolized by the unwisdom of Sophia prior to her turning to the Light. As Sophocles says in the final lines of *An-
tigone:*

> Where wisdom is, there happiness will crown a piety that
> nothing will corrode. But high and mighty words and ways
> are flogged to humbleness, till age, beaten to its knees, at last
> is wise.

The sublime figure of Sophia did not disappear with the ancient Gnostics. An ever-mounting body of scholarly evi-

dence indicates that she remained the principal inspiration behind innumerable mystical symbolizations of the feminine wisdom throughout the ages. From the Shekinah of the Kabbalists to the mysterious feminine muse of the Sufi poets, and from the cult of the Virgin Mary to the crypto-Gnostic reverence of the woman practiced by the Troubadours and beyond, the hidden hand of Sophia is to be discerned. Neither is her undisguised Gnostic form without its votaries, for the current upsurge of interest in esoteric traditions has brought with it a slow revival of the never-quite-extinct Gnostic movement. Myth, poetry, liturgy and other modalities of Gnostic individuation are in evidence among today's Gnostics once more. Although in true Gnostic manner she shuns the limelight, Our Lady Sophia is alive and well today, and her archetypal power is still capable of inspiring and exalting those who revere her. The *gnosis kardias*, the ''wisdom of the understanding heart,'' is still awake and responsive to the ancient admonition of the Gnostics, those forgotten wandering minstrels of Lady Sophia:

> The day from on high has no night...Say then in your heart that it is in you who are this perfect day...That it is in you that this light, which does not fail dwells...Speak of the truth with those who seek it, and of the gnosis with those who in their error have committed sins...You are the children of the understanding heart...[17]

By way of a conclusion for this essay, and also as a proof of the continued presence in our day of the understanding heart, is a previously unpublished poem written by a present-day Gnostic poet, Linda S. Sang, entitled *Sophia:*

> O Light, have mercy upon me,
> For there is no virtue in the cup of forgetfulness,
> If chaos were only chaos,
> I might in time fall asleep upon the green grass.
> I might forget that perfect, symmetrical silence
> Where the angels sing hymns to Thee.
> Where every voice is a being, and every being a voice,
> Each tuned to its eternal note.
> Where the harmony of the fullness is silence,
> As the harmony of the rainbow is white.

Have mercy upon me, O Light,
For I have seen beauty by its own divinity destroyed,
And love by its deepest desire betrayed.
Day and night all the lovely abandoned things
Of the holy city cry out for redemption,
And a lost god looks out of every human eye.
I will never fall asleep again upon the green grass,
Hear my voice mingled with every prayer,
O Light, have mercy upon me!

References

1. C. G. Jung, *Collected Works*, vol. 4, Freud and Psychoanalysis. Bollingen Series, New York, 1961, p. 332.
2. *Evangelium Veritatis*, 17. 9-16.
3. *Gospel of Philip*, p. Logion 55.
4. *Pistis Sophia*, p. 56-59.
5. Ibid., p. 60-61.
6. Ibid., p. 67-68.
7. Ibid., p. 148-49.
8. Ibid., p. 162.
9. Ibid., p. 176-177.
10. Edward F. Edinger, "The Tragic Hero: An Image of Individuation," *Parabola*, Winter 1976, p. 66
11. *Gospel of Philip*, p. Logion 71.
12. Ibid., p. Logion 78.
13. *The Gospel According to Thomas*, p. Logion 22.
14. Ibid., p. Logion 70.
15. Ibid., p. Logion 114.
16. *Pistis Sophia*, p. 77-79.
17. *Evangelium Veritatis*, 19. p. 6-15.

3
Oya: Black Goddess of Africa

JUDITH GLEASON

The goddess Oya, of African origin, manifests herself in various natural forms: the river Niger, tornadoes, strong winds generally, fire, lightning, and buffalo. She is also associated with certain cultural phenomena among the Yoruba people (the first to worship her), notably with masquerades constructed of bulky, billowing cloth—ancestral apparitions—and with funerals. To the leader of the market women in Yoruba communities she offers special protection and encouragement in negotiation with civil authorities and arbitration of disputes. Thus, one may speak of Oya as patron of feminine leadership, of persuasive charm reinforced by àjé—an efficacious gift usually translated as "witchcraft." Although Oya is associated with pointed speech, most of what she's about is highly secret. Always vanishing, she presents herself in concealment. More abstractly, Oya is the goddess of edges, of the dynamic interplay between surfaces, of transformation from one state of being to another. She is a jittery goddess, then, but with a keen sense of direction.

To describe and elaborate upon Oya's various manifestations is inevitably to present an idea not commonly thought of when the word *goddess* is mentioned. Oya's patterns, persisting through many media—from air to the human psyche—suggest something like a unified field theory of a certain type of energy that our culture certainly doesn't think of as feminine. To speak of her thus integrally, it has been necessary to attempt to combine two ways of thinking: African and European. And, as the wind can be both playful and violent, so this religious idea of the persistence of Oya in radically varied contexts may be entertained variously: sometimes metaphorically, other times with a discursive earnestness that may offend both agnostic and believer in some other religious system.

But challenging the accepted view (in this case, of goddesses) is not tantamount to claiming the right to make others share one's vision; for this would mean attempting to seduce the world to madness. Simply to present the vision involves the painful recognition that a lot of hard work has to be done on its material. The chaotic has to become sequential. Symbols have to be modeled.[1] Containing walls of words must be built. The Yoruba have already formulated careful words about Oya and the other gods with whom she shares their cosmos. These words have been heeded throughout. Each section of the book presents a sacred, oracular text in translation with commentary. So however widely the argument may range—touching upon various fields of discourse, moving from continent to continent, however anecdotal and personal it may at times become, these "likely stories" from the Yoruba may act as philosophical fulcrum.

It seems appropriate to introduce the goddess to the reader through some of her traditional Yoruba praises, uttered by her votaries—those who take her part, depend on her, and hope in the utterance to render her benevolent to themselves. Oracular stories, to be found later on, praise her too. However, the diviners who recite them are concerned not only with getting people who ought to be worshiping her to do so, but with keeping Oya herself in line as well. The Yoruba oracle, known as Ifa, is a sort of regulatory agency created to foster a balance of forces in society, the universe, and the human soul. The worshipers of a particular god or goddess, by contrast, shamelessly extol his or her powers. They would, if they could, seduce the world to their own, their god's, own brand of madness.

Judith Gleason

Traditional Praises of Oya

I
Dark forest, deepest obscurity
which grabs and swallows you in the forest,
Wind of Death
tears the calabash, tears the bush.
Shango's wife
with her thumb tears out the intestines of the liar.
Great Oya, yes.

Only she seizes the horns of the buffalo,
Only she confronts the returning dead.

Swiftly she gets her things together, swiftly.
Oya, messenger, carry me on your back,
don't set me down.

She walks alongside violence
Ripeness of the afternoon
Powerful river
Fire burns; so does the sun.

She wakes up dancing with fire
Nine, the flashes of lightning
Secrecy sees her.
Fly to us, Oya.

Nine-headed apparition
tramples upon the evil mound
Until nightfall she supports her fighting child.
Lengthily she extends herself across the land.
We have threaded the needle of death in the house.

She burns like fire in the hearth, everywhere at once.
Tornado, quivering solid canopied trees
Great Oya, yes.
Whirlwind masquerader, awakening,
courageously takes up her saber.

II
Iya O, Oya O
Mother, Oya

It is not from today that she is honorable
but from long ago.
She arrives at Witch's house
dragging muddy feet.
Egun of Elegba, huge cloth,
she dares confine the elder to his room.
Flood who prevents everyone from leaving the house.
Iya O, Oya O
Mother, Oya
She's the one who employs truth against wickedness
She stands at the frontier
between life and death
Customs officer of multitudes!
Wife of Ogun
She picked up the drum to play and tore it to pieces,
She danced under the Odan tree and tore that to pieces.
Iya O, Oya O

She's the one who makes a pact
with someone wanting to bear a child
and doesn't break it.

She carries the lamp into the house
and strolls around leisurely
pacing in circles
waiting for the Creator to come.
Do you think you are safe in the house?
If you think too much about her
you probably won't run into her.
She quarrels with you and you never win.
Even if she doesn't quarrel with you
she'll terrify.
Everything she does is a big production.

Iya O, Oya O
If it's a whirling beat, she'll dance to it,
If it's Bembe, she'll dance it, O she'll dance it.
Who dances to Bata drums? O she dances to them.
Who dances to Shekere? O she dances to it.
Wife of Ogun, that's the one who dances it
whatever it is.

59

Judith Gleason

She has been performing Egungun masquerade
for a long, long time.

Oya had so much honor
she turned around and became Orisha.
Oya guards the road into the world
and out of it.
Oya, respect to the awesome!

III
Insatiable vagina
Wizard's medicine
Child who carries the corpse
Fighting Oya will come into her own
Fighting Oya will come into her own.

Sunrise that hits the sky, pa pa
Broom, which handles reluctantly
May she sweep in money!

Frowning canopy of huge tree
beholds the strong wind
Purifying stream of air
fought the lagoon
beat upon the mountain
Honest person who inhabits the sky
Honest person of the sky
cleaned out the swamp
leaped over the mountain
stripped off somebody's head.
Oya, don't take offense.
Eeepa! *Oya, please go easy!*

The first set of praises is excerpted from a collection made by Pierre Verger. I have translated them into English from his interlinear text.[2] The second set (Part Two) were sung by a small group of old women, clothed for the occasion in red and purple, in Ogbomosho, Nigeria, on February 15, 1977. It was Oya's day of the week, and they had gathered rather informally to do her homage in a compound housing her shrine. Bata drums, played by men, accompanied their singing and eventual dancing. The keeper of the important shrine where the praising occurred was also a man, who took nominal charge of the event, which effectively the women ran in collaboration.

Two special performances linger on in memory. Midway through the singing, a youngish woman dressed like a beggar in burlap appeared at the entrance to the compound. She entered shyly, then gallivanted crazily about for a bit. Her face was smeared with gray ashes. She was not mad; she was fulfilling an obligation. Long barren, this woman had begged Oya for a child. Oya spoke through the cowries and said that her wish would be granted but that she must promise for a year after the birth to perform like this every fourth day at the praise session: a fool for the goddess! The second haunting image was that of a very old, blind woman who had seated herself out of sight in the shadows of an adobe veranda that encircled the compound. As the praising broke into dancing, she got up from her stool and danced privately. She wore an old wrap and no blouse. Her feet, of course, were bare. The expression on her face remains indescribable.

The third set of praises was sung to me by Oya Kupolo, a young priestess of Oya, on February 17, 1983, in Ologbin compound, Oyo City. The first three lines of this sequence, a sort of introduction, mention three supernatural powers related to the type of Oya enshrined in that particular compound—witch, wizard, and collective family ghost—and to the three correlative types of medicine possessed by the Ologbin. From then on it is Oya herself who is praised—an Oya, however, of an especially martial sort. It was not Oya's day but rather that of another god, Ogun, hunter and warrior, Oya's first husband. . . .

Of the countless household and cult-house shrines containing the mystery of Oya, one might roughly sketch a composite. A covered earthenware vessel set upon the floor, in a corner, or upon a raised altar of some sort (perhaps a simple dais made of packed mud, perhaps the shelf of a common cupboard) contains her quintessential power—the heaviest form in which this may be grounded and held by human initiates. No stranger sees what's inside this receptacle, which might be painted a deep red or draped with variegated cloth. Affixed to this great pot or arranged nearby are the various symbols of the goddess: buffalo horns, locust pod or the larger seed-vessel of the Caribbean tree called flamboyant, fly whisk, saber or machete, perhaps a copper crown, a necklace of Oya's special beads (coral, or brown glass beads with a black and a white stripe, alternating with red beads, which "fix" their power), in New York a playful whirligig with bells upon it. Offerings of food might be set before or upon the altar—fried bean cakes and glossy purple eggplants, for example. With the ineluctable voice of objects these things also praise Oya. To my own altar I've added more toys for her to play with: a delicate wooden top painted deep purple and a red boomerang, light but lethal.

How does one fall into the worship of Oya? Yoruba sages say that when a person is born he or she "chooses a head," thereby becoming endowed with a portion of cosmic essence, which is the soul's matrix. Such primal substances of which our various heads are made can be experienced in their natural manifestations as water, wind, fire, tree, and so on. These environing forces are not worshiped as such but rather as loci of beings the Yoruba call Orisha *(òrìsà)*. These Orisha are equivalent to the *megaloi theoi* of the Greeks and to the *lwa* served by practitioners of traditional Haitian religion. They are numinous archetypal forces. They are wounds that heal us, sanctifying madnesses. The word *Orisha* literally means "head-calabash." Calabashes, which grow on trees in tropical climates, are used as containers—of water, of food, of anything that can be put into them: magical substances as well as humdrum items. Our heads, like calabashes, contain a modicum of sacred substance, shared with Orisha, whose portions are plenitude....

Old women, the grandmothers are a strong, affecting presence in religious places all over the world. They light the candles. They arrange the flowers. They sew the altar cloths, the vestments, the shrouds. When speaking of the Yoruba system of belief, it is important to point to the predominance of feminine symbolism as well. Already in speaking of shrines, of destiny, of the very gods, we have visualized a succession of opaque containers rounded about hidden matrices. The feminine is primary to the Yoruba imagination. Womankind, therefore, is regarded with ambivalence. Female passion, potentially overwhelming, in turn is contained by male structures of thought and language (including that of the Ifa oracle), which then by their own logic exclude women, except for occasional grandmothers, from enclaves and conclaves of authority. Even grandmothers are suspect. They might be of that breed of unseen female beings who before birth have chosen to use their special gifts for destructive purposes. A woman who has *àjé* won't admit it. Thus she cannot be overtly connected to her shadow-sisters. In true womanly fashion, she'll contain it. Secrecy is feminine. Secrecy too is primary in the Yoruba world-view. The old women praising Oya were very powerful.

How Yoruba women come to terms with this dichotomy is instructive to us whose society is premised upon metaphysical imaginings the opposite of rounded. From the pillar of flame to the latest guided missile, our icons thrust themselves upon the world, the sky. Even our bodies are no longer opaque to the prying gaze of scientific culture. So far are they from being considered prototypes of the sacred container that their very fullness has been aesthetically deplored. Thus rigorously we join in to flatten our tummies. And when we would go to work in man's polis, fashion designers coax us into business suits whose shape is the diametrical opposite of those wraps and blouses worn by women of Africa, who, whatever their problems, however discountenanced for becoming increasingly outspoken (in the face of a new multinational sexism), still prize whatever it is that makes them undeniably women.

What is especially interesting about Oya in human context is her refusal to stay out of the enclaves of cult and culture preempted by male authority. She has, potentially, a sharp tongue, which occasionally she wields like a sword. Now and again her mouth spits fire. Furthermore, though

she's rounded, though she might stay for a time in her corner (which is where her altars are always placed), suddenly she's storming all over the place, a revolutionary.[3] So she
has to be made part of the picture. Incorporated into the
establishment, how does she behave then? What part of her
boldness must she give up?

If excluded altogether, Oya turns unimaginably violent.
She has whirled her way into the Yoruba pantheon. (She
isn't natally Yoruba.) She has even managed to set herself
indispensably in the midst of the male ancestral cult. But
for millennia our monotheisms have ignored her type. Even
this "polytheistic paganism" that James Hillman advocates,[4]
tends to admit only more temperate Greek goddesses between the rather pristine sheets of its books and articles.
The inclement types require male friends, consorts, advocates.

Just as I was about to return to Brazil, source of its inspiration, to work on the final chapter of this book, the following words appeared in print to provide a social justification,
even urgency, I hadn't recognized. Christopher Whitmont
makes a brilliant connection between the inner turbulence
many of us have been experiencing and common concern
with the fate of the earth. Since his words provide Oya with
a context, I quote them here at length.

> The Goddess is now returning. Denied and repressed for
> thousands of years of masculine domination, she comes at a
> time of dire need. For we walk through the valley of the
> shadow of nuclear annihilation. . . . Amidst tremendous tran-
> sition and upheaval, the Goddess is returning. Traditional male
> and female roles in society are being challenged. The feminine
> call for a new recognition arises simultaneously with the vio-
> lence that threatens to get out of hand. This strange coinci-
> dence eludes our understanding. Here mythology
> unexpectedly comes to our aid. . . . The oldest deities of war-
> fare and destruction were feminine, not masculine. . . . These
> archaic goddeses had dominion over both love *and* war. They
> were credited with both chastity and promiscuity, nurturing
> motherliness and bloodthirsty destructiveness. But they were
> not at all concerned with conquest and territorial expansion.
> These were male obsessions. Rather, these goddesses
> monitored the life cycle throughout its phases: birth, growth,

love, death and rebirth. Evidently today our endangered life cycle needs divine monitoring. In the depths of the unconscious psyche, the ancient Goddess is arising. She demands recognition and homage. If we refuse to acknowledge her, she may unleash forces of destruction. If we grant the Goddess her due, she may compassionately guide us toward transformation.[5]

. . . . Oya is her simplest name. It is a verb form conveying her passage as an event with disastrous consequences. *Oya*, meaning "She tore" in Yoruba. And what happened? A big tree, as we already know from her praises, getting in the way of the storm, wildly agitated its branches. Perhaps its crown got lopped off. She tore. A river overflowed its banks. Whole cloth was ripped into shreds. Barriers were broken down. A tumultuous feeling suddenly destroyed one's peace of mind. *"Eeepa!"* one exclaims, by way of homage. *"Eeepa Heyi!"* What a goddess!

In Brazil to which she voyaged, along with other African gods, in the heads of worshipers chained in the holds of slave ships, Oya is preferably known as Yansan, which (again, in Yoruba) means "Mother of Nine." These progeny to which she gave birth are, geographically, nine estuaries where her river empties into the sea. But Brazil is far away from the brackish purgatory. The nine her worshipers are thinking of belong to the mystery play over which she presides. Behind the curtain of death she gives birth to nine anomalous beings whose youngest reenters our world with a strange voice, an odd shape, and power of chastisement as well as blessing. But on whichever side of the Atlantic, nine is always Oya's number: an arithemetical wonder, which, when multiplied by anything, always returns to itself in the magically added digits of the product. And this is how I heard her called for the first time, Yansan.

In 1967, in a Macumba cult house on the outskirts of Rio, an old woman possessed by what they call a *preto velho* (literally "old black"—the ghost of an African slave) suddenly rose from her chair, spun, stopped, and pointed directly at my face. "Yansan!" *(Iansã)* she cried. Thus, someone who had never quite known what to make of herself had been deeply claimed. To say that an iron shackle had been abruptly torn from her heart, however, would be melodramatic and not really accurate, pace C. G. Jung.[6] The process, though for many years unaccountable, was gradual. That voice of the former slave would not have been heard had not its auditor already been involved in researching the Brazilian career of a long-dead African queen. Now in hindsight, this queen, Agotimè, a short sequel to whose story will be given in the final section of this book, was a human counterpart of Yansan-Oya, the goddess.[7]

That Oya's cultural manifestations are African is important. Her blackness matters—historically, politically, kinesthetically, even ecologically and psychologically. Without attempting to seduce the mad, white world into sanity, it may at least be argued that rather than planning to dump nuclear waste upon the underpopulated African continent, our leaders would do well to spend some time there learning about human relations, about drumming and dancing, about natural healing practices, and, incidentally, about the joy of living. I cannot go along with a Dutch gentleman I heard lecture on venerating a Black Madonna who wasn't in any way black except for dark paint and a liaison to the ''darker'' (in his parlance), unexpressed side of his own inflexible upbringing. The Black Madonna is African.

At the museum of the Villa Giulia in Rome I saw for the first time a type of drinking cup (kantharos) that exactly portrays the juxtaposed identity informing the tortuous steambed through which flow words telling her story: Oya! Between bowl and stem are two carefully modeled heads, back to back. One is the portrait of a white woman, the other of a black. Their hair has been arranged in parallel loops; indeed, one brain seems to be flowing into the other, and back and forth. Only their faces, looking out in opposite directions, are different. Inside that antique cup continues to brim liberation.

Notes

1. This is an almost-verbatim quotation from Marion Milner, cited by Seonaid M. Robertson, *Rosegarden and Labyrinth* (Dallas: Spring, 1982), pp. 186-187.

2. Pierre Verger, *Notes sur le culte des orisa et vodun. Mémoires de l'Institute Francais d'Afrique Noire,* no. 51 (1957), pp. 414-421 *passim.* The recording of the second sequence of praises, those from Ogbomosho, was transcribed by John O. Ogundipe. The third sequence was written down as dictated by my informant, Oya Kupolo, and the spellings were checked by Joseph Ologbin.

3. ''Pero Oya, con ser tan revolucionaria y tan valiente...es muy mujer, muy amante de su hogar. Pasa años sin salir, metida en su rincon.'' Lydia Cabrera, *El Monte* (Miami: Rema Press, 1968, 1st ed., 1954), p. 223.

4. Notably in *Re-Visioning Psychology* (New York: Harper Colophon Books, 1977).

5. Edward C. Whitmont, *Return of the Goddess* (New York: Crossroad Press, 1982), p. viii.

6. ''With more foreboding than real knowledge, most people feel afraid of the menacing power that lies fettered in each of us, only waiting for the magic word to release it from its spell....'' C. G. Jung *Collected Works,* 8, paragraph 405.

7. Agotimè (see Gleason, *Agotimè* [Viking Compass Books, 1971], like Oya, became involved in establishing a male ancestral cult in order to enable her son to become king. The psychology of woman as enabler (in Oya's case, of her consort, Shango) is discussed in Part Two. Agotimè too was revolutionary; her lover (the hypothetical Vivaldo) was a leader of a slave revolt, organized, curiously enough, by Malians. Finally, Agotimè's passion was the forest. When her cult-founding was done, she went off into Amazonas with her semimythological Tupi hunter. While working on *Agotimè* I had no knowledge of Yansan, only her name. For Agotimè was a Gege (Dahomean); therefore I studied the Gege cult in São Luis Maranhão. Similarly, while working through Oya's material, I didn't think of the parallel. Only now that the work is done have I done so— which makes one pause to wonder at the force of these archetypal configurations.

4

The Unknown Goddess

BEATRICE BRUTEAU

If, like St. Paul in Athens, we will walk about the city of
our soul, we may well stumble upon an altar inscribed *Ag-
nostai Theai*, ''To the Unknown Goddess.'' There may be
no worship offered to her there any more, or it may be of
so secret a nature that the common people of our city—our
everyday thoughts—are quite unaware of it. But the presence of the Goddess herself has never departed from her
holy place in our consciousness, and now, as we enter what
many feel to be a ''new age,'' we sense that the Goddess
is somehow making her way back to us. But in just what
guise is so far unclear.

The feminine principle has been recognized by humanity
in various aspects. In times long past we have paid her
homage as the source of life, the sustainer, the healer, the
enlightener, the one who receives in death, and the giver
of immortality. She has been courted as the protector of love,
the image of beauty, and the object of desire. She has been
subordinated to male divinities, relegated to an auxiliary
position, the relative and supporting role appropriate to a
secondary and derived being. In this guise she easily became
the scapegoat for the ills and evils of humanity, the personification of temptation, sensuality, and sin. Her essence has
even been reduced to passivity, irrationality, and darkness.
At this point a strange positive appreciation of the dark, the
irrational, and the unconscious arose; it was said to be a
necessary complement to the light, the rational, and the conscious.

In our time we find these two images of the feminine the most popular: on the one hand, the combination plaything/consumer/supporter of everyday life, and on the other hand, the mysterious dark, irrational, unconscious aspect of ourselves from which issue "feelings," hunches, affections, and other unaccountable experiences. We admit the need to "get in touch with our feelings," to accept the rather murky traffic on our unconscious level, and to experience our bodies without guilt; and all this we attribute to the feminine principle, and suppose that we are acknowledging its sovereignty and paying it honor by so doing.

For my part, I feel uneasy with this image of the Goddess. I do not think we have gotten to the real root of her femininity in these descriptions, or that we have given due credit to our own aspirations toward creative novelty. Thus I believe that the Goddess is unknown in at least three senses: 1) in the obvious sense, in which the Goddess herself, by virtue of Her Godhead, is necessarily ineffable; 2) in the sense that we do not know what the identifying quality of the feminine principle is; and 3) in the sense that we do not know what particular aspect of herself the feminine will manifest in the new era which we are entering. Of course, if we understood something of (2), we would be better prepared to deal with (3). And perhaps we may gain some light on (2) by looking at an approach to (1).

A fascinating instance of the ancient worship of the Goddess, in which her ineffability was (we may interpret) realized, is that of the double Goddess whose mysteries were celebrated at Eleusis. I find this example helpful in the present inquiry because it suggests, I think, a tentative answer to the question of (2), and this in turn may point a direction for our speculation about (3). Eleusis is also appropriate because it makes contact with our own nebulous sense of the "return" of the Goddess.

The Anodos

The "return" of the Goddess is not a new idea. In the ancient world it was a symbol of a deep and powerful event in people's lives. The *anodos*, or "way back" or "way up," was told of the Goddess in many of her forms in classical Greece, but the most important of these "returns" was that recounted in the myth of the two Goddesses, Demeter and Persephone.

According to the myth, Demeter (Grain-Mother), who is responsible for the fruitfulness of the earth, has lost her daughter, Persephone, because the latter has been abducted by Hades and carried off to the underworld. In her grief Demeter has neglected the crops and wandered about the earth seeking her daughter. At length she learns that Persephone is in the underworld and finds the "way down" to that realm, where she visits and beholds her daughter. Demeter's descent is followed by her return, celebrated by the ancients in a magnificent festival. Persephone also is said, in a Homeric hymn, to return to the upper air, riding in the chariot of Hades as Queen of the Other World.[2]

When Demeter and Persephone, who is also called Kore (Maid, Virgin), are reunited they act as one Goddess; for instance, in their dissemination of the cultivated wheat culture to the world, thus bringing civilization. In many representations of them, it is difficult to tell them apart, and images of a single Goddess are not readily identified as mother or daughter. The fact seems to be that Demeter and Kore are the two faces of a single divinity who is also reported to undergo multiple transformations. As Jane Ellen Harrison says, "Demeter and Kore are two persons though one god."[3] The mythological tradition, says C. Kerenyi, "permits the soul to hold mother and daughter together and causes them to be identified with one another."[4]

The real meaning, then, of the *anodos*, which we also are expecting as a "return" of the feminine principle, may actually be the *reunion* of the two aspects of the Goddess, the *finding* of Kore by Demeter. Perhaps it was this reintegration of her being which the Goddess commemorated and celebrated in the mysteries established by her at Eleusis. And perhaps it was because the initiates, who had prepared themselves by fasting and silence even as Demeter had, and like her, had drunk the *kykleon*,[5] also "found" and were reunited with their own lost "Kore," that the Great

Mysteries continued in force for nearly two thousand years without ever betraying their secret.

The secret of Eleusis was not only a secret of which it was forbidden to speak *(aporheton)*, but a secret which could not be spoken *(arrheton)*. The secret was the Kore herself, the *arrhetos koura*, the "Ineffable Maiden," the only deity to be so called.[6]

Is it possible that we can find here a hint as to our own Agnosta Thea, the feminine principle which is rising again in our consciousness? Harrison insists that Demeter and Kore are not so much mother and daughter as mother and maiden, two phases of one being, and also notes that Demeter tends to be associated with the things of this world, while Kore belongs to the kingdom of the spirit and is concerned with things "beyond." The "mother" aspect of the Thea is our everyday world, our "mater-ial" and multiple world, our technical world, our restless world in quest of its "maiden" aspect, integral being and meaning.

Now we can begin to see why the "mother" and the "daughter" are such ambiguous figures. The mother seeks the maiden as her own earlier state, her original being, her source. But as her final integral meaning, the maid is her offspring, her fruit, her goal. (At Eleusis the building in which the mysteries were celebrated was called the Telesterion, from *telos*, "goal.") For us, the manyness and the oneness of our lives mutually imply one another, as experience and theory, individuals and community, variety of activities expressing one personality, and in many other ways. Especially in our evolutionary view of our world we see development taking place, both in ourselves singly and in the history of our humanity, as periods of integration alternating with periods of wandering, each giving rise to the one which follows it as it had itself grown out of its predecessor. If we feel that we are again approaching a time of the "return" of the Goddess, it is because the pressure on us to integrate our lives and find a principle of unity to give us a deep and organic meaning has again become urgent. We need to experience our source.

In the Eleusinian image, Kerenyi sees Demeter as seeking a part of herself when she searches for her daughter, and he argues that the duality of the "questing one" and the "found one"—the division of the original Goddess into mother and daughter—has "opened up a vision of the *feminine source of life*" to all of us, men and women alike.[8] We may say that we are all seeking our original virginal, i.e., unitary or whole, self, and are saved when we are reunited with it.

The many gods preside over the many departments of life, giving alternately, as Swinburne says in his *Hymn to Prosperpine*, "labour and slumber," prototypes of all the finite "pairs of opposites." But only the unnameable Mistress, the Ineffable Maiden, gives death, that is, the absolute stopping of all the finite forms, thus entrance to the infinite. She is the Queen of the world beyond.

Demeter/Kore is the image of creative manifestation and return to unity, the eternal communion of the many and the one. When the restless wandering has achieved its goal and been reunited with its own source, then the one and the many and the whole marvelous movement between them can be summarized in the single ear of wheat shown the initiates in silence at the conclusion of the Great Mysteries.

The Root Meaning of Femininity

Kerenyi stresses his view that the mysteries enabled both men and women to become reunited with the feminine source of life. In the interpretation which I have suggested, the feminine is a dynamic union of the one and the many, a process in which the one ever becomes many and the many are ever reunited with and in the one. This process constitutes wholeness, and it is this wholeness which, I would suggest, is the root meaning of femininity.[9]

We are used to contrasting masculine and feminine as active and passive, bright and dark, positive and negative. I propose a different set of pairs: specialization and generalization, partiality and wholeness, analysis and synthesis. The two aspects of our consciousness do have a complementary relation to one another and do alternate in their emphasis in our lives. However, by putting the contrast in this way, I believe we can see more readily why we all feel that the feminine is our source and why reunion with it is what makes us feel complete, whole, and "at home at last."

We begin from a consciousness of wholeness; later we develop differentiations within this wholeness, we learn to analyze and categorize, to contrast and separate. We fragment our experience and concentrate on specializing in some chosen aspect of it. But eventually we begin to feel out of balance and to crave a reintegration of our lives, the finding of our original unity, the "maiden" aspect of ourselves. We wander and weep in our search but at length find her and are satisfied.

Another image of this is, of course, Odysseus, who goes forth on adventures and then wanders in his efforts to return home. "Home" is where the Woman eternally is, and rest is obtained only when he is again united with her.

Viewed historically, this cycle is a spiral. The Goddess—our feminine wholeness—is abducted, carried underground by the masculine principle of specialization. At the turning point of this eclipse, the feminine and the masculine are joined, and the Goddess returns, bringing the masculine principle, Plouton, and all his riches with her. But she does not come back the same as she went. Lost as a simple child, gathering flowers, she returns a Queen, ruling souls and bestowing immortality. Following this return, a new round is to be expected. The Goddess may give birth to a son who will in turn engage in various deeds, only to seek *his* completion again in the feminine. And so we move back and forth from focusing on specific matters, analyzing and classifying, to embracing all in an integral vision, an intuitive glimpse of the meaning of the whole of life. Each analysis begins from the higher level gained by the previous synthesis, and each succeeding synthesis incorporates the riches won by its antecedent analysis.

Looking back over our recent history, we seem to identify our masculine moment with the rise of individualism, especially with industrialization, and perhaps with the culture of the printed word. Thus we experience our contemporary movement away from the world so defined into something new, as a movement toward the feminine again. Roger Wescott, for instance, says that our sense of individualism was exaggerated in Renaissance and romantic Europe:

> Such hyperindividualism results not only in reduced cooperativeness (which is now putting such a strain on the social integration of the industrialized countries) but also in a lamentable narrowing of our awareness.[10]

Marshall McLuhan declares that "print created individualism and nationalism in the sixteenth century" and established its characteristics of "uniformity, continuity, and lineality" as the norm for human consciousness, hereafter known as "rationality." Any consciousness that did not conform to these principles was dismissed as "irrational" and identified with "illusion." For Wescott it is "the individual alertness of the waking state" that is the accepted norm in our culture. The fact that it alone is regarded as "real" by most people—dreams, trance, and cosmic or collective consciousness being classified as "mythical"—is in itself evidence of the "devolution" of our culture.[12]

But "mythical" is just what the new consciousness is, according to McLuhan. "Myth *is* the instant vision of a complex process." At the present time, he says, "we *live* mythically but continue to think fragmentarily."[13] And Wescott sees, with cautious optimism, a trend away from the artificial institutionalism of the past, which served in its day as a "behavioral chrysalis" protecting us during the difficult transition from the instinctive level of an earlier culture to the freedom of the new culture we are now called to enter.[14]

Henri Bergson had made a similar contrast. Tracing the progress of the *élan vital*, he distinguished instinct, intelligence, and intuition. Instinct "goes straight to the heart of life, through a divining sympathy or sure feeling for the vital." However, it is restricted to immediate and practical needs and does not give rise to invention. Higher than it is *intelligence,* which is creative but works only in terms of "the discontinuous, immobile, spatial world," represented by "concepts, words, and the structure of the positive sciences."[15] If a return to the power of instinct is to be had without surrendering the freedom of intelligence, a synthesis of the two is required. It is found in intuition, an "instinct that has become disinterested, self-conscious, capable of reflecting upon its object and of enlarging itself indefinitely."[16] In sum, "the *current of life*. . .is known by intuition, the *current of matter* and its practical extensions by intelligence." Re-enforced by intelligence, says Bergson, intuition reaches out to comprehend reflexively the cosmic *élan* itself, and this act constitutes *philosophy.*[17]

Neofeminism

If our review of the way to realization of the ineffable Goddess as reunion in dynamic harmony of our own multiplicity and unity has helped us to find the identifying quality of the feminine as the wholeness of process, we may now hazard a few guesses as to how the return of the Goddess may make itself felt in our own turn of evolution's helix.

McLuhan has argued that the previous (I will call it the masculine) era of mechanization was characterized by fragmentation, centralization, and superficiality. The new age of automation and the electric media, he says, is actually (although this is not apparent at first) characterized by integration, decentralization, and participation in depth. Human relations and social structures are much shaped by the very means of communication, so that the quality of the medium itself is the most important "message" that it has to convey. Of the various media, the "hot" forms of the past, with the "high definition" through abundance of specific data of a single type, are "exclusive," limiting themselves and their receivers to only certain consciousness states. The new "cool" forms, with the "low definition" or ambiguity, calling for audience participation to fill out the meaning, are "inclusive," tending to take in the whole of life and integrate it in some comprehensive experience.

Somewhat parallel to Bergson's triplet of instinct, intelligence, and intuition, McLuhan seems to have in mind the nonindustrial cultures, the industrialized and literate cultures, and the post-literate culture. The nonindustrialized cultures, he points out, have no specialist habits to overcome when they are introduced to the new "instant" and "totalizing" electric media of communication. They even have enough left of their traditional oral culture, with its own "total, unified 'field' " character, to make the new world familiar to them. Our recent literate culture, however, finds the new totalizing communication strange and threatening. As a specialist technology, it had "detribalized" us. The non-specific electric technologies of the present and the future will "retribalize" us, says McLuhan.[18]

This "retribalization" I wish to call *neofeminism* to distinguish it from our original tribal consciousness, or paleofeminism. I believe this is important because there is a tendency to reduce the aspirations of the evolutionary spiral to the simple oscillations of a pendulum, and in our case this would mean a retrograde movement indeed. In particular, I mean that the resurgence of feminism now should not be interpreted in terms of a renewal of the bodily, the sensual, the irrational, the emotional, the dark, the unregulated, the unconscious, and the occult. If the "everwomanly" is to "carry us on," as Goethe perceived, it must carry us forward, not back. Like Persephone returning from the underworld, it must come laden with the riches of its abductor, full of the fruits of rationality, intelligence, and literacy. This is why it is important to establish a highly general interpretation of the feminine principle, one which can be verified both in the paleofeminine era of the far past and the neofeminine era of the near future.

But just as neofeminism is not a swing of the pendulum back to the old connotations of femininity, neither is it a movement against the masculine moment of consciousness. Much less is it a movement against men. The first thing that needs to be clearly understood whenever one speaks of the new feminine consciousness, or neofeminism, is that it is not a consciousness or a movement for women alone but for women and men together. It is precisely *separation* and *exclusivism* that neofeminism rejects. It aims to overcome the internal and social alienation from which we suffer and to reunite us with ourselves, with each other, and with the whole world.

Robert Ornstein points out that while the "awareness of separation" was necessary in a more brutal age, the "analytic mode" is no longer so advantageous. Furthermore, "the existence of an individual and separate consciousness does not rule out the possibility of the simultaneous coexistence of another level of organization." He foresees for us "a shift toward a consciousness of the interconnectedness of life," a "shift from the individual, analytic consciousness to a holistic mode, brought about by training the intuitive side of ourselves." This is often called the "ego death" in esoteric traditions, he notes.[19]

Roger Wescott, remarking that ego may well be a "detour in the development of mind," can add to this that "alienation" is not to be eradicated by mere "altruism," because both are sprung from the same root: the perception of the world as composed of "others" *(alii).*[20]

We must reorder all our perceptive faculties so as to emphasize the wholeness rather than the otherness. Before we can love our neighbor as our self, we must *see* our neighbor as our self. Neofeminism is not so much a release of the affections as it is a reorganization of the power of seeing a new patterning of our world view. It is an integral (intellectual/affective) *intuition* of a holistic reality.

The feminist movement, therefore, if its deepest implications are to be successfully brought to the surface and made to play their role luminously and powerfully, must be seen as a *salvation* movement. It is not inappropriate that it should have social, economic, and political movements as its worldly components, for it is proper to this feminine consciousness that embodied expressions of its meaning should always be present together with its spiritual reality: that is, that the one and the many should remain in dynamic intercommunion. But neofeminism is essentially a movement toward the "ultraconscious" state, characterized by both "a feeling of transcendental love'' and ''a quickening of the intellect.''

In this the neofeminine consciousness resembles the intuition spoken of by Bergson. It is like instinct, or paleofeminism, in being unified, direct, immediate, full of feeling, sympathetic, and vital. But it is also like the intelligence, or masculinism, in being alert to distinction, capable of discursive and indirect reasoning, disinterested, and controlled. And it has a new quality of its own in its penetrating vision, the holistic insight that comprehends many experiences in one meaning. It will be again philosophy, as Bergson said, the love of wisdom, but a wisdom and a love appropriate to our own time, assimilating and elevating all that has preceded us. When we are reunited with the ''maiden'' of our era, it will be a new experience of salvation and homecoming, reminiscent of those that have gone before but rejoicing in its own unique quality, another face unveiled of the Unknown Goddess.

References

1. Cf. Acts 17:23.
2. C. Kerenyi, *Eleusis:* Archetypal Image of Mother and Daughter, tr. Ralph Manheim (New York: Bollingen/Pantheon, 1967), pp. 43-44, 146-47, 149.
3. Jane Ellen Harrison, *Prolegomena to the Study of Greek Religion* (Cambridge University Press, 1903), pp. 272-74. Cf. Kerenyi, p. 30.
4. Kerenyi, p. 33.
5. The *kykleon* was a barley ''mixture'' which may have been somewhat fermented. Kerenyi, pp. 177 ff.
6. Kerenyi, pp. 24, 26.
7. Harrison, pp. 274-76.
8. Kerenyi, pp. 145, 147.
9. For a more detailed analysis of the feminine as the union of one and many, see the author's ''The Image of the Virgin-Mother,'' *The American Theosophist* 61 (1973), pp. 308-15. On ''wholeness'' as the defining character of the new consciousness, see ''The Whole World: A Convergence Perspective,'' *Anima*, October, 1975.
10. Roger W. Wescott, *The Divine Animal:* An Exploration of Human Potentiality (New York: Funk & Wagnalls, 1969), p. 22.

11. Marshall McLuhan, *Understanding Media:* The Extensions of Man (New York: McGraw-Hill, 1964), pp. 19-20, 14, 15.
12. Wescott, p. 22.
13. McLuhan, p. 25.
14. Wescott, pp. 214-15, cf. p. 21.
15. James Collins, *A History of Modern European Philosophy* (Milwaukee: Bruce, 1954), pp. 835-36.
16. Henri Bergson, *Creative Evolution* (Mitchell tr.) II, p. 186.
17. Collins, p. 837.
18. McLuhan, pp. 8, 23-24, 27.
19. Robert E. Ornstein, *The Psychology of Consciousness* (New York: Viking, 1972), pp. 139, 177-78.
20. Wescott, pp. 228-29.
21. Marilyn Ferguson, *The Brain Revolution* (New York: Taplinger, 1973), p. 86, quoting Stanley Dean from *Behavioral Neuropsychiatry.*

5
The Buddhist Female Deities

ELEANOR OLSON

Until the early years of the Christian era, the male principle reigned supreme and unchallenged in both Buddhism and Brahmanism. The Hindu deities who were inherited and taken for granted by Buddhists were almost exclusively masculine. The Buddhas and Bodhisattvas—the ''gods'' so to speak—belonging to early Mahayana Buddhism were entirely masculine.

The first feminine deities to enter Mahayana Buddhism were Tara and Prajnaparamita. Tara, the Savioress, appearing in the second century, is the epiphany of the Great Mother whose worship had in ancient times extended over a vast Afro-Aegian-Asian territory and who has always been worshipped by the pre-Ayran population strata of India. Prajnaparamita, ''The Perfection of Wisdom,'' appearing in the fourth century, is the personification of the sutra of the same name.

The Prajnaparamita Sutra consists of discourses addressed by the Buddha to Subhuti and other celestial beings, believed to have been hidden away in the custody of the *nagas* (serpent demigods) until mankind was sufficiently enlightened to comprehend them. In the second century of the Christian era, the Prajnaparamita Sutra as expounded by the Indian sage Nagarjuna became the Madhyamika or ''Middle Path,'' the basic text of all the schools of Mahayana. In this famous sutra, which preaches the essential sameness

of all opposites and the voidness of all concepts and phenomena, the Buddha declares again and again that Prajnaparamita produced all the Buddhas and is their mother
and instructress.

> For she (The Perfection of Wisdom) is their mother and beget-
> ter, she showed them the all-knowledge, she instructed them
> in the ways of the world. From her have the Tathagatas come
> forth. For she has begotten and shown that cognition of the
> all-knowing, she has shown them the world for what it really
> is. The all-knowledge of the Tathagatas has come forth from
> her. All the Tathagatas, past, future and present, win full en-
> lightenment thanks to this very Perfection of Wisdom. It is in
> this sense that the Perfection of Wisdom generates the
> Tathagatas and instructs them in this world....How does
> Perfect Wisdom show up the world for what it is? She shows
> that the world is empty, unthinkable, calmly quiet. As purified
> of itself, she shows up the world.[1]

Prajnaparamita symbolizes the supreme liberating wisdom
which is the full consciousness of the Absolute, called
Shunya, the Void. She is the divine mother of the infinite
space. Her *mantra* (invocation) has the wondrous effect of
opening the mind to enlightenment.

During the first millenium of the Christian era, the mys-
tical-occult development called Tantrism swept over India,
obliterating many of the differences between Hinduism and
Buddhism. Many Hindu deities were admitted to the Buddhist pantheon as Bodhisattvas and Dharmapala (Defenders
of the Doctrine). In the later Tantric Buddhism, especially
the Vajrayana (Diamond Path) which has survived only in
Tibet, each male divinity is endowed with a feminine partner, as in Hinduism, but the philosophic meanings are different. In Hinduism the feminine deity is the active partner, the *shakti* (power or energy) of the Lord Shiva, who
without her would have remained in the deep sleep of the
Absolute. Buddhism reverses these roles in accordance with
the mystic philosophy of the Prajnaparamita. The feminine
deity is not shakti but *prajna* (wisdom), which is equated
with *shunya*, the Void. Prajna is the quiescent, the passive,
the contemplative. The Buddhas and male deities are the

Mandala of Vasudhara. Courtesy of The Newark Museum

Kwan Yin. From the collection of Kathleen Alexander-Berghorn. Photo by Gregory Berghorn

Yum Chen (Prajnaparamita). Courtesy of The Newark Museum, Newark, New Jersey

active partners, symbolizing *karma* (compassion) and *upaya* (method or skillful means), the essential characteristics of a Bodhisattva. The mystic union of the world's dualities and especially the inseparable union of wisdom, the feminine principle, and compassion, the male principle, is vividly symbolized in Tibetan art and ritual, most potently perhaps by the vajra and the bell, and by the sacred embrace of the deities, called in Tibetan *yab-yum* (father-mother). With the aid of these symbols the meditating adept transcends the dualities within his own nature. The final synthesis of compassion and wisdom is his realization of the Absolute.[2]

In Vajrayana, each deity has his place in the divine hierarchy, his mantra, his *mandala* (sphere of influence, symbolized by a cosmic diagram), his deputies and messengers. Each is recognized by his post, body color, number of heads and limbs, *mudras*, garments, emblems, ornaments, and accessories. All the above must be clearly and precisely visualized by the adept in order to bring the deity into manifestation.

Each deity has peaceful and fierce aspects. In peaceful aspect, the deities, whether masculine or feminine, wear the crown, jewelry, and flowing scarves characteristic of a Bodhisattva. They stand or sit on lotus pedestals and have halos and auras of light rays. In their fierce aspect, they tend to be dynamic in pose and heavy in stature, treading on demons, frowning, having fearsome emblems and ornaments, enveloped in flames.

Prajnaparamita is described as young, serene, grave, and majestic, her golden body emitting millions of rays of light which fill the whole universe. In Tibetan Buddhism, where she is the mystic partner and mother of the *Adi* (first) Buddha, she may be two or four-armed. One hand holds a volume of the sutra which she personifies. Prajnaparamita's worship extended to Java, and she enjoyed great popularity in Cambodia where she had a Tantric form with eleven heads and twenty-two arms. In Japan she is called Hannya.

The noble Tara is described as the "color of the moon, calm, smiling, senuous, radiating five-colored light...."[3] In this, her white aspect, Tara sits in Buddha pose, her right hand forming the mudra of charity or gift bestowing, and her left hand raised, holding the stem of a lotus blossom (her distinctive emblem), which blooms above her shoulder. She has seven eyes of wisdom, one in the center of her forehead, the palm of each hand and the sole of each foot. The White Tara also has a dynamic, slightly fierce form with a thousand arms, heads, eyes, and feet, called Ushnishasitatapatra, the Goddess of the White Parasol. The Green Tara is equally well known, and there are red, yellow, and blue Taras corresponding to the sacred colors of the five Buddha families. Filled with love for all beings, Tara (whose name is derived from the root *tri*, ''to cross'') carries her worshippers safely across the ocean of phenomenal existence. Tara is not worshipped in China and Japan, but in Tibetan Buddhism her popularity rivals that of Avalokiteshvara, the male Bodhisattva of Compassion. ''The first Dalai Lama (1391-1475) would do whatever he did,'' according to a Tibetan authority, ''only after he had prayed to the Holy Tara, and thereby his active power to augment the aims of the teachings and of beings became as great as infinite space. Indeed, the majority of holy men in former times took the holy Tara as their highest deity, and by the power of their prayers the quality of their understanding of the precepts was greatly increased in the stream of each of their hearts. . . .''[4] Tara, like all the high feminine deities of Vajrayana, is addressed as mother of all the Buddhas and Bodhisattvas.

In China and Japan, where the worship of the consorts was never adopted, the male principle is considered of primal importance since no woman without gaining masculinity through incarnation may enter the Pure Land, Amitabha's Western Paradise of Sukhavati, or hope to attain Buddhahood. Tara, in the ancient incarnation as the Princess Moon of Wisdom, is said to have defied this dogma with the following words: ''Since there is no such thing as a man or a woman and no such thing as a self or a person or awareness, this bondage to male and female is hollow. Oh how worldly fools delude themselves! . . . Those who wish to attain supreme enlightenment in a man's body are many, but those who wish to serve the aims of beings in a woman's body are few indeed; therefore may I, until this world is emptied out, serve the aim of beings with nothing but the body of a woman.''[5]

All the Indian Buddhist feminine deities were brought to Tibet with the entire Buddhist tradition between the seventh and the twelfth centuries. Due to Muslim invasions, Buddhism died out completely in India at the end of the twelfth century. Since the Chinese occupation of Tibet in the mid-twentieth century, lamas in exile have introduced the full range of the teachings to the outside world for the first time.

Several feminine deities were introduced to Central Asia, China, Java, and Cambodia with the Mantrayana school of early Tantric Buddhism in the eighth century. In China, the school called Mi Tsung (Secret School) or Chen-yen (True Word), had a meteoric career, but it soon lost its separate identity. This happened through its merging with other Buddhist schools, especially the meditative Ch'an, which had been brought to China by Bodhidharma in the sixth century. In the early ninth century, Kobo Daishi (Kukai) brought Chen-yen Buddhism to Japan, founding the still-flourishing Shingon school, and popularizing a number of feminine deities. As with so many other aspects of Buddhist culture, we must look today first to Tibet, and secondly to Japan for Buddhist feminine deities. Prajnaparamita, whom we have discussed, and Sarasvati, Vasudhara, Marici, and Hariti seem to be the principal goddesses known to both countries.

Sarasvati, the goddess of music, poetry, and learning, especially invoked for the gift of speech and eloquence, is portrayed as a beautiful young woman with a lute. Her Tibetan form may have two, four, or six arms. In Japan where she is called Benzaiten or Benten, she is the embodiment of ideal womanhood; most of her shrines are on islands (the principal one is Enoshima). She has a serpent mount, and is the only feminine deity among the popular Seven Gods of Good Fortune.

Vasudhara, goddess of abundance, is the embodiment of youthful charm and grace. Her Tibetan form, like that of

Sarasvati, may have two, four, or six arms; her distinctive emblem is a spike of grain, but she may also hold a vase, book, and jewel. The Japanese call her Kichijoten, and represent her as a court lady in ceremonial dress.

Marici, goddess of the dawn, invoked each morning at sunrise by the Tibetan lamas, is multiheaded and limbed in both Japan and Tibet, and sometimes rides in a chariot drawn by seven swine, possibly inspired by the seven horses that draw the chariot of Surya, the sun god.

Hariti was formerly invoked in China to cure disease. In Japan, where she has both a gentle and demonic form, she is venerated as a protector of the Saddharma Pundarika sutra. She is shown with a child in her arms, and often with her special emblem, a pomegranate. In Tibet she is little known as a goddess, but in accordance with the Buddha's command, it is customary to offer to Hariti and her five hundred demon sons some of the daily nourishment of which one partakes—a practice which is also followed in Japanese monasteries. In India she was a *yakshini* or "cannibal demon," who stole and ate children until cured and converted by the Buddha.

In China and Japan the only goddess whose popularity equals that of the masculine deities is Kuan-yin (Japanese Kannon), who is actually Avalokiteshvara, the male Bodhisattva of Compassion. Since the twelfth century, Kuan-yin has appeared (always in China, and usually in Japan) as the goddess of mercy. The worship of Avalokiteshvara was introduced to China at the end of the first century A.D.; to Japan early in the seventh century; and in both cases soon after the introduction of Buddhism itself. He is the son of the glorious Amitabha (J. Amida) Buddha, presiding at Amida's right hand in Sukhavati, the Western Paradise. The goddess Kuan-yin wears a high headdress or crown and flowing robes. Her chief emblems are a vase of heavenly dew and a willow branch. Like Benten, she often stands on a dragon, and her shrines are associated with islands, caves, and the sea. She has many forms, including one with a thousand arms. In China especially, where she superseded Hariti in the T'ang dynasty (607-906) as the giver of children, she

*Sarasvati. Courtesy of The Jacques
Marchais Center of Tibetan Art,
Staten Island, New York*

*Vajravarahi, a Dakini. Courtesy of
The Newark Museum*

*Lhamo (Kali). Courtesy of The Jacques
Marchais Center of Tibetan Art*

is often shown, like the madonna of Christianity, with a child in her arms. The child, however, is not her own, but one that she is ready to give to mothers who pray to her for offspring. All this is in accord with passages in the Lotus sutra which expressly state that Avalokiteshvara will appear in feminine form when circumstances are appropriate, and that "if a woman, desirous of male offspring...adores the Bodhisattva Avalokiteshvara, she will get a son...or if a woman is desirous of a daughter, a girl shall be born to her."[6]

As a great Bodhisattva, Avalokiteshvara may manifest in any form suitable to his beneficent purposes. The educated Buddhist says that the true Kuan-yin is by nature sexless and formless, but is capable of assuming or appearing to assume all forms. Fenollosa expresses this view when he states that " a great Bodhisattva is in its own nature indeterminate as to sex, having risen above the distinction, or rather embodying in itself the united spiritual graces of both sexes. It is a matter of accident which one it may assume upon incarnation. It just happens that T'ang thought, or preferred to think, of Kuan-yin as a great demiurge or creator, while Sung preferred to lay stress upon the element of motherhood."[7]

The chief mother-goddess of Hinduism, the wife of Shiva, enters Tibetan Buddhism in her destructive aspect as Kali as late as the fifteenth century, and soon merges with indigenous Tibetan deities of like nature. Palden Lhamo, "The Glorious Goddess," is worshipped primarily as a wrathful protectress, enveloped in flames, riding her mule over a sea of blood, and using the flayed skin of her son as a saddle blanket. She is the only feminine deity among the "Eight Terrible Ones," a group of the most powerful Dharmapala (Defenders of the Doctrine). As chief guardian goddess of the Dalai Lama and the Tibetan government, she is said to have appeared to the first Dalai Lama at a sacred lake near Lhasa where she solemnly vowed to watch over him and all his successors. When the Dalai Lama dies, it is here that the regent sees a vision of the new Dalai Lama's birthplace.

Palden Lhamo is surrounded by her emanations or deputies: the Four Goddesses of the Seasons ride a deer, camel, buffalo, and mule respectively; the Twelve Jewel Goddesses and the Five Sisters of Long Life ride various mounts including a deer, garuda, lion, and wild ass.

The glorious goddess's two attendants are animal-headed dakini, which brings us to a special class of supremely important Tibetan feminine deities of Indian origin, the *dakinis* or *yoginis*, who are the mystic partners of the *yogins*. They dance through space, imparting secret wisdom and magic power to the adept. In Tibetan art they are seen dancing the yogic dance which destroys erroneous beliefs.

The five highest dakinis are the feminine partners of five Herukas of Shivaite form, also called high patron deities and Yi-dam, or tutelary deities. They are the fierce aspects of five peaceful Buddhas called *Jinas*, conquerors or *Dhyani* (meditation) Buddhas, each of whom heads a family of deities. Dynamic and multi-limbed, clasping their prajnas in deep embrace, they represent the process of becoming a Buddha. The five dakinis are the supreme instruments of liberation, each dakini transmuting one of the five basic human weaknesses (delusion, desire, aversion, malignity, and jealousy) into a corresponding aspect of divine wisdom. With the aid of his lama, his yi-dam, and dakini, the adept makes his final leap from the bondage of the limited human ego to the freedom of Buddhahood. The holy triad—Lama, Yi-dam and Dakini—corresponds in Vajrayana to the Three Jewels of orthodox Buddhism—Buddha, Dharma and Sangha—in which every Buddhist takes his daily refuge. The deities can be brought into manifestation only by the lama (spiritual teacher). They are actually only forms of himself. The yi-dam and dakini are the most potent deities and the most profound mystery of Vajrayana.[8]

The gods and goddesses of Vajrayana are not arbitrary creations, but manifestations of the universal Void which occur spontaneously or are consciously produced during the meditations and the rituals. At times looked upon as external entities, in a deeper sense they are known to be patterns of redemption experienced inwardly on the path to enlightenment. The purpose of the Buddhist mystic is to unite within his own being the male and female aspects—compassion and wisdom—and all the illusory opposites of the phenomenal world, a reconquest of the completeness that preceded all creation.

References

1. Edward Conze, tr. and ed. *The Perfection of Wisdom in 8,000 Lines,* Ch. XII, Four Seasons Foundation, Bolinas, 1973, pp. 172-73, 179.
2. See John Blofeld, *The Tantric Buddhism of Tibet,* New York, 1970; S. B. Dasgupta, *An Introduction to Tantric Buddhism,* Calcutta, 1950; Lama Anagarika Govinda, *Foundations of Tibetan Mysticism,* New York, 1960; D. L. Snellgrove, *Buddhist Himalaya,* New York, 1957.
3. Stephan Beyer, *The Cult of Tara,* University of California Press, Berkeley, 1973, p. 105.
4. *Ibid.,* p. 14.
5. *Ibid.,* p. 65.
6. Alice Getty, *The Gods of Northern Buddhism,* Oxford, 1928, p. 80.
7. Ernest Fenollosa, *Epochs of Chinese and Japanese Art,* London, 1912, Vol. I, p. 124; R. F. Johnson, *Buddhist China,* London, 1913, p. 276.
8. See Beyer, *op. cit.;* Govinda, *op. cit.;* Snellgrove, *op. cit.;* Blanche Christine Olschak in collaboration with Geshe Thupten Wangyal, *Mystic Art of Ancient Tibet,* Switzerland, 1973; R. A. Stein, *Tibetan Civilization,* Stanford, Cal., 1972.

6

Isis: The Goddess as Healer

KATHLEEN ALEXANDER-BERGHORN

I am Nature, the Mother of All
Mistress of the Elements,
Sovereign of the Spirit
Queen of the Dead,
Queen of the Immortals,
The single embodiment of all goddesses and gods.
My will governs the movements of the stars,
The winds of the seas,
And the dread silence of the underworld.
I am worshipped under many aspects,
Known by countless names.
I am Isis.[1]

She was invoked in the ancient scriptures as Lady of Healing, Restorer of Life, Source of the Healing Herbs, the Great Sorceress Who Heals.[2] Her worship originated in ancient Egypt and spread from the Middle East to Asia Minor, Europe, and Great Britain, extending in time from the dawn of recorded history to the fifth century C.E.[3] Ancient, yet ageless, today Isis is reawakening in the hearts of women as we rediscover our own healing powers.

A Goddess of myriad facets, Isis was revered as the creator and sustainer of the cosmos, the source of life by whom all living beings are nurtured and to whom they return in death. She is often represented in Egyptian art as holding the *ankh,* the sacred symbol of life, denoting her identity as the Lady of Life,[4] the personification of the life force itself.[5] Her compassion was believed to be as infinite as her wisdom, and she was especially revered as the divine physician with the power to heal the body, mind, and spirit.

Although Isis was regarded as the universal Mother, she was the patroness of women in particular. As the Giver of Life,[6] who presided over both birth and death, she was the protectress of women in childbirth and the comforter of the bereaved. Isis' very human emotions and the qualities of love, compassion, tenderness, and perseverance which she exemplified endeared her especially to the hearts of women. In Isis, women found a source of support and inspiration for their own lives. Isis proclaimed herself in ancient hymns as the Goddess of women and endowed women with power equal to that of men.[7] She has been called one of the first exponents of women's liberation.[8]

Women in ancient Egypt enjoyed a high status in society,[9] reflecting the sovereignty of Isis in the spiritual realm. The introduction of the worship of Isis to Greece and Rome coincided with the greater emancipation of women in these rigidly patriarchal cultures.[10] The religion of Isis was open to all, regardless of sex, race, or social class. Her devotees included slaves and prostitutes, as well as the wealthy and aristocratic.[11] Oppressed peoples discovered special refuge in Isis, who promised salvation to all who turned to her in love and faith. Women participated fully in her worship, both as priestesses of her temples and as initiates of the most sacred and secret mysteries of the Goddess.[12] Thus Isis was responsible not only for bestowing healing on individuals, but represented a significant force for healing the oppression and injustices of patriarchal society as a whole.

Among the oriental mystery religions competing for supremacy in the declining years of the Roman Empire, Christianity emerged victorious. Tragically, the worship of Isis was ruthlessly suppressed by the early Christian patriarchs. For nearly two millennia, Western women have lacked a positive image of their own innate divinity and healing power. Historian Sarah Pomeroy has speculated, ''One cannot help wondering about the nature of the subsequent history of Western women if the religion of Isis had been triumphant.''[13] The implications of this question for the history of women healers are especially significant. As Barbara Ehrenreich and Deirdre English have noted, ''The status of women healers has risen and fallen with the status of women.... To know our history is to begin to know how to take up the struggle again.''[14] Isis stood for the equality of women[15] and manifested the healing powers of womankind to an exceptional degree. Knowledge of the ancient worship of Isis as the divine healer can help to make us aware that healing ''is part of our heritage as women, our history, our birthright.''[16]

Ancient Egyptian scriptures emphasize Isis' greatness as a healer, a role which revealed the full measure of her wisdom, love and compassion. She was revered as the Lady of the Words of Power, whose ''incantations destroy diseases.''[17] Isis' renown as a healer was so great that even Ra, the highest of the gods, was said to have called upon her to cure him of a deadly snakebite. Isis agreed to save him, on the condition that Ra reveal to her his secret name, the source of his power. Skilled in preparing healing ointments, Isis expertly ground a mixture of various seeds and juniper berries to a fine paste, which she then mixed with honey.[18] As she applied this balm to the snakebite, Isis intoned the secret word of power that she had learned from Ra. The dying god's pain disappeared and he recovered, but Isis had forever surpassed him in wisdom and power, usurping his place as the supreme divinity.

Isis' tender compassion for human suffering is revealed in another story of her greatness as a healer capable of restoring life to the dead. During her solitary wanderings, Isis sought refuge at the home of a noblewoman who, failing to recognize the true identity of her divine visitor, shut her door in the face of the Goddess. Soon afterward, the woman's son was fatally stung by a scorpion. Isis was moved with pity to save the innocent child, notwithstanding the insult she had received from the boy's mother. Hearing the woman's cries of lamentation to which no one else was responding, Isis called out to her, ''Come to Me, for My speech hath in it the power to protect and it possesseth life.''[19] Then Isis laid her hands upon the lifeless child and commanded the poison to leave his body, proclaiming, ''I am Isis the Goddess and I am the Lady of the Words of

Power, and I know how to work with words of power, and most mighty are My words!''[20] The child was thus restored to life, through the love and mercy of the Goddess.

Ancient women turned to Isis as an understanding Mother who, although divine and immortal, had personally experienced loss and grief. Isis had overcome death itself through the redeeming power of her love, restoring to life both her husband Osiris and their son Horus. After Osiris was murdered and dismembered by his evil brother Set, the inconsolable Goddess searched tirelessly for the scattered fragments of her husband's body. Having gathered together all the pieces she could find, Isis enfolded Osiris within her gently beating wings, breathing life back into him. Isis conceived her son Horus through this union, but bereavement came to her once again when her child was killed by a deadly scorpion. Isis not only resurrected Horus from the dead, but made him immortal through her gift of the elixir of life. The devotees of Isis found great comfort in these narratives of Isis' miraculous healing powers, confident that the loving Mother of all living beings would show similar compassion for the suffering of her human children. Her healing of Horus was regarded as a promise of the salvation which Isis offered to all. According to the ancient scriptures, ''Everyone who is under the [physician's] knife shall be healed likewise.''[21] An invocation to the Goddess dating from the sixteenth century B.C.E. calls upon her unfailing motherly concern: ''O Isis...heal me...as Thou hast saved and freed Thy son Horus.''[22]

Miraculous healings were attributed to the intercession of Isis, through whose mercy the blind regained their sight and the crippled walked again.[23] Her name itself was believed to possess divine power, and healing was performed in the name of Isis, the source of life and wholeness. As the embodiment of divine wisdom, Isis presided over all the arts and sciences, and was revered as the inventor and patroness of the medical arts in particular. The most learned of physicians, Isis understood the healing properties of plants and knew the secrets of the preparation of effective medicines to alleviate the sufferings of humanity. In ancient Egypt, plants believed to possess medicinal value were sacred to Isis, the supreme apothecary and mistress of herbal lore.[24] The priestesses of her temples helped to disseminate the healing wisdom which was regarded as the gift of the Goddess herself.[25] Isis shared her learning with women through her priestesses, who dispensed medicines for healing and for the protection of women in childbirth, preparations to calm crying babies, methods to predict the sex of the unborn child, and knowledge of both contraception and fertility.[26] Pregnant women identified with Isis through an incantation calling upon the gods to prepare the bed for childbirth, affirming that the request was made by the Goddess herself.[27] Marion Weinstein suggests that initiates of the Mysteries of Isis emulated the Goddess by learning to work with words of power, which she believes were affirmation techniques used for healing and self-transformation.[28]

The personal presence of the Goddess in dreams was experienced by her devotees as a powerful healing force, capable of restoring health to those whose lives had been despaired of by their own doctors. Those seeking a cure would often spend the night in her temple, for Isis was known to appear to the afflicted in their sleep, enfolding them in her healing wings of love.[29] Isis brought comfort and hope to the heart as well as renewed strength to the body.

The healing power of Isis was not confined to her temples alone. Isis the healer was the patron Goddess of the Greek city of Philippi.[30] As the divine physician, she was the guiding inspiration of the renowned medical school at Alexandria, one of the greatest centers of learning in the ancient world.[31] The Temple of Isis Medica, located near Alexandria, was also dedicated to the Goddess in her aspect as the divine healer. This temple was destroyed in the fifth century C.E. by Cyril, Archbishop of Alexandria, who denounced Isis as an ''odious demon'' and ordered that a Christian church be built over the ruins of her shrine.[32] Such desecration was a common practice during this period, when the early Christians were trying to obliterate every trace of the Goddess whom they regarded as a dangerous rival. (It is interesting to note that Cyril also ordered the murder of Hypatia, the famous woman philosopher of Alexandria. He was officially canonized in 1822.[33])

Isis could not be eradicated, however. Her presence continued to make itself felt, thinly veiled but recognizable, in Christian art and worship. Many art historians feel that Christian representations of the madonna and child are based on familiar Egyptian images of Isis suckling her son Horus. The practice of dedicating *ex-voto* offerings is another vestige of the Goddess in contemporary Christian worship. These symbolic representations of different parts of the body healed through divine intercession found even today in Catholic churches (especially those dedicated to the Virgin Mary) perpetuate a traditional custom in the ancient temples of Isis.[34] M. Esther Harding has suggested that some of the Black Virgin shrines of Europe, still centers of pilgrimages for those seeking healing, have grown up around ancient images of Isis, who was often represented as black.[35] Even the Christian angels recall the figure of Isis, the compassionate and protective Goddess with healing in her wings.[36] The esoteric mysteries of the Goddess are also preserved in symbolic form in the Tarot deck, in which the High Priestess card represents Isis.[37]

Today women are rediscovering Isis, recognizing her in the images that have come to us and celebrating her continuing presence in our lives through the creation of new rituals and works of art inspired by the Goddess.[38] Each of us can personally experience the healing presence of the Goddess within us. ''All women are Isis and Isis is all women.''[39]

Realizing our identity with Isis, we can begin to overcome the centuries-old suppression of our innate healing power. Under patriarchy, women healers have been denigrated and even burned at the stake as agents of the devil[40] instead of being revered as embodiments of the Goddess and channels of her healing power. To this day, the majority of women involved in the health care professions are subordinate to men, and women who try to practice the healing arts which were traditionally sacred to Isis, such as midwifery and herbal medicine, are vigorously opposed by the predominantly male medical establishment. Our spirituality is indeed political. By reclaiming Isis as our own, through identification with her attributes as the archetype of woman as healers, we begin to repossess our own heritage as healers.

Notes

1. These lines are adapted from Isis' famous speech in *Metamorphoses* by Apuleius, in which the radiant Goddess rises from the sea and directly addresses her devotee.
2. E. A. Wallis Budge, *The Gods of the Egyptians* (New York: Dover Publications, 1969), vol. 2, p. 214.
3. Common Era (C.E.) or Before Common Era (B.C.E.) are terms sometimes used by historians instead of Anno Domini (A.D.) and Before Christ (B.C.).
4. Budge, vol. 2, p. 214.
5. R. E. Witt, *Isis in the Graeco-Roman World* (Ithaca, New York: Cornell University Press, 1971), p. 35.
6. Budge, vol. 2, p. 216.
7. Sharon Kelly Heyob, *The Cult of Isis Among Women in the Graeco-Roman World* (Leiden: E.J. Brill, 1975), p. 52.
8. Ibid.
9. Merlin Stone, *When God Was A Woman* (New York: Harcourt Brace Jovanovich, 1976), p. 36.
10. Sarah B. Pomeroy, *Goddesses, Whores, Wives, and Slaves: Woman in Classical Antiquity* (New York: Schocken Books, 1976), p. 225.
11. Witt, p. 23.
12. Heyob, pp. 110, 130.
13. Pomeroy, p. 226.
14. Barbara Ehrenreich and Deirdre English, *Witches, Midwives, and Nurses: A History of Old Women Healers* (Old Westbury, New York: The Feminist Press, 1973), pp. 4-5.
15. Pomeroy, p. 226.
16. Ehrenreich and English, p. 3.
17. Budge, vol. 1, p. 380.
18. Stone, Merlin, *Ancient Mirrors of Womanhood: Our Goddess and Heroine Heritage* (Village Station, New York: New Sibylline Books, 1979), vol. 2, pp. 80-81. (Hereafter referred to as *Ancient Mirrors*.)
19. Budge, vol. 2, p. 207.
20. Ibid.
21. Budge, vol. 2, p. 211.

22. Witt, p. 186.
23. Ibid., p. 189.
24. Ibid., p. 313.
25. Stone, *Ancient Mirrors,* vol. 2, p. 79.
26. Ibid.
27. Heyob, pp. 50-51.
28. Marion Weinstein, *Positive Magic: Occult Self-Help* (Custer, Washington: Phoenix Publishing, 1978), p. 205.
29. Witt, p. 191.
30. Ibid., p. 192.
31. Ibid., p. 189.
32. Ibid., p. 186.
33. Barbard G. Walker, *The Woman's Encyclopedia of Myths and Secrets* (New York: Harper and Row, 1983), p. 420.
34. Witt, p. 196.
35. M. Esther Harding, *Woman's Mysteries: Ancient and Modern* (New York: Harper and Row, 1971), pp. 185, 187-8.
36. Witt, p. 33.
37. Sally Gearhart and Susan Rennie, *A Feminist Tarot* (Watertown, Massachusetts: Persephone Press, 1981), p. 6.
38. For example, see Dion Fortune's two novels about an ancient priestess of Isis in modern England, *The Sea Priestess* and *Moon Magic,* Linda Ann Hoag's poem ''Isis at the Supermarket'' (*Heresies,* vol. 2, no. 1, p. 39); and the beautiful Isis poster by the Women's Graphics Collective, Chicago.
39. Dion Fortune, *Moon Magic* (New York: Samuel Weiser, Inc. 1978), p. 189.
40. Ehrenreich and English, pp. 6-20.

Isis Healing Meditation

Go to a quiet place where you can be by yourself and not interrupted. Sit in a chair, set your feet flat on the floor, rest your hands on your thighs, let your back be straight, and close your eyes. Center and relax yourself by taking deep, slow breaths. Visualize yourself surrounded with radiant white light.

When you have finished these preparations, start imagining yourself journeying to a Healing Temple to receive healing for yourself. When you arrive, stand before the Temple's main doorway, and examine its shape, size, color, and design. Now, reflect on the healing you need and seek. When you feel ready, go through the doorway and enter the Temple.

In the center of the Temple is the Great Goddess Isis. She stands facing you. Her winged arms are outstretched. She is radiant. Healing Love energy emanates from Her body and fills the Temple. She welcomes you and asks you to speak about the Healing you are seeking. You tell Her what you want to receive Healing for. Then she tells you to come forward and receive Healing in Her embrace. You step forward, and she holds you to Her heart, gently enfolding you in her winged arms and in Her Love and Healing Power.

Now, experience Her energy flowing throughout your whole being as you chant ''Isis, Isis, Isis'' over and over. Let your consciousness merge with Hers. Absorb as much Healing energy as you sense you need, then imagine Her opening Her arms and stretching them out at Her sides again. Picture yourself standing before Her with your own arms outstretched and give thanks to Her. As you visualize this, rise up from the chair in which you have been sitting during this meditation and stretch your arms out. Open your eyes and feel Isis Healing energy radiating from you as you look around the room. Then, hold your hands to your heart and affirm to yourself that you will allow the power of this Healing meditation to flow through your daily life.

—Selena Fox, Circle Sanctuary

7
Rediscovering the
Feminine Principle

JOAN CHAMBERLAIN ENGELSMAN

Twenty years ago such an anthology as this would have
been unnecessary because everyone would have been more
or less in agreement as to what the feminine principle was
and what it meant. At least this would have been the case
with reference to Western thought which developed from
Greek philosophy and the Judeo-Christian tradition. In fact,
most philosophers and theologians have held the same view
for over two thousand years. This tradition states that the
feminine principle is the principle of nature as versus the
principle of mind, which is masculine. This system fosters
a duality of human existence in which the feminine stands
for passivity and receptivity, for the physical dimension of
life, or matter; for darkness and emotionality. Of course,
these qualities always stand in contrast to their opposites
which constitute the masculine principle of activity, reason,
and light. Thus Aristotle was able to assert that the woman
plays no role in conception other than to be receptive to the
creative male sperm and to supply the body or matter which
will house the human spirit or mind during its stay on earth.
This means that the body is either a prison for the soul or
it corrupts the soul through sensual pleasure, and therefore
is often described as evil. Thus, human nature or physical
nature is seen as something to be overcome.

On the other hand, this same feminine principle of nature
has also been romanticized. Particularly since the Enlighten-

ment there have been those who have glorified man in his "natural" state. Some recommend a "return to nature" and others extol sensual pleasure and the irrational or Dionysiac forces of life. For these philosophers the feminine principle is seen in a more positive way, although it still represents passivity, darkness and passion.

This general understanding of the feminine principle is reinforced by a complex set of symbols and myths which appears in all forms of art and literature, as well as in religion and psychology. The earth, the moon, caves, bowls, caldrons, trees, vines, grain, mountains, rocks, fire, water, and wind have been used as symbols of the feminine at one time or another. Usually these symbols represent the woman as mother—the one who gives birth—or the woman as bride— the one who inspires. The negative aspects of these figures are personified by the witch: the old witch who devours children, such as the witch in *Hansel and Gretel;* and the young witch who lures men to their death, like the Sirens or Lorelei. These symbols are so universal that they appear as archetypes in Jung's psychology, and even Freud believed that these mythic themes were ingrained in the unconscious of Western man.

Now, however, this meaning of the feminine principle is being challenged. Because of the woman's movement, women in particular are beginning to reexamine the symbols and myths which undergird their treatment and position in society. This reexamination will require a new look at traditional material to see whether or not it 1) truly represents the feminine, and 2) if it has been correctly understood. Women feel this is particularly necessary because for 2500 years the creators and interpreters of culture have been male philosophers, theologians, politicians and artists.

One way to begin this process is to reexamine the great virgin goddesses who once personified the feminine principle. Before the beginning of the Christian era the Western world was experiencing another age of anxiety. The formal state cults of Greece and Rome were unable to cut through the sense of malaise and dis-ease that permeated the civilized world. As a result, more and more people sought aid

101

and comfort from the great mystery religions of the day. These religions were oriented toward the individual and the individual's hope for immortality and life after death. A Homeric hymn to Demeter regarding the Eleusinian mysteries said: ''Blessed is he whose eyes have seen them; his lot after death is not as the lot of other men!'' There were many such religions, but two of the most popular involved the Greek goddess Demeter and the Egyptian goddess Isis. Despite the syncretistic tendencies of that time, these two religions were different, and each grew out of its own indigenous country. Nevertheless, there are deep similarities between them. These similarities seem to derive from the fact that both goddesses are women and therefore reflect what human beings naturally tend to regard as the feminine dimension of the divine. This is particularly so since these same characteristics can be found in almost all great goddesses regardless of nationality or period.

The story of Demeter and Persephone is widely known. In one version or another it appears in almost all collections of Greek mythology. Unfortunately, the version which served as the basis for the Eleusinian mysteries is not so readily available. The myth as told in the Homeric ''Hymn to Demeter'' is far more than a simple story to explain the changing of the seasons. It is probable that Demeter began her existence as the goddess of the harvest, but the mysteries celebrated in her name flourished long before the Golden Age of Greece. In the mysteries, Persephone is abducted by Pluto and carried off to the underworld to be his wife. When Demeter discovers Persephone is missing, she seeks the help of Hecate, the moon goddess, who continues to be related to one or the other of the goddesses throughout the story. When Demeter learns what happened to her daughter, she flies into a rage at Zeus who arranged the marriage. In her anger she leaves the home of the gods and wanders the earth mourning for Persephone. When Zeus refuses to listen to Demeter and to return her daughter, Demeter causes the earth to be barren, thereby making it impossible for mortals to make offerings to the king of the Gods. This attracts Zeus' attention and he agrees to restore

Persephone to her mother. In the meantime Persephone has eaten one pomegranate seed and therefore must spend part of the year with her husband. However, apparently as a result of her stay in Hades, Persephone is no longer a frivolous child; she has matured and become a great goddess in her own right. Now she is queen of the underworld, the "dreaded" Persephone.

It is easy to see Demeter as the Classic *Mater Dolorosa,* the mother who mourns and grieves over the death of her child. Bereft of youth and beauty, she wanders over the earth hoping to find her child and to be reconciled with her. However, in the case of Demeter another dimension is added to this picture—Demeter's rage. This rage stems from the forcible separation of mother and child and is directed primarily at the gods. It is her anger, not her grief, that moves Zeus to modify his agreement with Pluto. This combination of grief *and* rage is usually absent in later prototypes of the *Mater Dolorosa* such as the Virgin Mary where the image is exclusively one of a grieving parent. In most cases the quality of rage is split off and projected into a witchlike figure. Clearly, the fact that Demeter retains both emotions indicates the power and awesomeness of this great goddess who embodies both the negative and positive qualities of the maternal.

The figure of Persephone, or Kore, is equally ambivalent. She is forever youthful and beautiful, playful and alluring. However, she journeys to the depths and returns radically changed. Now she is equal to her mother in power and will "reign over everyone who lives." It is probable that, at Eleusis, Persephone came to be identified with the human soul which survives death. The cycle of death and rebirth no doubt originated in the succession of the seasons, but it became the symbol for the rebirth of the human soul and the mysteries of this rebirth were initiated by the goddesses.

The myths of the Egyptian goddess Isis are probably less well known. Although her cult is at least as old as Demeter's, she did not become widely known until the Hellenistic period when, under the Ptolomies, religion became a matter for export. From then until their final repression by the Christians in the fourth century, the mysteries of Isis spread throughout the Mediterranean world until every major city in the Roman Empire had its own shrine. Images of Isis have even been excavated as far north as France and England. The myth of Isis and Osiris has been preserved in Plutarch's *Moralia,* and the rituals and the process of initiation are told by Apuleius in *The Golden Ass.* From these sources it is clear that there are similarities between Isis and Demeter, most notably in the wanderings of Isis in search of her dead husband Osiris. However, equally important is the dimension of her character that emerges from other sources. In these she is connected with Maat, the goddess of world order and justice.

Maat is one of the most important figures in Egyptian mythology. She is a goddess in the normal sense, complete with cult and temple. However, she is also a basic value, the principle of the proper order of things both in nature and in society. She was created before the world and through her the world itself was created. Therefore, it seemed to be more important to "keep Maat" (that is, to obey the law) than to worship her. Maat herself assists in this endeavor by guiding, instructing, and inspiring the Egyptians, and after death she is the principle by which they are judged. She is the personification of wisdom and therefore there are many similarities between Maat and Sophia, the Jewish concept of wisdom which is described so forcefully in the book of *Proverbs.*

In the Hellenistic period the attributes of Maat were absorbed by Isis. In one of the aretologies, or Praises of Isis, she says of herself such things as: "I gave and ordained laws for men, which no one is able to change....I divided the earth from the heaven....I order the course of the sun and the moon....I made strong the right....I assigned to Greeks and barbarians their language....I established penalties for those who practice injustice" (*Hellenistic Religions: The Age of Syncretism,* edited by Frederick C. Grant, pp. 131-33). Clearly, Isis is the goddess of law and order. However, in the same aretology she also says of herself, "I make the navigable unnavigable when it pleases me." This provocative statement establishes Isis as the goddess of disorder as well. Thus she, like her sister Demeter, integrates two opposing principles which in later periods became separated. For instance, even in the Jewish wisdom-literature Sophia is solely the figure of the world order and righteousness; the qualities of chaos and disorder are projected onto other figures such as the Strange or Foreign Woman.

Even this brief resume of Isis and Demeter reveals some aspects of the feminine principle as it was understood at the beginning of the Christian era. First, both goddesses have a strong relationship with the earth. Demeter was the goddess of the harvest and Isis was the Goddess of the Nile. Despite the development and elaboration of their characters and attributes, this essential affinity with the earth, this quality of rootedness remained part of their nature. Even the goddess-like figure of wisdom retains her connections with the practical and manual arts. Wisdom is not mastery of abstract theories but rather knowledge of the ways of man, God, and nature.

Second, the goddesses are concerned with persons, particularly persons in a family setting. Demeter searches for her daughter and Isis searches for her husband/brother Osiris. Isis also has a son, Horus, who plays an important role in her myths. In his book, *The Mothers*, Robert Briffault suggests that the concept of the brotherhood of man was originally a teaching of the goddesses. It would certainly be in keeping with their concern for the individual in the intimate setting of the family.

Third, the goddesses represent the presence of opposites within a single personality. For instance, the goddesses display both love and rage, the constructive and destructive forces of the universe. This aspect of their character is clearly visible in the myths of Demeter and Isis: confronted with the loss of their loved child or husband, both grieve and rage. The contemporary work of Elisabeth Kübler-Ross is a reminder of how intertwined these two emotions are within anyone facing death or enforced separation. In addition, the goddesses also demonstrate the qualities of rootedness and wandering. Demeter and Isis are strongly identified with a place (Eleusis and Egypt), yet both are connected with wandering and searching. As *Mater Dolorosa* they leave the world of gods and live among human beings. As such they are readily available to the people and can act as intermediaries between them and the gods. Even though during their travels they frequently conceal their divinity, they still establish the mystery religions and confer immortality on mortals. Finally, the goddesses represent both world order and world disorder. The connections between Isis/Maat and world order have already been mentioned. It is interesting to note that to this day "Justice" is still personified as a blind woman. The chaotic or antinomian aspect of the goddesses is less well known. Nevertheless, Demeter's disregard of the will of Zeus and Isis' ability to make the navigable unnavigable when it pleases her are evidence of this dimension of their personalities.

This analysis of the great virgin goddesses of the ancient world reveals an understanding of the feminine principle substantially different from what we know today. How or why this original meaning was corrupted or perverted is hard to determine. It may have resulted from reducing the power of the goddesses by splitting up their attributes and assigning them to a variety of goddesses; or from reinterpreting their myths so they reflected the concepts of Greek philosophy; or from the repression of the goddesses and the destruction of their cults after Christianity became the dominant religion of the Roman Empire. Certainly all three methods were used to support a growing patriarchal bias which some thinkers believe came as a reaction to an earlier age which was dominated by the Mothers. Whether or not this is true, it is clear that the patriarchal bias was firmly entrenched by, if not before, the beginning of the Christian era. From that point, a new construction of the feminine principle and the repression of the goddesses who embodied the old was inevitable, until even the watered down version of the feminine principle was subordinated to the masculine principle.

The history of the repression of living women is now being written and patriarchalism, which often reached the level of misogyny, is now being checked by legal means. However, the domination of the masculine principle has done more than truncate the lives of women in society. It has elevated certain traits to the level of philosophical absolutes, and as absolutes their power has grown corrupt. Society as a whole becomes truncated when the mind is glorified at the expense of feeling; when activity alone is honorable; when the rational denies the existence of the irrational; and where the will of man is imposed on all nature. Such distortions eventually produce a host of problems, not only on a personal level, but on a global level: aggressive national policies which could lead to nuclear destruction; devaluation of nature or ecology which results in the starving of billions and the possible destruction of the atmosphere; the breakdown of the family and the absence of intimacy which leads to anxiety and sensationalism; and the mechanization of life and a vain intellectualizing uninformed by wisdom and a caring for the human condition.

Obviously, many people are concerned about these and similar problems, but it would be naive to ignore their relationship to a masculine principle gone wild. Therefore, at the same time as pragmatic attempts are being made to prevent global disaster, attention should be given to reordering the philosophical and religious values which undergird our culture. No doubt the reclaiming of the feminine principle as it once was and the establishing of that principle as equal to, and compatible with, the masculine principle will be part of that reordering. There are many people today who speculate about and yearn for a new age. It is just possible that after 2500 years the turning of this axial age will hinge on such a renewal of the values of the feminine.

8

The World Mother

GEOFFREY HODSON

Christianity, Hinduism[1] and other great world faiths all teach that there exists a Being here on our earth who embodies in perfection all the highest attributes of the feminine aspect of both the creative deity and the human race, including human motherhood. She, the all-compassionate One, gazes with infinite tenderness and concern upon life on earth. What must she see? A frankly ruthless and nakedly cynical violation and desecration by humanity—chiefly, though not entirely, by the male—of everything holy and beautiful for which she stands. She must see everywhere throughout the world irreverence, abuse and cruelty—the continual infliction of unnecessary suffering upon humans and upon the animal kingdom.

If it were not that she must also know that this epoch is a phase out of which there will grow a nobler, a fairer, a

---

1. In Hinduism, the Supreme Deity is worshipped in both Masculine and Feminine Aspects, is regarded as Universal Father of the World and Universal Mother. The Feminine Aspect is worshipped under many names and in many forms. She is chiefly known as *Jagadamba, the World Mother,* and this concept includes also the *Shakti* (expressed energy) Aspect or Compliments of the Trimurti. These are Parvati, the Complement of Shiva, Lakshmi of Vishnu, and Sarasvati of Brahma. All women are regarded as representatives of the *Jagadamba* who is the Mother of all mothers, the Divine Queen of the Kingdom of Motherhood, woman's highest ideal.

kinder and a more gentle civilization, surely her heart would be unbearably torn by what she must see. If we add that in her divine love she voluntarily remains near to humanity, that she is not only an outside observer, not only a great Spirit removed from us, not only an ascetic adept who long ago attained to a spiritual mountain top, but that in a mysterious way she is actually present within our hearts, and especially within the hearts of every woman and child, what an almost unbearable experience such nearness to humanity would be!

I am myself profoundly convinced that such a Being exists and that, beyond human understanding, she is the perfected embodiment of all that is highest and noblest in womanhood. Her heart, I believe, is filled with love and compassion for us all and, while she does see our sins, she does not condemn us. Rather does she draw nearer to enfold us in her arms of love, even while we transgress.

St. Catherine of Sienna, when for a time she had lost contact with her Lord and in her own eyes had fallen deeply, asked, ''Lord, where wast Thou amidst all that failure?'' In what is called the mystic locution, when the devotee communes with God and hears his voice, the Lord answered, ''Daughter, I was there with thee in thy heart.'' So she, the Mother of the World, is here with us in our hearts, as well as brooding maternally over all humanity.

Let us now look at our world and see some of the problems with which we—and so the World Mother, since she is one with us—are confronted. . . . The world she loves and serves is also deeply sullied by violence, organized crime and vice, such as drug peddling, even to children and adolescents, and prostitution. Other evils deeply affecting the progress, happiness and health of humanity, particularly the birth of a new and nobler race with which process the World Mother may also be presumed to be concerned, consist of monopolies, cartels, price fixing, corruption in public, professional and business life, soil exploitation and timber denudation. All these bring gain to the few but result in poverty, and in some parts of the world in famine, to the many. . . .

Such are some of the plainly discernible phenomena of the particular phase of evolution through which humanity is now passing. In consequence, most people go on living their everyday lives half frightened, half indifferent, not daring to think into the future and, as Thoreau said, ''in quiet desperation.'' So we, the people of the world see—as she, the World Mother, must also see—the ghastly, tragic comedy that is being performed on the international, national, political and economic stages, where the fate of humanity is being largely decided and individuals find themselves relatively helpless. No wonder disillusionment, bitterness and cynicism characterize the thinking and the outlook of youth and adult alike.

Hence the deep significance of those movements which focus attention on certain aspects of this problem, particularly those concerning the birth of a new and higher race and the life and work of women in the world. There are all too few of such movements on earth, born out of tenderness and compassion for humanity, out of a spiritual vision and a recognition of the existence of a feminine principle in God, in all nature and in humans.

If I may here introduce a personal note, I well remember how the vision of the veritable existence of the World Mother first dawned upon me many years ago. I think I was privileged to see her, however faintly, not only as an ideal or even as one in the succession of personifications of the mother aspect of Deity, but also as a wondrous living Being, the exquisite jewel in the hierarchy of Earth's adepts, the World Mother for this epoch, the Star of the Sea, as she is severally named....As a result of such experiences, I feel that I came to know at least that she exists and a little of what may be seen in her eyes and in her heart—a divinely tender, maternal solicitude for all humanity. I learned, I think, that childbirth should ideally be as conscious as possible, though never at the cost of undue pain: for certain expansions of consciousness can then be experienced which can effect, can exalt, the consciousness of the mother and through her that of the whole race.

How may she be truly envisaged? While the beautiful ma-

110

donna blue is probably universal, the form in which she presents herself is apparently adapted to those who see her. Possibly their own minds shape the vision of her into a familiar form. . . .For us Christians, she in her compassion may deliberately adopt the madonna form so that we might recognize her.

A Chinese lady once invited me to her home and showed me her beautiful garden. Among the trees were statues of Kwan Yin, goddess of wisdom and compassion, the feminine logos of Chinese Buddhism. My hostess said to me, "I have had thirteen children, and on more than one occasion Kwan Yin herself saved my life. When the pangs of birth became unendurable and I would die, I saw her there beside my bed. She stretched out her hand towards me, and immediately the pain was eased and the lost poise and steadiness restored, not once, but many times."

Thus I have come to believe, even to know, that there is such a wondrous and glorious Being on our earth as the World Mother, that she is very near to human mothers during pregnancy and at the time of birth. I have also learned that she ever seeks human agents and human helpers who will serve in her name and endeavor to live in her presence. While women especially represent her, she also needs men of honor to be her knights, ever ready to fight for the weak and the exploited and to guard with knightly loyalty all women and children, as true knights should. . . .A great Mahatma once wrote: "Not till woman bursts the bonds of her sexual slavery, to which she has ever been subjected, will the world obtain an inkling of what she really is and of her proper place in the economy of Nature."[2]

All nations have recognized, honored and worshipped this maternal principle in nature. All their exoteric religions have personified it as a Goddess, an archangel mother of universes, races, nations and humans. These personifications of the World Mother are among the very noblest concepts of the human mind, which in creating, reverencing and serving them reaches its highest degree of idealism,

---

2. *The Paradoxes of the Highest Science,* by Eliphas Levi, p. 171.

devotion and religious self-expression. Such reverence, such devotion and such worship as are offered to World Mothers are therefore worthy of the deepest respect and—gross superstition apart, ever to be resisted—may usefully be encouraged. For through devotion, human beings may be reached from on high. Through aspiration, highest love and supplication, we are susceptible to both our own spiritual Self and the influence of the adept ministrants of humanity. The madonna ideal, for example, has been and still is of incalculable value in consoling, purifying and ennobling humanity. Through it, a realization of the mother-love of God has been brought within reach of millions of suffering and aspiring people. The concepts of Kwan Yin, Isis, Ishtar, Parvati and other Goddesses are similarly founded upon the existence, nature and function of the same great Being. . . .

Such are some of the thoughts and the ideals which have awakened in me since I passed through those experiences many years ago, followed as they have been by others. Is it not worthwhile to be associated with such an ideal and with such a work as hers? I feel strongly urged to appeal to those similarly moved, that they will participate and contribute to the best of their ability that her work shall not only live on and prosper, but that it shall enter on a great era of activity in her name, which is the name of compassion, wisdom and universal love.

II

Psychological Perspectives

9

The Sadness of
the Successful Woman

JUNE SINGER

Why should a woman who has achieved most of what she wanted, or thought she wanted—romance, a good job, a measure of power—come to a psychotherapist for help? Many of the women with whom I work in therapy these days are in middle life, but younger women, as well, need to be aware of the problems of this age group because they will most probably have to face them. I am aware that my sample of the female population is skewed because the people who seek out an analyst are, as a rule, suffering to such a degree that they are willing to undergo a long, deep, and demanding process of soul-searching. These women differ in two ways from the general female population: first, they are aware that their suffering may have to do with something within themselves (which is not to exclude factors in the outer world), and second, they are willing to submit to the possibility of profound changes in themselves, whatever these may cost in terms of commitment, work, time and money.

I would like to give you a composite profile of the woman who comes to me suffering from what I can only call "the sadness of the successful woman." She is somewhere between thirty and forty-five. If she is married, she says that her marriage is a problem for her. If she is not married, not being married is a problem for her. On the one hand she is afraid that she may be too dominant in her relationship with a male partner, and that he will not be able to cope with her powerful energy. On the other hand, she is afraid that if she doesn't express herself in her personal and professional life as well as she is able, she will feel frustrated, diminished, and untrue to her deepest self. If she has chosen a man who is willing to further her and support her goals, even at times at the expense of his own, she fears that she will emasculate him and then dislike him for his weakness. If she has chosen a man who is bent on fulfilling his own ambitions, she wants to provide the necessary support system for him, yet resents having to sacrifice some of her own needs in order to be available for him.

Children are inevitably an important part of this woman's life and consequently a source of deep concern to her. Since only women have the capacity to bear a child, it becomes primarily a woman's concern whether or not to raise a family, and if so, when. Of course men ask these questions, too, but a man can more easily evade them. A woman cannot. Deciding not to have a child, not to go through this specifically feminine experience, has a profound effect on a woman's psyche. Pregnancy has a profound effect on a woman's psyche, also. So do miscarriage and abortion, childbirth, breastfeeding, using a nursing bottle, or having to choose between breast and bottle. All of these experiences or the absence of them have made their mark on woman's psyche.

Our composite "successful woman" initially tried to approach these issues in the same rational way that men do. She decided what would be best for her on the basis of reasonable considerations; she weighed the pros and cons of her decision and then acted, or refrained from acting, with what she regarded as "full knowledge of the consequences." But when it came down to the actual experience, it was not what she thought it would be. There was nothing rational about it. It was pure feeling. Something rose up in her psyche, something so deep, so elemental, that there are no words for it. It was felt bodily, it was felt in the unconscious, and only gradually did it seep into consciousness to color the very fabric of her life, so that there was no mistaking it.

The biological clock is another woman's issue. No man watches the erratic flow of the menses at menopause and feels the embarrassing hot flushes signaling a woman that her childbearing years are nearly over; that what was so casually postponed in favor of "higher priorities" will never happen now, or that if it does, there will be greater risks attached. These are matters a woman doesn't talk about much, except perhaps to her therapist, but they rest like heavy stones on her heart.

Let us suppose that this composite woman is one of the luckier ones. She has managed to marry well, has a pleasant home, and two or three healthy children. She has been able to go back to school or to get a position with good prospects for advancement. Many of her friends feel less fortunate and envy her. The woman tells her therapist, "Everyone thinks I have it made, but I'm not really happy. My life is hard and I'm very tired. I don't feel fulfilled either in my work or with my family. Nothing goes the way it should, or if one thing is right, the other is wrong."

This woman belongs to the first generation of those reared in an atmosphere more enabling for the working woman than in times past. She and her sisters went to college and were able to major in something other than teaching or nursing. They continued on to medical school or law school, or they earned degrees in business administration or finance. They have now completed the initial phase of working in the world, and many of them have achieved executive, managerial, and professional positions, with all the powers and responsibilities attached. Their problems, as they have presented them to me, are first and foremost women's problems. It is true that they are also problems of men and of society, especially its legislation, management, and labor aspects. But even if men and labor and management and society chose to disregard or to disown these issues, they would still exist for women. This is because women are intrinsically different from men. It may be argued that women as a group are equal to men, or superior to men, or inferior to men. But that women are *different* from men is beyond dispute. Biologically, women are different in structure and potentiality. Psychologically, women's values tend to be differently ordered, so that their priorities may not line up in the same way that men's do.

I want to move now to another level. Is this general unhappiness, this subclinical depression, merely a phenomenon of our times? Or are its roots deeper?

I believe we are facing an archetypal problem. It is archetypal because it stems from a pattern in the unconscious that affects people of every culture and every age, for practically all human beings are nurtured by women, reared by women, love women and are loved by them, and have women for partners and friends. From earliest times, feminine sensibilities have added a touch of gentleness to life, a certain dimension of caring. If these qualities are not present in our lives, there is likely to be a silence of the soul. Yet some women are saying today that despite their success in the world, or perhaps because of it, they have lost touch with their "femininity,"—and then they are likely to add, "whatever that is." If we can explore the archetypal basis of the unhappiness of the so-called successful woman of our culture, we may be able to discover its depth and meaning instead of being swept away by it.

It appears to me that all cultures support values that, objectively seen, are in direct opposition to each other. Most cultures, including our own, tend to emphasize one set of paired values, while the other set remains relatively unconscious, acting as the opposite or shadow of these. The same is true of individuals. Most of us find that in our own lives one of these sets of values is in the foreground of consciousness, while the other is more or less relegated to the unconscious—emerging only at certain special times, and often with considerable effort. A set of paired values that is particularly characteristic of a society of educated and informed urban Americans could be designated *individual identity* and *relationship*.

Our society places a particularly high emphasis upon personal identity. The hero myth is the main archetypal story in our culture. A man of honor, a knight, a "warrior" in Carlos Castaneda's sense, must adhere to certain standards. He must use all his strength and will to prove his excellence.

He must achieve the goal he has set for himself, despite the consequences. Odysseus must take every twist and turn of the archetypal journey no matter how many times Penelope, waiting at home, has to embroider and pick out the stitches of the enormous piece of needlework she is making.

Today's entrepreneur lives, eats, and sleeps his personally conceived enterprise in order to give it his very best. He needs and wants a woman to take care of his household and to provide emotional support for his efforts while he is establishing his place in the world. The career woman, who is striving to get ahead and whose position demands a great deal from her, also needs emotional and practical support. She regards herself as extremely fortunate if she has a partner who can provide the kind of support that men tend to expect from women as a matter of course. In a culture that places a high premium on identity, career-oriented individuals put themselves on the line. They risk failing to accomplish what they have set out to accomplish, and having to face the shame of not being what they thought they were. Shame, then, is the great terror for the identity-oriented person in our culture.

Some people in our society are not so much concerned with personal identity as with participation in a group. Relationships or membership are their overriding interests. Children are taught to think of others before themselves. Businesses are run by encouraging people to feel that their efforts ought to be directed toward cooperation in the development of a better product rather than toward individual excellence, individual skills, or individual accomplishment. Personal goals are subordinated to the general welfare, with the reward being that if the enterprise is successful, all the members who have contributed toward it will prosper. Personal satisfaction comes from winning the esteem of co-workers or from family members, as the case must be. One should be understanding rather than outstanding.

In a society or family where the relationship values are stressed, people fear being thought uncooperative, unhelpful, and uncaring. Guilt is the great terror, the guilt of not having met the expectations of others. ''I am not fulfilling my obligations. I am selfish. I will end up being lonely and despised.'' This is what some people tell themselves when they are trying to live up to the demands of an environment in which relationship is the highest value.

So shame is failing to meet one's own expectations, while guilt is failing to meet the expectations of the group. Shame is the unwanted dark side of the culture of identity, and guilt is the shadow side of the culture of participation. They each have a different effect upon the individual.

One who experiences shame feels like an outcast from society, absolutely valueless. ''I am not the person I thought I was,'' could be one of the most damning phrases ever uttered. A permanent state of shame is a living hell. The person in the identity-oriented culture is most afraid of a kind of psychic death, an annihilation of that very identity which was so prized, without any possibility of resurrection.

Guilt is painful because the person who incurs it fears being judged by the laws of society, of being rejected by not living up to them. The person from the relationship-oriented culture is most afraid of the need to confess the wrongdoing. But here, at least, there is hope, through repentance. Renewed conformity secures membership in this group.

In our society we have of course been exposed to both identity-oriented and relationship-oriented values. Our individual paths may have led us to emphasize one or the other during the first half of life. But when situations change, as they tend to do at mid-life, the opposite set of values comes into play. It is then that we must face a host of new choices. This can be a challenge or a threat, depending upon how we have prepared ourselves for it. What can happen to our ego-ideals as we face each of these cultural sets of values in later life? If we were mainly identity-oriented, the image of what we wanted to become was elevated, and our ambitions were tailored to fit this ideal. Conversely, if we were relationship-oriented, the ego-ideals of youth, of what we wanted to become, are abandoned in the face of the perceived reality that there are others in this world who need to be considered before ourselves. In both cases, we will have to admit the opposite side as we become older.

Clearly, both sets of values exist in every culture, in every work setting, in every family, and in every person. As society continually forces choices upon us, these values frequently conflict with one another. Which will attain priority in any given situation—the preservation of one's personal autonomy or the necessity for cooperation with a group of which we are members? No wonder that we are concerned as to whether these two polar opposite agendas can ever be blended into some kind of harmony.

Before we can explore this conflict, it seems to me that we must approach it historically. This is not a new dilemma, even though it seems especially pressing upon people today at mid-life. The set of values where identity is primary has nearly always been associated with the masculine principle. Identity reigns in a highly stratified society, with those who have successfully forged an identity being able to rise to positions of higher power. This has usually occurred in a patriarchal society, with men primarily in the positions of power. Why men? Simply because a man who is ambitious and career-oriented can rush headlong into his work and the adjunctive activities that support it without having to stop to have babies and or to stay home when the baby sitter doesn't arrive—it is not necessary to extend the list. Today it is accepted that women will work, not only to add to the family income and make it possible for the entire family to enjoy a higher standard of living than would be possible otherwise, but also to find an identity of their own outside the home and family. But I believe that for most women the value of personal identity is most satisfying within the context of a fulfilling relationship.

Traditionally, the set of values having to do with Eros, with relationship, has long been associated with the feminine principle. The kinds of societies and settings in which relationships are highly prized tend to be dominated by matriarchal values. These values include membership in a group, a sisterhood, a family; and the membership is of a different sort from that in the groups to which men typically belong.

If the identity-oriented attitude is more characteristic of

the masculine in our culture, then the feeling function, at its best, its most developed, allows us to trust people once they have been assessed and found "all right." The feeling function makes possible a certain kind of relationship which could be characterized as "defenselessly bonded." That means that we are able to be vulnerable, to allow our weaknesses, fears, and liabilities to be seen. How difficult this must be for one to whom identity is all important!

If the relationship-oriented attitude is more characteristic of the feminine, the shadow side or unrecognized aspect is a longing for unlimited power. Just because woman is, by nature, cyclical in her functioning and at times does not have the capacity to function in a fully extraverted way, she longs for that complete freedom which, she imagines, belongs to the male. She may then deny her true femininity and attempt to handle her relationships in a more pragmatic manner, choosing those which will further her ambitions and either neglecting or delegating to others the more nurturant tasks.

It is surely evident that many women today are sliding into the culture of identity, and therefore exposing themselves to shame, the terror of that orientation. In the early days of the women's movement we were discovering our inner strengths. We were moving into higher education in ever-increasing numbers. We were taking more responsible jobs. Now, a generation later, we and our younger sisters have begun to assume positions of power. But, unlike men, we have had to make certain choices along the way. Women's choices are structured largely by relationships. Conversely, relationships among men tend to be structured largely by the choices they make.

It seems to be that the deepest psychic conflicts come about when one is living in a way that is strongly one-sided, biased either toward identity or toward relationship. I am speaking now of the women today who are considered successful in the so-called man's world and who also have been able to maintain a home, a husband, and children. These women tell me that they are beginning to feel that they have sacrificed too much for the sake of establishing their identity in the world. It has been harder for them than they ever thought it would be, because they have had to do nearly everything that men do and more besides, for women still carry the primary responsibility for sweeping the hearth. Such women are suffering from a particular form of depression. I believe that they are mourning for their lost femininity.

These women refuse the symbolic message of their depression, which is a longing for the harmonization of the opposites within themselves. The way of life they have chosen does not validate the feminine self. By "feminine self" I include the totality of a woman's conscious and unconscious views of herself. These women suffer from the refusal or the impossibility of living it out. They oscillate between despair and guilt: despair that they can never be fully secure in the world of patriarchal values, and guilt that even if they do achieve recognition in that world, a very important part of their being, their Eros, will have to be sacrificed in the process.

The position of an ego turned toward goals of identity, recognition, and power gives rise to a shadow, an inferior unconscious counterpart which refuses meaning and represses feeling. The woman in this position can easily become dominated by the patriarchal values around her. The result is a consciousness that is marked by enslavement to a driving ego. Such a woman sees the feeling values as retrogressive. She may become a mother who is able to be absent from her child, a woman who is rigid and distant. Within herself she is a mass of contradictions. The feminine self, which by definition includes the totality of a woman's being, flounders on the maternal function—which is seen by this woman as a threat to her identity and indeed to her psychic survival.

The archetypes of Identity and Relationship are ever present and active within this woman, as they are for everyone—whether we acknowledge this inner conflict and try to heal it or choose a single path and suppress the path not taken. For the two opposites in the psyche will not always rest easy with each other. At times the need for personal identity, the need for following the dictates of one's own particular soul, will be in the foreground of consciousness. At such times another person—a love partner, a child—will be seen as an obstacle to one's fulfillment and will be resented. But immediately as this is felt, guilt sweeps over one. ''What am I doing to the ones I care for?'' The rejected feminine impulse comes rushing up from the unconscious to disturb the flow of consciousness toward the well-ordered personal goals. Then Love or Eros or Relationship will seem most desirable, and the whole inner turmoil will switch over into its opposite. Personal identity will seem relatively unimportant now. ''What is the good of fame and fortune if I come home to an empty house and if no one really cares whether I live or die?'' ''Why am I placing all these unreasonable demands on myself, demands for excellence, demands for perfection? What is it all worth in the end?''

And so the woman who has it made swings between the two opposing sets of values that she sees as part and parcel of what society imposes upon her. But is it true that society has imposed these? No one can deny that all of us are to a very large degree conditioned by society. Our conditioning begins when we are born, when we begin to gain a sense of the expectations of mother, and later of the wider world. Still, if we can believe that we are something more than our conditioning, that we come into this world with a psyche that is imprinted with archetypal patterns, then we have some choice as to what patterns we will live out, what we accept and what we reject out of that which is offered to us. Can a free society impose anything upon anyone unless that person tacitly agrees to it? Tacitly and perhaps unconsciously? When we begin to see how we have learned to follow the crowd without giving it a thought, we may discover that after all we do have some choice in the matter.

I have struggled for a long time with this issue, this conflict, as I have worked with analysands and in my own life as well. Lately I have come to something like a tentative resolution. It is in the realm of feeling, and surely far from rational. It comes of a recognition that life in this body on this earth is short. As we get older we become ever more conscious of this simple fact. It will soon be over anyway. There is not much left of it, perhaps only twenty years, perhaps only ten, perhaps there is only tomorrow. Will we then spend these few precious days bouncing back and forth between the guilt of having been insufficiently loving and the shame at not having achieved all that we were capable of achieving? Will we spend this precious time wishing that we were better at the one or at the other?

I think that what we need to do is to practice for the last act of our earthly drama, the one that is most certain and for which we are least prepared. I am talking about the act of dying. It will go something like this: Imagine that you are on your deathbed. You feel life slowly ebbing away from you. You don't have any more energy to do anything. Your desk is piled high with unanswered letters, unfinished tasks. It really doesn't matter much. Either someone else will pick them up or they will remain undone. In the long run it will make little difference. No one will know that the idea you meant to work out never came to expression. No one will feel poorer for it. Then there are the people in your life. If you loved them well, they will grieve for you and miss you. Over time the poignancy of your relationship and your absence will fade and only a soft glow will be left. There will be those whom you did not care for enough, those whom you rejected, those with whom there is still unfinished business. It doesn't matter now. There is only one thing you can do about it, and that is to let go. Let the tasks of this world slip away. Let your very identity slip away. Let your loved ones mourn you for a little while and then go on their way. Let go of everything, your home, your possessions, your feelings, and your thoughts. Allow yourself to drift.

You will begin to feel lighter. You will lose the heavy load you have been carrying. That heavy load was your sense of self-importance. It was your feeling that everything you did had intrinsic importance, therefore you had to do it fully and perfectly no matter what it cost. You realize how temporal it all is when you are facing your death.

This conflict between relationship and identity is a conflict through which we all must live. It can be healed only by a recognition of our own limitations, by moderation in all things, and by accepting ourselves as we really are. This requires that we recognize that the personal identity that is so precious to us is not something we can hold onto and possess once and for all. Our nature is dynamic and growing, everchanging. We only know who we are by observing ourselves and by paying attention to the responses we evoke in other people. Personal identity does not exist in a vacuum. It is affected by relationships and events in the world. At the same time, who we are, how we express our system of values, plays a significant role in how we affect the small world in which we live.

What I am advocating—to practice dying—is not an easy thing. We may experience letting go of our own sense of self-importance, but that moment is quite ephemeral. We tend to forget it too easily. Awareness of the approach of death can be a beautiful thing, a frame into which we can put the work of art that is our life, our personal masterpiece. This awareness can help us to be content to do a little less, to do it a bit more slowly, with care and with love. The inclinations toward identity and the impulses toward relationship can both be served if we do not require that each be done to perfection. A wise person once said that the goal of the masculine principle is perfection and the goal of the feminine principle is completion. If you are perfect, you cannot be complete, because you must leave out all the imperfections of your nature. If you are complete, you cannot be perfect, for being complete means that you contain good and evil, right and wrong, hope and despair. So perhaps it is best to be content with something less than perfection and something less than completion. Perhaps we need to be more willing to accept life as it comes. When we think about it, do we have another choice?

We cannot know whether we have twenty years or forty or only a day in which to accomplish whatever it is that life offers as its agenda. So perhaps we should not strive so much for the applause, but rather for the pleasure and the grace of the dance.

10
A Higher View of the Man-Woman Problem

ROBERTO ASSAGIOLI AND
CLAUDE SERVAN-SCHREIBER

For spirits when they please can either sex
assume, or both; so soft and uncompounded is
their essence.
> *John Milton,* Paradise Lost

The first time that I saw Roberto Assagioli was about two years ago, at his home in Florence, in the old house where a large part of his life has unfolded. He showed us into his office, cluttered with books and papers to such a point that he had to move a pile over so that my husband and I could be seated.

For a long moment we looked at each other, all three of us, without speaking. Assagioli smiling, his eyes, astonishingly vital within a face lined by great age, moving over us, going from one to the other. Was he submitting us to an examination? It was instead the opposite. He was allowing us to discover him leisurely, to establish a connection with him, without us even realizing this was happening. It was a climate of communication where words find their place later, while something like a current was developing between us. His face was shining with an extraordinary, radiant inner joy, such as I have never encountered in an octogenarian, and rarely in men much younger. This message of joy, perceived immediately, communicated immediately, is the finest memory which I keep of the numerous meetings which we later had with him. "All is possible and accessible *to you:* joy, serenity, I offer them to you as a gift."

Roberto Assagioli and Claude Servan-Schreiber

I did not expect to find in Roberto Assagioli the echo of my own concern in a particular, specific area: the psychology of women within a world in which their roles, their functions, lead them to undergo first a conditioning, then an oppression which often they do not yet recognize. In the eyes of the feminist that I am, the father of psychosynthesis has therefore an additional merit: an amazing capacity to adapt to changing attitudes, which comes to him from his will to understand others and from his love of scientific truth, even if different from past beliefs. On the subject of women, he had in the past been limited; and he knows it and frankly admits it. He had been influenced by cultural prejudices denoting as "feminine nature" that which is largely the product of a social system. But later he freed himself, in this respect, from the weight of his upbringing, his environment, his age. He quickly became interested in the new existential research into the nature of women which is our liberation movement. At his age, and for an Italian, this is a double achievement! Especially if one judges according to his conclusions.

There is not, and there cannot be a general psychosynthesis of women or, for that matter, of men. There is only, for each individual, of either sex, a personal, unique journey, toward the development of all his emotional, mental and spiritual faculties. "The human being," he said, "today is no longer defined by any of his roles. I believe in the primacy of the human being not conditioned by his sex." Can there be a more beautiful message? Here, more fully, is what he said to me on the subject:

Assagioli:

We cannot accurately speak of women and men *in general*. Each one of us is a human being before being 'man' or 'woman.' And each one of us, man or woman, has roles and functions to fulfill, individually, interindividually and socially. Here is where the differences begin. These are most emphatically not *differences in value, only differences in function*. The human being is never defined by any of these roles. Women, as human beings, can accept or not accept traditional feminine roles. It is not necessary that a woman accept the role of wife or of mother. She can choose another vocation. It is not a 'must,' a necessity. It is a free choice.

"Woman therefore is right in demanding that she be treated as a human being and not as a 'mere woman,' as simply a woman and only that. She is right for refusing to be identified with a certain image of woman. She is a living being, with all the dignity and the potential of a whole human being. All attitudes which limit the possibilities of woman are mistaken. Women have the right to demand respect and parity with men. And the same, of course, is true for men.

"Each of us can equally choose to play different roles. For instance, a woman can decide to play the role of spouse or of mother, or both. She can carry on a creative, social or business activity. She can choose one role, or she can alternate several of them, perhaps during the same day, perhaps over longer periods of time. This is the free choice of a human being. I believe in the primacy of the human being unconditioned by his or her sex.

"The differences between men and women are clearly found reflected in our environment—in the family and in society—and it is here that we must work to eliminate their unfair and harmful crystallization into rigid stereotypes and prejudices.

"But it is important to realize that these differences exist also *within* our psyche, in the depths of our unconscious and, just as much, in the collective unconscious of humanity, where they appear through some of the most powerful archetypes. So there are universal masculine and feminine principles, which manifest themselves in quite diverse ways through different individuals. In other words, while masculine and feminine principles do exist in the universe, different people experience them and describe them in different ways—as is equally the case with beauty, truth, harmony, goodness, justice or any of the other universal principles.

"The point is not to try to define what these principles are, but to distinguish, in our consciousness and in our relations with others, 'masculine' and 'feminine' from 'man' and 'woman.' We need to recognize that *both* the masculine and feminine principles exist in their own rights, and that they are present—although in unique forms and different proportions—in *every* man and in *every* woman.

"Within each human being is a percentage of psychological masculinity and a percentage of psychological femininity, completely independent of the sex of the individual. Each person is a unique combination of these energies. When we look at women *on the whole,* we find that they are more attuned to the feminine principle, have greater access to it and have a higher percentage of it in their psychological make-up. And similarly, men are more attuned to the masculine principle. Of course this is a generality. People are unique. Some men are psychologically more feminine than many woman, for instance.

"Take the example of the French novelist George Sand (the pen name of Baronne Dudevant) and Chopin. They were lovers, and he, physically, had the 'man' role and she the 'woman' role. But psychologically he was feminine and she was masculine. She dressed like a man, wrote in a vigorous style—and smoked cigars! In her personality, masculinity predominated, while Chopin was imaginative, sensitive.

"There is therefore a difference between physical sex and psychological characteristics. Over the years, I have met many who feared—or even believed—themselves to be homosexuals just because they did not recognize this distinction.

"Only by accepting both the masculine and feminine principles, bringing them together, and harmonizing them within ourselves, will we be able to transcend the conditioning of our roles, and to express the whole range of our latent potential.

"As this is true for the individual, so is it true for society. From the social standpoint, there is a great need in present society for the expression of the feminine principle. Society needs women to contribute the higher aspects of their femininity—altruistic love, compassion, the sense of and respect for life—with which they are usually more familiar and which they can often express with greater facility than men. It is therefore desirable for women to be involved in social and political life. If they so choose, they can do this while they continue to play traditional feminine roles in the family, or they can give themselves completely over to activities such as social service, renouncing the traditional family roles. They have the full right to do it. Society must respect and appreciate their valuable contribution.

"The fact that a woman may dedicate herself much of the time to certain roles must not prevent her from considering herself equal to men. It is not at all a question of superiority and inferiority. Masculine and feminine psychological characteristics, even though dissimilar, are of the same value. This is a statement of fact.

"Women are right to protest and to rise against the long-standing prejudicial attitudes of society. But in the protest one can lose perspective. One can be destructive and not constructive. Psychologically and historically, conflicts and exaggerations can be understood. The ideal would be for them to remain within boundaries that are constructive as well as just.

"For example, some women go to the opposite extreme of current social stereotypes. Rather than balancing and integrating their feminine energies with their masculine energies, they may virtually deny the feminine in themselves. A woman may reject traditional feminine roles in order to prove to men that she can play masculine roles. Here exists the danger of the masculinization of women. Ironically, this attitude can proceed from the unconscious evaluation of the masculine principle and masculine roles as inherently superior to the feminine. But there is no such inherent superiority. What is needed is an honoring and valuing of the feminine principle, and the ways and roles through which this energy can be expressed by both men and women. Masculine roles are neither better nor worse than feminine roles. They are both needed and are of equal value.

"A controversial question is whether the fact that women frequently have certain functions better developed and men others is the product of nature, or of education, or of social pressure. In my opinion all three factors are present, in different proportions, in each individual.

"While this is an important *social* problem, fortunately, from the *individual's* standpoint it can be largely sidestepped. He or she need only consider how he or she is *right now*, and how he or she *can improve*.

"For example, if a woman has had fewer opportunities or incentives to express her ideas, her thoughts, it does not seem to me to be necessary to spend much time and energy to search to understand why, who is responsible for this, and so forth. Quite simply, if this function is insufficiently developed, *she can develop it*. And the same is true for a man who has not developed his feelings, or his intuition. (Needless to say, there are men who need to develop their intellect, and women who need to get in touch with their feelings and cultivate their intuition.) The point is to recognize the strong qualities and the deficiencies in each person— which are not 'faults' but qualitative, relative deficiencies— and to bring them into a condition of harmony and balance. This is what I call a psychologically and spiritually practical approach.

"Let us come now to the couple. A couple founded on a basis of fundamental equality, respect, reciprocal appreciation as human beings, can work out the psychosynthesis of their particular couple together. Each one can work on his [or her] own psychosynthesis, and each one can also collaborate in the psychosynthesis of the other, helping the other to achieve psychosynthesis by helping strengthen his [or her] less developed functions. Then once they have done this to a certain point, they can truly act as a couple by combining and complementing their qualities and functions in all situations: in their marriage, their role as parents, and in their social activities.

"For each function to be developed training is needed— often including specific exercises. The process is analogous to the training of muscles: if one wants to play a certain sport, he finds someone who is competent, gets trained and afterwards continues to train himself. If a man recognizes that his emotional and imaginative sides have been neglected, he can cultivate them. If a woman finds that her mind is not as active as she would like, she can train it. One has to 'cultivate one's garden' by planting different flowers. A woman or a man can do it alone, but it is often more effective, much easier and more enjoyable to do it together as two people.

"When we come to particular problems, many difficulties may emerge, and in each specific case we can apply a therapy. I speak of 'therapy' here in the broadest sense of the word, because none of us is one hundred percent healthy in the higher psychosynthetic sense. In difficult situations a benevolent and wise therapist or counselor can be of great assistance: someone impartial, kindly, comprehensive, who helps the two members of the couple to become more aware, who explains the situation, who indicates possible solutions and helps to choose the means to attain them.

"For each couple the situation is different. Each human being is unique. Thus unique multiplied by unique gives unique squared; this is a fundamental principle of psychosynthesis. Each case is unique, each situation is unique. Each couple is unique. Each family is unique. We need to focus on the unique existential problem of a certain situation, rather than on generalities, and afterwards to choose techniques which are most adequate for resolving the problems of that particular case. This eliminates the fictitious, inauthentic problems. It may be called the psychoanalytical phase: the discovery of the obstacles to constructive work. And the obstacles are for the most part those which we spoke about before: erroneous attitudes of men and of women. I believe therefore in the equality of value, and in the differentiation of functions *up to a certain point*. Collaboration, integration on a base of equality.

"In education, the child needs a maternal environment and a paternal environment. Much harm is done in education when the paternal influence is missing. But if for some reason there is no father, the woman can take the paternal role also. It is difficult, but she can do it, if she wants to. And the same for the man: if the woman is not there, the father can take on the maternal role also. We can perform any role that life requires of us or that we decide to play. The same is true for work. In a large variety of situations, there is always in the human being the latent possibility to do anything within reasonable limits, to choose freely, to deliver himself from social pressures, prejudices, obstacles in order to reach his higher goals.

"We are now in a period of crisis and profound changes. I believe that woman is evolving perhaps more rapidly than man. For him, the task is to discover the real human being beneath masculine limitations—to be not only a 'masculine-man,' but a *human being*, who plays masculine roles—and if he chooses, feminine ones. We know that historically there were matriarchal civilizations and patriarchal civilizations; the ideal would be a new synthetic civilization, that is neither patriarchal nor matriarchal, but one that is psychosynthetic, that is to say, a civilization in which the highest and best qualities of each are manifested.

"This would be something new. In all historical civilizations and cultures there has been a preponderance of one or the other element. But in this new civilization and the emerging global culture, for the first time humanity is sufficiently developed to make a planetary, global pattern, incorporating the very best of all men and women. I think that this planetary psychosynthesis, this psychosynthesis of humanity is possible and needed. Each particular problem will then have its frame of reference in the greater whole, and conflict can be replaced by harmonious integration and cooperation. All of this is within our reach—for not only is it very beautiful—it is very *human*."

11

Sex-Based Superiority Complexes: A New Perspective

GINA CERMINARA

Thinking in reincarnationist terms in the area of sex results in some important clarifications, psychologically and ethically, as we have seen.

But perhaps the most important and drastic outcome of our thinking in this way is the realization that by the fact of sexual alternations, *the absoluteness of the sexual cleavage between men and women disappears.*

We are spirits, Cayce tells us, entrapped and enclothed in bodies.* The spirit is in the image and likeness of God; and the spirit must therefore include both polarities within itself even as God does; it is bisexed or androgynous in its essence, and it takes on a specific biological sex only in human embodiment.

This concept has important and tremendous results both for our understanding of men and women, and for our evaluation of each other.

With regard to our understanding, it seems likely that we will be led to see that the polarity of the body conditions the psyche. In an obvious way, of course, the body's sex

---

*Edgar Cayce was a renowned medical clairvoyant who diagnosed and prescribed for illnesses while in a trance, a state in which he also communicated philosophical teachings and gave advice. The transcripts of his "readings" are still being researched and much of the material has been verified as being correct.—ED.

determines the biological and social role that one plays in life, and thus conditions the whole life experience; but more subtly than that, it would seem to have an effect upon abilities, personality traits, and large areas of mental and emotional life.

The way the body conditions the psyche is comparable, perhaps, to the manner in which clothing affects us. Every woman knows, certainly, the psychological effect of the clothing that she wears. A pair of heavy oxfords, a short woolen skirt, and a cardigan sweater, for example, give a woman's psyche an entirely different "feel" than high heeled silver slippers and a bouffant low-cut evening gown. Men do not experience as much as women, perhaps, these subtle psychological differences that clothes impart because, for one thing, men's clothing, in modern times at least, is not so varied, and for another, men's success in life is not so dependent upon the success of their personal appearance. But men experience enough of a psychic difference between the wearing of dirty old fishing togs and a tuxedo to know that clothes *do* affect one's morale, self-esteem, self-estimate, and consequently have ramifications in one's conduct and speech, even if only in minor ways.

How much more profoundly, then, must the sex of the body affect the psyche! And its sex, let us remember, includes more than the conspicuous or "primary" sex differences, concealed by fig leaves or draperies, and its positivity or receptivity with regard to the sex act. It includes also the "secondary" sex differences—the body's hardness or its softness, its straightness or its roundness, its distribution of hair and of muscle and of flesh. And it includes, in fact, every cell of the body, because of the direct distribution into the blood stream of differently sexed hormones, so that the body's sex is actually an all-pervasive and not merely a mechanical and localized difference. These differences cannot but condition profoundly the life-feeling of the entity inhabiting it.

Certain traits of character and capacities of mind might well be facilitated or inhibited by the sex of the body one happened to be in. For example, both on mental tests and in actual life performance, entities in the male polarity show higher capacity for mathematics and mechanics, and entities in the female polarity generally show higher capacity in language and social understanding.

These distinct differences may be acquired rather than inborn: that is to say, they may be—and probably are, in large part—the direct result of environmental influences and the pressures brought to bear because of what we think men and women *should* do. But if there is any inborn difference, then this difference *cannot* inhere in the soul as a soul, because all souls are androgynous and have been in bodily form in both sexes many times.

The difference might then arise from the polarity or the constitution of the male or female body as such. For example, dexterity of the fingers is greater in female bodies than in male because of the female's smaller fingers. Color blindness, which is much more prevalent in males than in females, is traceable to sex-linked genes. Mathematical and mechanical abilities are not so obviously related to a male body as is finger dexterity to a woman's smaller fingers, or color blindness to sex-linked genes; but perhaps, in some yet unknown way, there is a relationship just as distinct.

The body's sex, then, would seem almost like a modality or mode of being—comparable perhaps to major and minor modes in music. In the minor mode, as in the major, certain notes and intervals *must* appear by virtue of the mode, and other notes and intervals cannot. Each has its own distinctive feeling and force and beauty; neither could, by any stretch of the imagination, be called superior to the other.

And this brings us to what is perhaps even more important than the matter of how the body conditions the psyche, namely the matter of evaluation, and the notion of superiority on the basis of sex. According to the reincarnationist view, any notions of superiority or inferiority in the basis of sex must of necessity disappear. They must disappear for two reasons: first, because they are untenable, and second, because they are so karmically dangerous.

If I have been both a man and a woman, and you have been both a woman and a man, how can either of us claim to be superior because of our sex? Superior to whom? When? The alternation of roles obviously gives us a fluid situation rather than a static one; only a moron could maintain that people sitting on the left side of the bus are the absolute superiors of those sitting on the right, when at any time in the course of his life he might be under the necessity of sitting on either one or the other side, and when all persons who ride the buses experience the same necessity. Thus any superiority attitude is seen to be, in the last analysis, absurdly untenable.

But more than untenable, both logically and psychologically, it is actually downright dangerous.

Since the time of the psychiatrist Alfred Adler, we have heard much of the inferiority feeling, and how important it is to overcome it. But the superiority feeling has not been so much discussed, despite the fact that it is equally as unhealthy as the inferiority feeling, and can lead to many terrible aberrations of conduct.

Wherever there is strength, wealth, beauty, power, talent, or excellence of any kind, the superiority feeling can easily develop, and many women have certainly been as guilty of it as men. But history shows us that in almost every civilization of which we have any record, men *as a class* have been much more guilty of it than have women.

It is easy to see why this is so. In primitive, materialistic societies, might makes right, and the strongest can easily impose his will on the others. Because of their superior size and muscular strength, and also because of their greater biological freedom, men have easily established a dominant position over women, and have perpetuated it by laws, customs, and superstitions of infinite variety and even—ironically and tragically enough—by religion.

However much the great world scriptures may have been "inspired," nonetheless they were obviously filtered through the male brains of their transcribers, and their male-dominant sentiments are very apparent in the texts.

Hindu, Buddhist, Muhammadan, Judaic, and Christian scriptures, to mention only a few, all show this distinct bias. "Women are as impure as falsehood itself," writes Manu, the Hindu lawgiver; ''Day and night women must be kept in dependence by the males of their families.''

The Buddha only reluctantly, and after much persuasion, allowed women to become members of his monastic order—and then only on condition that a woman devotee, no matter how many years of service she had given to the order, would defer to a male monk, even if he had become one only yesterday.

Among the Jews, the rabbinical prejudice prevailed to the effect that woman is not capable of profound religious instruction. Better burn the Law, was their teaching, than teach it to a woman. How can man that is born of a woman, asks Job, be clean? And while Christ seemed to have been free of male-domination sentiments, both the Old and the New Testament writers, especially Paul, were not. The psychologically damaging effects of their own fear and distrust and disparagement of women are incalculable in the world of men and women today.

Until very recently, women all over the world have had little better status in many places than property and animals, and in almost all places have been regarded as inferior beings. Both laws and customs have operated almost entirely in the favor of men and to the disadvantage of women; she has been denied education on the grounds of inherent mental inferiority and the right to vote for the same reason; she has in many places no right to own property, or to obtain a divorce for just cause, even though her husband could divorce her for any reason whatsoever; adultery has been overlooked entirely in the case of men, and punished with severity ranging from stoning to death to ostracism in the case of women; she still receives in many places—including the United States—less pay for the same job that men do; she is still barred, openly or through subtle subterfuges, from many positions and professions. It has only been in the last fifty years that women have been gradually freeing themselves from these injustices.

''The saddest thing in life,'' runs a Japanese proverb, ''is to be born a woman.'' And if one reads thoughtfully the history of womankind, not only in Japan but in almost every country of the world, one cannot help feeling the poignancy of the saying. Women have suffered untold and untellable indignities, physically, emotionally, mentally, and spiritually because of men's compulsion to be superior; and they still continue to do so.

A situation such as this can only be accompanied by profound psychic imbalance and unhealthiness, not only in the victims of the subjection, but also in the perpetrators of it.

Philip Wylie makes this point with singular force in his brilliant novel on the relationship between the sexes, *The Disappearance.** He dramatizes the terrible dichotomy between man and woman by a science fiction kind of story in which, presumably because of atomic disturbances, all the men suddenly disappear from the world of women, and all the women disappear from the world of men. Separate, they try to continue life as they knew it; both men and women soon realize the indispensability of the other sex, and learn a new kind of respect for it. But mainly it is the men who must learn how deeply they have sinned.

His principal character, Gaunt, realizes this most intensely. He writes:

> [Man]... became so entranced with himself that he never found enough objects of odious comparison to satisfy the greed of his inner conceit. He went to war with other men exactly like himself, always on the grounds of their "inferiority." Not satisfied even by that, he declared another war on the still more similar half of his own tribe: woman. She was necessary to him, so he could not exterminate her, but he put her in her place to give his own a more exalted seeming....
>
> If the sexes so revile each other, how can a species love? How, if one sex regards itself as superior, can it refrain from detesting the "inferior" sex? And how in the name of nature and of God can beings regarded as inferior by their mates bear towards those mates a whole affection? Creativeness is not possible where the creators are at such odds, and have been for hundreds of centuries. A hate of life is inevitable.

In debasing and vilifying woman, Gaunt concludes, man has debased and vilified himself. But the added dimension

---

*New York: Rinehart & Company, Inc., 1951

of reincarnation shows us that the manifestations of a superiority complex have serious psychological consequences, not only to the present personality in the confines of the present world scene, but also indefinitely into the future. From the evidence of the Cayce files, whatever we do to another, ultimately comes back to us; as we sow, so shall we reap; as we mete, so it is measured out to us again.

The karmic law is inescapable. If the ego waxes fat, it can only mean that it must later be slenderized, through suffering; if an ego exploits its position, and treats others with contempt, with selfishness, and with tyranny, then some day it will receive the same kind of treatment itself.

Women who are suffering today, even in modern relatively enfranchised America, because of the brutality, selfishness, and subtle or obvious tyranny of some man, may find it a source of some comfort to think that they are paying the just price for their own brutality, selfishness, or tyranny of ages ago when, as a man, they treated some women in the same callous manner.

And men of today who can see any reasonability whatsoever in the reincarnation idea should seriously take stock of their own behavior and their own subtle attitudes as well as of the legal and social behavior of all men towards all women; for if they do not, they are inviting, for some future experience of their own, as women, exactly what they are giving out today, as men.

We can have a healthy, wholesome, sane civilization on this planet only when all ego-inspired notions of superiority shall have disappeared among men and women, and the more cosmically necessary view of our complementary nature has taken its place.

141

12

Is the Animus Obsolete?

MARY ANN MATTOON AND JENNETTE JONES

Since Jung's enunciation of the animus concept in the early decades of the twentieth century, this concept has come to occupy a central position in Jungian writings on the psychology of women. In recent years a number of books and articles reflect a renewed interest in the animus as the unconscious "inner masculine" in a woman's psyche.[1] To the writers of these works and, no doubt, to many of their readers, the existence of the animus is self-evident.

At the same time that the animus has achieved the status of dogma within the Jungian community, the concept is virtually unknown to non-Jungian psychotherapists and has come under attack from feminists who judge it from new perspectives and evidence from psychology and anthropology. Indeed, for feminist writers who know of the animus concept, it is likely to head their list of objectionable Jungian ideas and may cast a pall over the whole field of Jungian psychology. Even if they do not know the animus by name, many feminists reject the closely associated concepts of "masculine" and "feminine" qualities. These concepts seem to imply that certain characteristics belong to one sex by nature, that men are naturally assertive and initiatory whereas women are naturally passive and gentle. Such a rigid view of the sexes implies a hierarchy in which "feminine" is less valued than "masculine," and manifestation of cross-sex qualities is considered a debasement.

The problem is not that Jungians and feminists have fundamentally different goals for women's development. The two groups agree that women and men are inherently of equal value and that persons of both sexes can be psychologically mature only when each is self-defining, that is, when each determines her or his own values and goals. The two groups' descriptions of the process of psychological growth for women, however, turn on different understandings of the "feminine" or "masculine" nature of women. As self-defined feminist Jungians, we believe that the time has come to reexamine the animus concept in the light of recent criticism, and ask: Is the animus (concept) obsolete? We consider it important to question the validity and usefulness of the concept, whatever the answers hypothesized by us and other Jungian theorists.

In this article we follow three main lines of inquiry. First, we review the challenges to the animus concept that are important for Jungians. The central question emerging from these challenges seems to be: Is a view of women's psychology that was developed in a very different social context appropriate in our own time and place?

Second, we argue that the answer to the feminist objections lies in a more complete understanding of the nature of the animus. The concept did not spring full-blown from the head of C. G. Jung but, rather, was shaped in significant ways by women analysts, especially his wife, Emma Jung. The antagonism to the animus theory by feminists might be much less if Emma Jung's version of the animus, informed by her own experience as a woman, had been more widely available outside Jungian circles.[2]

Third, we cite anthropological and psychological data that support the concept in response to those that seem to undermine it and accompany these data with accounts of the subjective experiences of women.

Finally, we make suggestions about the ways in which the animus concept may contribute to understanding and aiding the psychological development of women.

Challenges to the Animus Concept

Numerous feminist writers have pointed out that Jung's views on male-female differences reflect the biases of his day, which now are regarded as sexist.[3] One of these views is that women are less capable of objectivity and independent action than are men. For example, Jung stated (in a passage often quoted by his feminist critics): ''No one can get around the fact that by taking up a masculine profession, studying and working like a man, woman is doing something not wholly in accord with, if not directly injurious to her feminine nature.''[4] Later in the same paragraph he added insult to injury: ''It is a woman's outstanding characteristic that she can do anything for the love of a man. But those women who can achieve something for the love of a *thing* are most exceptional, because this does not really agree with their nature.''

Feminists are joined by anthropologists and psychologists in challenging the equating of women's competence (in logos matters) and assertiveness with an unconscious, hence underdeveloped, part of the female psyche; to identify these qualities as animus or masculine may be to say that they are inappropriate for women. If Jungians wish to continue to use the concept of the animus as a phenomenon of normal psychology, we must demonstrate that it is consonant with the strivings and achievements of psychologically healthy women in the late twentieth century.

Also subject to challenge is a corollary of the animus concept: What our culture calls ''feminine'' is innately characteristic of women more than of men. Anthropological evidence, some of it gathered by Margaret Mead a half-century ago, throws considerable doubt on this assumption. In 1931 Mead began the research in the highlands of New Guinea, which was published in 1935 as *Sex and Temperament in Three Primitive Societies*.[5] (1931 was the year that C. G. Jung published an expanded German-language version of his essay ''Mind and Earth''; in it he posited the animus as ''the masculine archetype in woman.''[6] And in 1931, Emma Jung lectured for the first time on the material that became her published essay on the animus.) Mead's study of sex and temperament, now important mainly for its historic interest, was the first anthropological statement of what has become a familiar theme among feminists: that ''masculine'' and "feminine" attitudes and characteristics vary from one culture to another.

Among the Arapesh, both men and women were nurturing and non-agressive—qualities we see as feminine. Among the neighboring Mundugumor, both sexes were "masculine"—warlike and fierce. In a third tribe, the Tschambuli, the roles were reversed from those in our society: Women were competent, practical, and assertive; men spent their time adorning themselves, strutting about, and gossiping. Comparison of these three societies provides evidence that the "masculine" and the "feminine" are, to a very great extent, artifacts of culture.

Mead's early insight on the cultural relativity of "masculine" and "feminine" behavior has been elaborated and refined by more recent research on the status of women, and some anthropologists go so far as to abandon the term "gender" altogether, speaking only of masculine and feminine "roles," that is, socially prescribed behavior. This position, which ascribes virtually all sex-specific behavior to cultural learning and almost none to innate biological differences between men and women, does not accommodate the idea that "masculine" and "feminine" principles are innate and archetypal, a theme that we address later.

Psychologists, too, have argued extensively against the idea that most sex differences in personality are innate. Although biological differences are undeniable, most of the personality differences result from the divergent ways that girls and boys are treated by the adults around them. For example, girls tend to be rewarded for dependency, boys for being independent. And girls are punished consistently for aggressiveness, while boys are offered channels for their aggressive tendencies. Such findings cast doubt on the innateness of greater male activity as well as female passivity.

The discipline of (non-Jungian) psychology offers the further criticism that the animus concept is essentially arbitrary. These psychologists point out that the animus is not an organ or part of the brain, but a hypothetical construct—a set of mental contents that have been grouped together but have no necessary connection with each other. Although Jung saw the animus qualities as belonging together on a deep archetypal level, other observers may assign the same contents to different groupings. Even in Jungian terms, some "animus" contents, such as assertiveness, could be assigned to the cluster of traits we call "ego," while others, such as exaggerated self-criticism, could be grouped with so-called shadow contents. Thus, the attitudes and behavior often assigned to the animus can be explained without recourse to an archetypal masculine principle in women.

Another alternative psychological concept is that of function types. The "irrational opinions" that Jung cited so often as characteristic of the animus may stem from an underdeveloped thinking function more than an inferior masculine component in a woman's psyche. Probably no one can dispute the observation that women are capable of illogical and dogmatic thinking. But is such irrationality limited to women? Obviously it occurs also in men. Thus, it cannot be attributed always to the animus, which is said to exist only in women.

If fewer women have developed thinking functions, the cause probably lies more in their education than in their genes. Psychological research has demonstrated, for example, that girls and boys are about equal in mathematical achievement until they reach puberty. Although their hormonal balances change at that time, their environment changes even more. Many girls begin to discover that they are less acceptable to adults and to their peers, especially males, if they excel in mathematics and science. Thus, it is not surprising that, driven by their need for acceptance, they begin to fall behind in those areas of study, never to recoup their losses. (Some American schools have begun to reward girls for excellence in mathematics and to provide role models for developing their scientific ability, but courses treating "math anxiety" are still needed by many female students.)

What View of the Animus is Being Challenged?

Most of the explicit criticisms of the animus concept have been aimed at Jung's own formulations of the idea. He did not present a thorough theoretical statement, although he devoted a chapter in each of two volumes to the concept: ''Anima and Animus'' in *Two Essays on Analytical Psychology* (Volume 7, first published in 1916) and ''The Syzygy: Anima and Animus'' in *Aion* (Volume 9-11, first published in 1950). The rest of his comments on the animus are scattered references throughout the *Collected Works.* Many of these statements are incidental to discussions of other topics and are embedded in particular contexts, which may subtly alter Jung's meaning. The statements they contain are based on intuition and clinical observations, in a particular time and place, of Jung's female analysands. These women tended to be of similar ages, educational levels, and professional backgrounds. Before attempting to judge the adequacy of the animus concept, it is important to reach a deeper understanding of it than its challengers have done and to view it in historical perspective. We begin with a brief review of Jung's formulations of the concept and trace the main themes of its evolution through the contributions of other Jungian theorists.

Jung's View

Perhaps Jung's most consistent definition of the animus is that it is the unconscious, archetypally based masculine part of a woman's psyche. He took the position that women's consciousness is innately governed primarily according to the feminine principle (eros), which he described as relatedness and conciliation, while men's is governed innately by the masculine principle (logos), a combination of structure and discrimination. Despite the gender-related distinction, *Jung saw the masculine and feminine principles as equally valid and complementary, albeit contrasting.*

For Jung the concept was virtually self-evident and empirically based. He pointed to the existence of a minority of male hormones in females and of female hormones in males; he reasoned that the psyche is likely to have a corresponding minority of opposite-sex qualities. Moreover, he found examples of the animus even before he identified the concept. Very early in his career he noticed such figures, for example, in Miss Frank Miller's fantasies, which he reported in his 1912 book, *The Psychology of the Unconscious* (later, *Symbols of Transformation*, CW5); only later did he develop the concept of the animus. Therefore, he maintained, the concept could not have contaminated his observation of Miss Miller's images.

As an unconscious content the animus, according to Jung, is a "projection-making factor." Thus, the animus of an individual woman tends to determine what kind of man she will admire, become attached to, or fall in love with. As a source of projections, the animus is what Jung called the "soul-image." The first carrier of this image is often a girl's father, whose influence—for good or ill—often shapes much of the content of her animus. The animus is plural, however, and thus can be projected onto males of a variety of temperaments and qualities.

Jung often characterized the animus as spirit. In his essay on the anima and animus in *Aion*, he referred to spirit as "philosophical or religious ideas...or rather the attitude resulting from them." Spirit also includes intellectual and cultural concerns.

Probably the key role of the animus, for Jung, is in the individuation process. It contributes to the process in two ways: as a component of the unconscious psyche and as a mediator to the unconscious. As a component of the psyche, the animus is the masculine principle, which Jung saw as a necessary ingredient of psychic wholeness. As a mediator, providing access to the contents of the Self, the animus contributes to a woman's capacity for reflection and self-knowledge. (The corresponding process in a man is that of the anima connecting him with his emotions.)

What Is Wrong with Jung's Presentation of the Animus?

Jung developed the animus concept at a time when the position of women in the Western world was lower than it is today; this was even truer in Switzerland than in the United States. The relative effectiveness of the women's rights movement in the two countries is an indication of the difference. In the United States the movement fought successfully for a constitutional amendment providing woman suffrage in the United States by 1920. The Swiss segment of the movement was so ineffective that few cantons allowed women to vote before the 1970s. The objective status of Swiss women surely must have affected Jung's thinking about female psychology.

There is doubt, also, regarding Jung's claim to empiricism in developing the animus concept. He weakened his claim by deducing the animus concept from the anima concept: ''Since the anima is an archetype that is found in men, it is reasonable to suppose that an equivalent archetype must be present in women.''[7] This passage implies that when one has observed men and found a contrasexual component, one can assume a comparable component in women, without taking the trouble to observe them.

The empirical basis of the animus is not established by dream images either, although Jung often cited them as ''psychic facts.'' Women clearly have male figures in their dreams and fantasies, and these figures change or are succeeded by new figures. But Jung failed to show a clear connection between such figures and the attitudes and behaviors that he identified as manifestations of the animus. Not every male dream figure is a reflection of an individual woman's animus. When a woman dreams, for example, of a man who is making a speech to an adoring audience, how does she know whether the image is an undeveloped aspect of her own psyche or simply her unconsicous perception of the largely male-dominated world that both oppresses and entices her? Either interpretation is possible, according to Jungian theory. In the ''subjective'' view, the dream figure is part of the dreamer's psyche; in the ''objective'' view, part of the outer world. Thus, the clinical evidence (from dreams) challenges the concept of the animus as readily as it supports it.

The archetypal basis for the animus is asserted but not explained in Jung's writings, despite his frequent mention of mythological animus images. That is, he did not establish the general applicability of the animus concept to the psyches of women. He hypothesized that the animus "is one of the archetypes which arrange human figures in dreams."[8] Evidently he deduced, from the ubiquity of male figures in women's dreams, that such figures are archetypal. However, ubiquitous images are not necessarily archetypal, even if their sources are unknown to the dreamer. And calling a hypothesized phenomenon "archetypal" does not establish its validity.

Another difficulty with Jung's description of the animus lies in his inconsistency in dealing with the question of whether a woman has a soul. On some occasions he denied the existence of woman's soul, seemingly on the basis of certain logic: Anima is soul; anima (in Latin, a word of feminine gender) is the unconscious feminine; a woman's unconscious is not predominantly feminine; consequently, a woman does not have a soul.[9] Yet he stated repeatedly that woman has a soul, it has a masculine character, and its name is "animus."[10] A further complication is added by Jung's occasionally stating that "soul" and "spirit" are synonymous, while at other times distinguishing between them: Anima equals soul and animus equals spirit. Evidently, he used a given word differently in different contexts. (Part of the confusion seems to stem from the fact that Jung wrote mostly in German and often used the word "Seele," which can be translated as either "psyche" or "soul." Nevertheless, he often wrote in English, in which he was fluent. For English-language readers, at least, his imprecise use of terms has occasioned considerable perplexity.)

The uncertainty about woman's soul and/or spirit gains significance because Jung sometimes treated animus (the logos in a woman) as inferior to anima (the eros in a man). "In men," he wrote, "Eros, the function of relationship, is usually less well developed than Logos. In women, on the other hand, . . . their Logos is often only a regrettable accident."[11] Surely a quality that is less well developed is preferable to one that is a regrettable accident!

Although one can dispute the fairness of placing retroactively a sexist label on such statements, they clearly leave little room for individual differences. Jung gave insufficient

recognition to the fact that women vary greatly in their capacities and in their aims, including the degree to which consciousness is "feminine" and the unconscious "masculine."
There seems to be general agreement today, in contrast to
Jung's statements, that degrees of "feminine" and "masculine" vary in each individual (of either sex); each woman
has some masculine qualities in her consciousness as well
as some feminine qualities in her unconscious. Indeed, the
variation is so great and so complicated that it casts doubt
on Jung's basic premise that women have predominantly
a "feminine" consciousness, with a primarily "masculine"
unconscious—the premise on which the animus concept is
based.

Another challenge to the animus concept concerns the
idea that a woman's projections onto men are virtually identical with her animus, especially in romantic attachments.
A study by Aron and others (1974) found that women as
well as men tend to marry persons with whom they have
relationships that are similar to those they had with their
mothers.[12] Thus, it appears that male figures are not the only
determinants of a woman's projections onto men.

Unfortunately lacking in Jungian theory on the animus is
an awareness that the projections of lesbians onto men may
differ from those of heterosexual women. To our knowledge,
the psychological literature does not yield empirical research
on this question or even conceptual discussion.

Jung seemed to think that many problems of women result
from *too much animus.* Although he attributed spirit and soul
to the animus and insisted that it takes "plural" forms, he
described it primarily in negative terms, frequently using
adjectives such as "dangerous" and "disturbing to the
ego." Most characteristic are his references to "animus possession" and the opinions that, he claimed, the animus puts
into the mouths of women. Jung designated these opinions
sometimes as "irrational," often as "prejudices." At least
27 such statements occur in the 10 volumes of *Collected Works*
in which the animus is mentioned. (By contrast, his descriptions of the man's anima are quite balanced: She makes him
moody at times, but at other times she helps him to be cre-

ative and related to the inner and outer worlds.) Thus, a woman's attempts at logos concerns (philosophical and religious ideas, structure, and objectivity) must produce results that are awkward, rigid, and dogmatic.

Jung never clarified why he assigned so many negative qualities specifically to the animus. Many of his descriptors are characteristic of unconscious contents in general; they can be applied just as appropriately, for example, to shadow qualities or specific complexes. Irrationality that is disturbing to the ego can be rooted in any complex, and thus it can be attributed to the shadow as plausibly as to the animus.

Jung's largely negative description of the animus, moreover, contrasts with his usual characterization of archetypes as bipolar (positive and negative). His frequent mentions of an animus "problem" are not accompanied by mention of a positive aspect, such as "capacity." Some positive views are implied, and the importance of the animus in the individuation process is explicit, but the impression remains that a woman's manifesting an animus is at least mildly disgraceful.

Emma Jung and the Animus

If Jung's original statements about the animus had cast the concept in its final form, we should have to side with his critics and pronounce it obsolete. Fortunately, some women analysts have been able to rework the idea in order to give a far truer reflection of their own experience. In so doing they have avoided some of the more obvious pitfalls of sexism and also have brought their readers closer to psychological truth.

By far the most important of the early molders of the animus concept was Emma Jung, whose original lecture on the subject was published later as a monograph, *Animus and Anima*. Although a few non-Jungian feminists have read the monograph, its circulation outside Jungian circles has been limited.[13] Wider availability of it might have mitigated some of the feminist hostility to the animus concept. Unlike her husband, Emma Jung could report on the animus from her own subjective experience; she concluded that, for many women, the problem is *not too much animus, but too little.* Hence, she wrote about the animus as a many-faceted psychological factor that takes different forms and thus applies in different ways to a variety of women.

Emma Jung identified different forms of the animus and described their positive and negative aspects. The forms that she described are patterned on various meanings of the Greek word "Logos"; power, deed, word, meaning. Corresponding to each form are kinds of images that appear in a woman's dreams or influence her projections onto males.

An animus image of power may be a physically powerful man, a sports hero, or a soldier. In his positive form he gives the woman the energy to achieve, to be active in her own behalf. The negative side is the tendency to dominate; its personification could be a dictator or a malevolent king.

Closely related to the animus of power is the animus of the deed. The dream image is a man of action, perhaps an explorer or an astronaut. The positive expression of this inner masculine figure may include a woman's effective leadership in social reform. The negative side is an exaggerated concern for rules and abstract justice; it could be personified by a harsh and arbitrary judge.

The animus of the word may appear positively as a poet. A woman in whom such an animus is active may be articulate, even eloquent, in expressing ideas. In its negative form such an animus may be represented by a fire-and-brimstone preacher. The woman may be afflicted by the unfounded opinions against which Jung railed. The fourth form of the animus is that of meaning, which may be imaged in dreams as a priest or a philosopher. A woman who is affected positively by such an animus is passionate in her quest for the spiritual dimension of life. The negative form can be dogmatism, which may be "frozen meaning."

In this monograph Emma Jung showed clearly that the animus has many possible manifestations, which change from one into another and take positive and negative forms at different times and in various individuals. But perhaps her most important contribution, for our purposes, is the observation that women in whom the animus appears overpowering and largely negative need to develop and differentiate the positive inner masculine, rather than trying to minimize or suppress the negative.

Other Jungian Views

As Jungian psychology has matured, a number of theorists have introduced and supported additions and modifications to the theory of the animus. Emma Jung is not alone, even among highly traditional Jungians, in her view that the positive aspects of the animus are at least as important as the negative. Irene Claremont de Castillejo, for example, wrote (in a book that has been distributed more widely than Emma Jung's): "My purpose is to show that the animus...is not only irritating and destructive but is of the utmost value, and is essential for any creativeness on [a woman's] part."[14]

Emma Jung is not alone either in seeing the animus in developmental terms. Polly Young-Eisendrath, for example, hypothesized five stages: (1) alien other; (2) father, god patriarch; (3) youth, hero, lover; (4) partner within; and (5) androgyne. She sees these stages as an "experiment in clinical thinking rather than an empirically sound paradigm."[15]

Some Jungian theorists have differed markedly from Jung's view. Their major focus relevant to the animus is on whether it is soul, spirit, or both. James Hillman stated clearly that even if anima is "the archetype of the feminine," as Jung declared, a woman has a soul—an anima—which needs to be cultivated in the form of fantasy and imagination.[16] He seems to agree with Erich Neumann that masculine qualities function similarly in both women and men, that is, contributing to the development of the ego.[17] (In contrast, E. C. Whitmont averred that women's egos are feminine and that the understanding of Neumann's view by many Jungians is "uncritical...and superficial.")[18] If the animus is a characteristic of men as well as women and has a large, conscious component in both sexes, the concept is much broader than in Jung's view.

Marion Woodman also challenged Jung's conceptualization from a different perspective, stating that spirit is not exclusively masculine but may be also feminine in character:

> Without the feminine spiritual experience of surrender, conception, and giving birth (both in men and women), the human link which connects us to our deepest psychic roots is missing. It is through the feminine modality that the Incarnation can take place—the spirit can be received and born out of the flesh.[19]

Such an experience is sometimes metaphorical, but it can be intensely emotional and, therefore, have a bodily component as well.

Other Jungians have provided suggestive evidence that animus development may vary from one woman to another. For example, Linda Leonard described the father who is more of "puer" and distinguished him from the "senex" father.[20] Thus, the animus that is influenced by the personal father may take different forms in different women.

Most writers have emphasized the influence of the father and other males on a woman's animus, but we find that the mother's psychology may be relevant also. The negative, critical animus, for example, may be carried and transmitted by a mother whose masculine side has received too little nourishment. Consequently, some women notice that their animus images correspond to their mothers' repressed and distorted masculine qualities more than to their fathers' characteristics.

Jungian psychology has always used mythological images for archetypal phenomena, but current writers are enriching the repertoire, sometimes to increase our understanding of female psychology. Jean Bolen, for example, specifically challenged the general applicability of Jung's animus theory by positing a psychology of women based on archetypal images of women. In her view, the virgin goddesses of Greek mythology—Artemis (Goddess of the Hunt and of the Moon), Athena (Goddess of Wisdom and Crafts), and Hestia

(Goddess of Hearth and Temple)—personify many of the traits that Jung identified as animus qualities: "the independent, active, nonrelationship aspects of women's psychology."[21] Thus, some of the qualities Bolen attributes to women's consciousness match some of those that Jung dubbed masculine and largely unconscious.

The Animus Is Not Obsolete

Despite difficulties with the concept, our view is that the animus remains a viable and useful concept. It has received support, at least indirectly, from the fields of anthropology and (to a lesser extent) psychology. Moreover, the concept is consonant with the subjective experiences of individual women. Our reasons for retaining the animus concept follow.

Masculine and Feminine Are Recognized Across Cultures

Cross-cultural research, from Mead's early work to recent studies, shows enormous variability in the personality traits assigned to men and women in different societies. This research emphasizes the plasticity of the human psyche: We tend to become what our culture expects us to be. Challenging this research are recent findings that indicate innate differences in male and female brains. The brains of infant girls seem to respond differently from those of boys to the same stimuli; the left hemisphere tends to be dominant in the girls, the right in the boys. At the same time, the differences are amplified by cultural expectations. Whether or not there are innate sex differences in the human psyche, anthropologists generally agree on several premises.

First, all cultures assign different roles to men and women. Indeed, in the simplest societies sex and age are the fundamental principles for organizing social reality, though the contents of the sex and age roles differ from one culture to another.

Gender differences also function to organize symbolic reality; thus, maleness and femaleness (or we might say the "masculine" and the "feminine") are projected onto the pantheon; they are expressed mimetically through ritual, and they are often projected onto nature itself. Consequently, earth, sky, sun, rain, moon, and forest may be associated with one gender or the other. In this way, gender, sexual opposition, and sexual joining (the "conjunctio") serve as metaphors for a wide range of social, natural, and spiritual experiences. This statement does not do justice to the range and complexity of pre-literate religious systems; it does suggest that the tendency to "genderize" the world is universal and may spring from a deep archetypal source.

A corollary of the above is that women, who give birth to children and are responsible for their early nurturance, are almost universally seen as closer to nature than men; while men, who operate in the public sphere of economic, political, and religious life, are seen as closer to culture. (Ortner has since modified this formulation, but in broad outline it still applies.)[22] Since cultural pursuits are generally more valued than those we share with lower animals, men tend to have higher prestige than women. (This occurs despite the fact that women's role as nurturer and early teacher is intimately tied to the transmission of cultural values.) A compensatory tendency, in many cultures, is to view women as higher than men in addition to being lower—the familiar "pedestal phenomenon." This tendency is due to the association of women and the feminine with much-prized social values, such as tribal unity.

Whatever the definition of masculine and feminine, feminine qualities are demanded of women; in them masculine qualities are disapproved and, consequently, tend to be repressed. These repressed qualities in a particular woman become her animus. These qualities are not necessarily undesirable in themselves, even though they are deemed inappropriate for women. Thus, the animus can have positive (individually and socially useful) qualities as well as negative ones. (The fact that the animus is often considered to be more negative than the anima may be due to the relatively lower status of women in many cultures.)

Specific qualities of the animus are reflected in a few psychological studies. Marilyn Nagy, a Jungian analyst, has combined cross-cultural data with research on the dreams of women in analysis.[23] She discovered that women at the time of their menses often have dream images of a strange man. These motifs parallel some images from myths of a variety of non-Western cultures. In the myths women, isolated during their menses, often encounter a demon lover or husband. Nagy's argument is that a woman's physiological change constellates the (demonic) animus. Since the corresponding myths are widespread, they suggest an archetypal dimension to the dreams.

Psychological studies that support the idea of the animus are scarce. However, one piece of research by a non-Jungian psychologist showed that "College women [have an image of an] ideal date." This study found commonality in many descriptions by women of their ideal date: a male who is "high on assertiveness and dominance."[24] A Jungian interpretation of this study is that the "ideal male" for an individual woman is her "positive animus" image, which is likely to be reflected in dreams, fantasies, and projections. Some of these animus projections are as specific as falling in love with a particular man; others are diffuse, such as the expectation that an ideal male will appear and make the woman's life complete. And in the middle range are legions of rogues and heroes who people the erotic fantasies of women.

Widespread Interest In Androgyny

The idea of androgyny reflects a widespread awareness that both "masculine" and "feminine" traits are potential or actual in each person. The fact that one category is dominant is due, in part, to the repression of the other. Thus, in women, feminine traits are better developed (more conscious), the masculine less so (more repressed). Because the repressed masculine is, by definition, the animus, evidence for a drive toward androgyny affirms the existence of the animus and the need to integrate its positive aspects while depotentiating its negative manifestations.

The increasing literature and research on this concept draws from both anthropology and psychology. In psychology, Heilbrun and Singer have described androgyny; Bem has measured it.[25]

In anthropology, research shows that in every human society the delineation of gender roles is narrower than the actual capabilities of the men and women within the group. Thus, just as biologically we have hormones related to contrasexual characteristics, culturally we have the potential for manifesting some of the qualities that ''belong'' to the other sex. Societal pressures, whether mild or severe, tend to repress not only the outer expression of contrasexual traits but even the awareness of them. The renewed interest in androgyny over the past 15 years may lead to a more conscious connection with the full range of our sexual and social capabilities.

In general, the tighter the definition of sex role and the more rigid the boundaries, the greater is the tendency for both men and women to express contrasexual tendencies symbolically, by projection, by fantasies about the opposite sex, or by patterned imitation and parody. Thus, Indian women of the Northwest Coast engage in play ''pot latches,'' hilarious parodies of the men's solemn ritual of gift-giving; and among the Iatmul of New Guinea, the women participated in a *naven* ceremony in which they aped the strutting and overbearing manner of the men. Modern American bacchanalia, in which male athletes dress in tutus, provide an example of contrasexual parody closer to home.

Subjective Experiences of Women

For many women, arguments from empirical evidence about the existence of the animus are beside the point; the animus is a familiar presence that is manifest in dreams, fantasies, and emotions.

Animus as Other

Since the animus is, by definition, of opposite gender from the ego, it represents some aspect of the ''not I'' or the ''other.'' Even if a woman is heavily identified with her masculine side, she still lives in her female body and in some important ways *is* her body, to which the masculine aspect of her psyche offers a contrast. But what is "other"? This varies enormously, of course, from one culture to another, and among individuals within a culture. On an inner level the same complementarity applies: The more a woman's ego identifies with a limited range of qualities defined as feminine, the greater will be her tendency to project her unexamined fears and undeveloped capabilities onto men, in her outer life as well as within. Thus, it is clear that one of the important developmental tasks for a woman is to become acquainted with her inner "other" and bring some of the qualities originally perceived as "masculine" into the light of her ego consciousness.

The way in which this process may occur is expressed in a series of dreams by a woman in analysis. The woman had had several dreams in which Abraham Lincoln figured prominently, as a strong masculine figure who presided over an inner civil war. The subject had been sufficiently impressed with these dreams to read a biography of Lincoln. She read that, during his prairie years, it was said of him that "Nobody had a strong right arm for chopping wood like Abe." Shortly after she read those words, she had the following dream:

> I'm in a rustic cabin or house where there is a political meeting going on. There is much milling about among the women. Then the guest speaker arrives and I'm to introduce her. We all go into the living room and sit down. The big point I want to make in my introduction, a point that I know is very important politically, is that this woman has a strong right arm, and can chop wood. This is terribly important, and I'm subliminally aware, in the dream, of a connection with Abraham Lincoln. I begin my introduction, and state that the speaker is a pioneer in this locality.

The dreamer felt that the strong (male) right arm for chopping wood reflected her projection of political strength onto a male "other." Attributing the strong right arm to a woman suggests that the quality of strength has been brought closer to the ego.

160

Male Figures in Women's Dreams

Although male figures are legion in women's dreams, the mere appearance of such figures is not necessarily evidence of the animus's existence. They may represent instead a woman's perception of objective (outer) men or their qualities. But when a male figure in a woman's dreams changes without a change in the actual man, the dreams often reflect inner change in the woman.

One kind of change may be from an image of a physically powerful man, through one with social or "word" power, to a more spiritual animus figure. This sequence is outlined by Emma Jung, and many women can recognize it, in a very general way, from half a lifetime or more of dreaming.

Another important change, which often occurs in psychotherapy, is the shift of the animus from negative to positive. One woman, whose experience is fairly typical, began analysis with low self-esteem. She absorbed verbal abuse from her husband and added her own self-depreciation to it. Thus, her inner negative animus and its image in dreams mirrored the destructive male in her life. As she began to develop psychological strength, she was able to take some of the energy that had empowered the negative animus and turn it into assertiveness and initiative, that is, her animus became more positive, although there was no corresponding change in her husband.

Emotions

Women experience the emotional force of the animus in different ways, but there seems to be some commonality in these subjective states. The negative animus is often perceived as a destructive force, which the conscious mind cannot control. It may fill one's whole being with malevolent energy or it may be, as one woman described it, "something that takes me by the scruff of the neck and shakes me." In any case, it comes unbidden and refuses to respond to commands from the ego.

In its positive form the animus may be experienced as a

feeling of unaccountable energy, whether for a relationship, an idea, or a project. In such an instance, the woman has a sense of being in focus, on target, all there. One woman reported two exhilarating experiences of positive animus energy. One involved successfully solving a complicated problem in statistics; the other occurred when she organized a complex family move, working for several weeks with unusual competence and energy. She saw these experiences as instances of animus activity.

Usefulness of the Animus Concept

Thus far we have indicated a number of problems with the animus concept and expressed our view that the evidence from other disciplines lends some indirect support to the idea. But the fact remains that outside the Jungian community no one seems to find the animus concept particularly exciting—except negatively—and no serious discipline other than Jungian psychology has adopted it as a useful tool for understanding women.

Then why do Jungians hang onto the idea with such tenacity? After talking with many women of various theoretical and political persuasions, we find that the chief value of the animus concept is this: It often helps women to understand themselves better. We suspect that much harm has been done in the name of "your animus," whereas an examination of "my animus" can be the beginning of wisdom. To suggest that the use of the term should be limited to members of the female sex is perhaps going too far. But it does seem evident that the animus is most dangerous when used as an accusation against others and most healing when claimed for oneself.

Indeed, not every woman needs to apply the concept to herself. Some have managed to develop their qualities of strength, focus, and assertiveness without ever labeling them, or imaging them, as masculine. For such women those traits are not "other."

But for the rest of us, many of the qualities we admire and

enjoy most in ourselves inhabit our dreams and fantasies in masculine guise. For those who find the concept useful, here are some of the ways in which the animus concept can help in charting the course for our own psychological development.

Awareness of the animus can be helpful to women in finding in themselves qualities and capabilities that they had attributed to men. In a culture that labels many positive qualities ''masculine,'' it is often easier for women to project these qualities onto men than to recognize them closer to home. We believe that it is essential for women to withdraw these projections and reclaim their own assertiveness, creativity, and ability to cope with the world. When we do so, the positive animus becomes more conscious—more under control of the ego.

Similarly, the negative animus can and should be brought home. Each woman must take responsibility for the monsters within, regardless of their gender. This process has particular significance for the more separatist wing of the women's movement, where women sometimes fall into the custom of projecting all selfishness, oppression, and brutality onto the male sex, at the cost of neglecting their own inner development.

The other side of this act of reclamation is to recognize the many ways in which our social institutions repress, brutalize, and trivialize women. There is little hope for women to develop their creative potential without support from their environment. And where repression of women's creative potential is systematic, over many generations, the bitchiness and witchiness of the warped animus have become so prevalent as to be considered normal, albeit unlovable, attributes of the female sex. One of the jobs of personal development, then, is to help create a social climate in which women—and men—are free to move beyond narrow stereotypes.

The animus is one pole of a dynamic inner process that is the key to a woman's individuation process. For many of us, to become aware of the animus, tame it but not obliterate it, to have the courage to kiss the beast and make him a friend, are the essential steps in the journey toward consciousness and wholeness.

Notes

1. Claire Douglas, "The Animus: Old Women, Menopause, and Feminist Theory," in *The San Francisco Institute Library Journal*, Vol. 6, Issue 3, 1986. In this article, Douglas has traced the history of writings on the animus.
2. Emma Jung, *Animus and Anima* (Dallas: Spring Publications, 1969).
3. Naomi Goldenberg, "A Feminist Critique of Jung," in *Signs*, Vol. 2, Issue 2, Winter 1976.
4. Carl Gustav Jung, *Collected Works*, Vol. 10 (Princeton: Princeton University Press, 1970), para. 243. [Hereafter, *Collected Works* will be signified by *CW* followed by the volume number.]
5. Margaret Mead, *Sex and Temperament in Three Primitive Societies* (New York: William Morrow & Company, 1935).
6. *CW* 10, para. 71.
7. *CW* 9, Part II, para. 27.
8. *CW* 9, Part I, para. 309.
9. *CW* 17, para. 338.
10. Examples found in *CW* 10, para. 83 and *CW* 16, para. 522.
11. *CW* 9, Part II, para. 29.
12. A. Aron et al., "Relationships With Opposite-Sexed Parents and Mate Choice" in *Human Relations*, 1974, Vol. 27, Issue I, pp. 17-24.
13. B. Gelpi, "The Androgyne" in *Women & Analysis*, J. Strouse, ed. (New York: Grossman, 1974). pp. 227-238.
14. Irene Claremont de Castillejo, *Knowing Woman: A Feminine Psychology* (New York: Putman's, 1973), p. 73.
15. Polly Young-Eisendrath, *Hags and Heroes: A Feminist Approach to Jungian Psychotherapy With Couples* (Toronto: Inner City Books, 1984), p. 39.
16. James Hillman, *Anima* (Dallas: Spring Publications, 1970), pp. 97-132.
17. Erich Neumann, *The Origins and History of Consciousness* (New York: Pantheon, 1964).
18. Edward Whitmont, *The Return of the Goddess* (New York: Crossroad, 1982), p. 83.
19. Marion Woodman, *The Owl Was a Baker's Daughter: Obesity, Anorexia Nervosa, and the Repressed Feminine* (Toronto: Inner City Books, 1980), p. 118.

20. Linda Leonard, *The Wounded Woman* (Berkeley: Shambala Publications, 1983).

21. Jean Bolen, *Goddesses in Everywoman: A New Psychology of Women* (San Francisco: Harper & Row, 1984), p. 10.

22. Sherry Ortner, ''Is Female to Male as Nature is to Culture?'' in *Woman, Culture, and Society*, M. Zimbalist-Rosaldo and L. Lamphere, eds. (Palo Alto: Stanford University Press, 1974), pp. 67-87).

23. Marilyn Nagy, ''Menstruation and Shamanism'' in *Psychological Perspectives*, Vol. 12, Issue I, Spring 1981, pp. 52-68.

24. J. Curran, ''Differential Effects of Stated Preferences and Questionnaire Role Performance on Interpersonal Attraction in the Dating Situation'' in *Journal of Psychology*, 1972, Vol. 82, pp. 313-327. (Cited by Kay Deaux in *The Behavior of Women and Men* [Monterey, CA: Brooks/Cole Publishing Company, 1976]).

25. See Sandra Bem, ''The Measurement of Psychological Androgyny'' in *Journal of Consulting and Clinical Psychology*, 1974, Vol. 42, pp. 155-162; Carolyn Heilbrun, *Toward a Recognition of Androgyny* (New York: Harper & Row, 1973); June Singer; *Androgyny* (Garden City, NY: Anchor Press, 1976).

13
Toward the Companionate
Man-Woman Relationship

DANE RUDHYAR

The word "liberation" has always been invested with a quasi-hypnotic emotional intensity and a magical meaning. It is nevertheless a negative term used by people who have become aware of being in a state of bondage and who, as a result, crave either inner freedom or outer sociocultural and political liberty. Unless one is vividly aware of being *bound*—whether by biological instincts, emotional yearnings, social tradition, cultural rules, or political laws—one does not demand and fight for liberation. The struggle for liberation at any level is often arduous and violent, because what binds a person or a class of persons almost inevitably resists change, the more so if it is institutionalized and supported by a dogmatic ideology or by what appears to be self-evident facts. In the fight, many essential issues are easily forgotten or brushed aside for later consideration. This is unfortunate because, as a result, a clear perception of what essentially is at stake is clouded by emotionalism and partisanship. As the battle rages, these basic principles and their embodiment in concrete personal and interpersonal behavior are ignored; either violence-prone passion, an Arjuna-type of despondency, or perhaps a dulling resignation prevails.

When there is a fight, there must always be at least two sides. Relationship is involved. It may be the positive relationship of love, or the negative relationship of war and hatred. In either case, the central issue is *the character and the intensity of the relationship.* Nevertheless, it is evident that the nature and temperament of the two or more individuals being related, and the level at which the relationship operates, are determining factors. What might usually be considered a highly spiritual relationship cannot exist between two personalities operating at a primitive level of development. The meaning of the term ''spiritual'' has an ambiguous character, which can only be clarified when one considers the level at which the relationship exists. There are indeed many levels of interhuman relationship. At each level a sense of bondage and yearning for liberation can develop. At each level what we may broadly call the creative process takes different forms, because the purpose and quality of the process change as the relationship moves from one level to the next.

The process of interpersonal relationship between man and woman operates at different levels of activity and consciousness within different sociocultural environments. The role woman plays in the process and the challenge men and women living in this period of basic human transformation face, as they relate intimately to each other, indicates the possibility of developing a new quality of relatedness, productive of inner peace, harmony, and illumination, rather than to the attainment of an ambiguous and ill-defined condition of ''freedom'' and ''equality'' by one side, which in some instances and from some special points of view may mean either woman or man.

The Man-Woman Relationship at the Biological and Social Levels

In the past, the character of the basic man-woman relationship has reflected the belief that human beings are not only able, but *meant* to operate primarily—if not exclusively—at two levels, the biological and the social levels. This is so even today for the majority of human beings in the world. Such a belief has been formulated in the statement that human beings are especially social animals. Animals may live in groups and often in large societies, but the socializing process in the human kingdom has produced results of extraordinary magnitude and with a revolutionary character. This has been caused by the fact that human beings have been able to transfer from generation to generation the knowledge born of repeated personal and group experiences.

The essential means used for communication and the transfer of knowledge has been an increasingly complex type of language, and symbolic representations of what eluded verbalization. Language and symbols have become the foundations for cultural, religious, and social institutions. On such foundations the development of personalized thinking led to the crystallization of the results of increasingly individualized experiences and biopsychological responses into a psychic structure we call the ego.

All over the world tribal groups—originally constituting social organisms with powerful social cohesion and differentiated group activities (clans)—developed their own language and their cultural-religious and social patterns on the basis of exclusivism and a sense of superiority. Tribal cultures operated within a limited geographical environment to which they were attached in a powerful, instinctual manner, somewhat as a growing embryo is attached to the mother's womb. The earth was regarded and worshipped as the great Mother; each tribal whole receiving nourishment from her, and drawing from its contacts with plants, animals, soil, and sky the basic elements needed to build complex systems of symbols and cultural patterns of acting, feeling, and thinking.

In such a situation existing on all continents, the fundamental factor is, in the strict sense of the term, *life*. Biological needs and their satisfaction dominate everything, including the forms of social organization. The term ''social'' is at first hardly befitting when referring to tribal ways and tribal thinking-feeling, yet we must use it to stress that even then human beings already operated at two levels, biological and sociocultural. They could therefore relate to each other, and men and women related to each other in two essentially different ways, though at first the difference was not too clearly defined. Gradually, a process of differentiation increased under a more and more dominant patriarchal system. Woman's characteristic type of work and consciousness was seen to most specifically and naturally refer to the biological level of productivity, while the levels of social and mental activity gradually became a field more or less exclusively reserved to men.

As long as the two levels were closely interrelated and human beings operating at both were bound by a common sense of rootedness in a common purpose and will, the man's role was not crucial in its basic implications. Women bore children and men usually fought against enemies and predators, but they worked together in the fields. They were both producers of concrete entities needed for the preservation and growth of the community as a whole. Everyday activities were determined by the elemental *needs* of life, whether at the strictly biological level or at a more psychic level of perpetuating a strong and unchallengeable feeling of communal identity and purpose.

The cities developed, and with them the demands for more complex and extensive forms of social organization. The social and the biological realms became increasingly distinct and separate, and likewise the roles of women and men. Social and political organization, commerce and distant travel, and an ever greater and more specialized development of the military became man's business; the home and the children became woman's business. Man became the provider of that mysteriously abstract and ubiquitous social power, *money.*

With money, and special capacities for dealing with the competition and pressure of society and politics, came prestige and social authority—and the power to make laws and to impose social and religious restrictive patterns upon biological processes. Male personages had assumed the role of founders and preservers of religious institutions. While in some ways these religions related the social to the biological level, they also increasingly sought to separate spirituality from biological fulfillment. Then woman and her biological role were made subservient to the organizing power of men, representing the absolute, all-encompassing power of a God in the form of supreme Creator—a Creator imagining or fashioning matter as he pleased—and womanhood became equated with cosmic matter.

What we see developing today is, on the one hand, an attempt to do away with what the *city*—a type of society based on a strictly social mode of organization and money-power—brought to mankind and, on the other hand, a persisting endeavor to reduce to a minimum the *biological* processes (artificial insemination, test-tube babies, the private home-life and feeding of a single family, children's education) and to give to woman a role in the *social* processes on a basis of asexual equality with men. We shall return to these recent developments, but we must first discuss other types of man-woman relationship derived from human needs and inner experiences transcending the biological and social fields of activity and consciousness.

The Psychospiritual Approach to the Man-Woman Relationship

What for many centuries and in most parts of the world has been defined and sanctioned as "marriage" refers almost exclusively—in principle even if not always in actual fact—to a relationship operating strictly at both the biological and the social levels. The purpose of marriage was to perpetuate not only the human race, but a particular culture, religion, and social order as well. Marriage between a man and a woman of different races, religions, and/or social classes was scandalous, and in most cases unthinkable. It was organized by the parents, and in many places the boy and girl either never or only briefly met before their marriage. It was then consummated as a religious sacrament, a social feast, and an impersonal biological act in the symbolic (and actual) darkness of the "generic unconscious"— the world of animal instincts. Except in the rarest cases, a man and woman did not marry of their own free will for the deliberate purpose of fulfilling each other *as individuals*

in an equality of sharing and free enjoyment of *all* their po-
tentialities of self-development. The marriage partners were
meant to perform archetypal roles—as husband and wife,
father and mother, son-in-law and daughter-in-law, etc.

In some societies, however, different kinds of roles were
considered possible which referred to spiritual or psychological values. In old India, for instance, the husband was
considered, at least potentially, as his wife's *guru*. To her,
he embodied the ideal of divine power and wisdom. He was
to perform the role of spirit mobilizing and fecundating matter, not merely at the biological level, but in a deeper, more
cosmic and *consciously* impersonal manner. It was only
through the man that woman could reach inner spiritual illumination; he was her inner light. And in a society rever-
ing such a light, it became almost logical—or at least
acceptable—that the wife should commune with that depart-
ing light at her husband's death, and throw herself into the
burning funeral pyre.

A somewhat reversed situation has occurred in our Western world—with fewer clear-cut variations than in some
other cultures—when at certain periods woman was idealized. In some instances, she was idolized as the source of
spiritual values, the symbol of a higher life, the mediator
between man and God, the "redeeming woman," or the
Muse inspiring the creative artist or poet. It was in the
remarkable culture developing in southern France during
the twelfth and thirteenth centuries that this idealization and
even adoration of women most definitely occurred. Other
cultures, especially in India, had known of a worship of the
Mother as a potent manifestation of the devotional spirit,
but as far as I know, the Western world and its Hebraic-
Greek tradition had not featured such forms of worship of
the embodied feminine aspect of the Deity. The use of
women as oracles in Greece did not have the same character.
The sybils were mediums rather than mediators or channels for divine creative power.

In medieval southern France, after the great collective fear
of the year 1000 when the end of the world had been expected, a male and muscle-dominated feudal society emerg-

171

ing from centuries of violence and crude living sought self-transcendence and cultural refinement through the idealization and worship of the feminine. Sex and war had to be purified and transmuted into pure love, poetry, and festivities by a spiritualizing alchemy of the feeling-nature of men. "Courtly love" developed, not so much as a spiritual-religious ideal—though it had its parallel in the growing worship of Mary as the Virgin-Mother of the incarnated God—but as an answer to a collective psychological and deeply psychic *need*.

This culture of love and beauty was soon to be drowned in the blood of the crusade against the Albigenses. In that infamous "crusade" conducted by the rulers of northern France with the full participation of the Pope, the culture of southern France—which extended also into Catalonia and part of northern Italy—was savagely destroyed. The Church's official motive was to stem the spread of a gnostic movement challenging papal authority and Catholic doctrine, but the French kings' purpose was merely to gain more power and wealth, and to expand their territory. The karmic result was the nearly disastrous Hundred Years War with England, and deep psychic scars in the body of the French nation which were gradually formed in the crucible of war, violence, and deceit.

We see a typical expression of this Mediterranean and also Celtic woman-idealizing culture in Dante's *Divine Comedy* with the quasi-sanctification of Beatrice, the beloved, as inspirer and guide in the spiritual quest. Later on we find the ideal reborn in the romantic culture in Goethe's celebration of "the Eternal Feminine that draws man heavenward," and in many poets' references to their inspiring Muse. Romanticism developed as a reaction against the proud classical rationalism, the scientific intellectualism of "the Enlightenment" in the eighteenth century, and the rise to power of a dull and crudely individualistic bourgeoise—thanks to the Industrial Revolution. Man instinctively saw himself caught in the merciless wheels of a society in which the male greed for power and the worship of money were beginning to dominate all social processes and the lives of human beings helplessly drawn to cities and factories.

In the psychology of Carl Jung the concept of the *anima*, and of the archetype of the Redeeming Woman, occupies a basic function. The *anima* is the ideal woman-image mediating between the ego (often the slave of a socially set *persona*) and the deep unconscious filled with potency for rebirth. For the ego-dominated, college-educated, and money-obsessed man, a woman can (and usually must) serve as the embodiment or "psychological projection" of all that subconsciously longs for spirituality and ideal love within him. She becomes for the extroverted man the inward way to the spirit. If the woman is not able to accept this psychological projection of the man's *anima*, the man's inner life may remain empty. Then the relationship between them cannot be truly fulfilling.

The anima-embodying woman—mystical beloved, Muse, or Redeeming Mother—is the polar opposite of the guru-husband regarded as a lord, teacher, or hierophant leading to the higher level of consciousness. In either case, one cannot speak of "equality" except at a superficial social level. There may be companionship, sharing of personal and social responsibilities, and productive love uniting two biopsychic polarities, yet these relationships have an essentially transpersonal and transformative character. They may have today a psychotherapeutic value as a means of overcoming crisis-situations, and in most cases some kind of crisis-situation is implied in the creative process, especially—but not exclusively—in the arts. A crisis-situation develops whenever an individual comes to experience an irrepressible urge to break through ego-bondage or subservience from a way of life that is felt to be meaningless. Such an urge may lead this individual to another person with whom a deeply transforming alchemical relationship may be formed. In such a relationship, a transpersonal flow of power or spiritual light is likely to operate, freely or spasmodically. The flow may occur through either the man or the woman, depending on who needs it most. And both may need it.

What I have called elsewhere the companionate order of relationship has, theoretically at least, a rather different character. It refers far more accurately to the coming together and commergence of two persons operating *at the same level* of activity and consciousness. The companions may be very different in terms of background and past endeavors, but essentially they come together as "equals." As companions, they "eat of the same bread" *(cum-panis)* and, as comrades, they are active in the same space or room *(camera* meaning "room"). Their consciousnesses operate in terms of nearly identical premises, and are moved by a similar vision of what they have to accomplish together.

Such a fundamental equality and cooperation existed at the strictly biological level in the ancient tribal community. But they gradually vanish, or at least lose their pure and wholesome character, when social forces and the development of the mind on a social (which means both religious and intellectual) level introduce patterns of differentiation separating the social from the biological, and the intellect from the feelings. The important point, however, is that equality and cooperation in the archaic state of tribal unity are instinctual and compulsive. "Life" rules every act. The human species, not the individual person, makes the basic decisions. There are indeed no true *individuals* at such a stage of human evolution.

The compassionate type of relationship *requires* conscious, self-determined, and relatively independent individuals, deliberately accepting responsibilities of their own choosing. Such individuals may form communities, but these communities would be basically different in spirit and psychism from the ancient tribes. The use by many young people of the word "tribe" when referring to their countercultural communes shows that they do not understand either what they are seeking or how different these loosely organized associations are from tribal communities—even from American Indian tribes. In many instances, these young people, male and female, are trying to effectively return to nature. But one cannot actually "return" to the past; one can only try to revitalize faculties and attitudes to life that have become partially paralyzed while another type of consciousness and other faculties were developing according to the planetary process of human evolution. If such a revitalization were to produce a paralysis of these recently developed mental and rational faculties, it would only mean that one kind of paralysis now succeeds another. The only valid goal is a total actualization of the human potential. It is the development of the whole person, in whom individual selfhood and the relatedness of conscious and unpossessive love are constantly *interpenetrating*.

"Interpenetration" is the keyword. The true companionate relationship implies an interpenetration of minds and feelings, and there can be conscious and free interpenetration only where the centers of consciousness are oriented toward a commonly accepted and intuitively envisioned goal. Because of this common orientation the companions are sustained by the same ray of spiritual light and power. That light is their shared sustenance, the "living bread" (*panis*) in the partaking of which they are truly companions. Out of their togetherness a "commonsoul" is being formed, very different from the commonwealth represented by the traditional type of marriage operating in societies where money, position, security, and self-perpetuation in a progeny are the basic ideals.

The companionate interpenetration of minds and souls that are self-consecrated in their common dedication to a transpersonal purpose, though individualized and matured by a life openly and courageously lived, is not a utopia; neither is it an easy achievement. It can only be actualized through the overcoming of crises of growth and particularly of ego-surrender. In many instances, one of the partners is likely to be more active or further along in the process of alchemical transformation than the other. It may be either the man or the woman in a bipolar union. The woman may need, at least for a time, the stimulation, inspiration, and leadership of a guru-type of man; the man may require the "redeeming" love and mediation of a woman accepting to be an *anima* figure for him in helping him to interiorize his consciousness and to realize both his own center and the presence of the "star" illuming their togetherness.

Creation always means transformation. And there can hardly be any transformation without relationship. The creative process is not to be separate from life itself. We speak of procreation and of artistic or social creation; we can also speak of the creation of the "immortal body" (Diamond

Body in Buddhism or Christ-body) of which mystics and occultists have spoken in symbolic words. In all instances and at all levels, relationship provides the substance of the process of transformation, and the quality of the relationship determines the level at which the process operates.

At the biological level, the relationship is instinctual and compulsive. At the social level, it is energized by the many-sided crises of personal relationship between the ego-conscious individual and society. At the psychological level, the transformation reaches beyond the personal stage and takes on an alchemical character. Yet it is always based on relationship, even if powered by the will or the conscious determination and biology-transcending love of the related individuals.

If one recognizes this to be a fact, the struggle for "liberation" acquires a new meaning. What has to be liberated is the ability to enter consciously, freely, and significantly into purposeful relationship at the highest (because the most inclusive) level at which an individual human being can operate in terms of his biological, social, and personal conditioning—his karma. Of itself, and sought for itself, liberation is an illusion—perhaps the greatest of all illusions. Most of the early Buddhists were lured by that glamor, seeking nirvana by destroying in them their capacity for relationship. They reached only a state of spiritual selfishness. They did not realize that, if Gautama renounced nirvana in compassion for humanity, compassion was for him greater than liberation.

Yet compassion requires inner freedom. The will to sacrifice oneself requires a self to be sacrificed. The pure love of the mystics requires the potency to love other human beings, for there can be transmutation only where there is vibrant energy to be transmuted. Of what use is it for a man to fight for a free society if he remains in his heart a slave to his ego and to the traditions of his past? Of what use is it for a woman to strive for social and biological liberation from a male-dominated way of life if she is not able to love and give total sustenance to the man with whom she may long to live in a companionate relationship?

III

Religious and Traditional Views

14
Maria Avatara

JAMES M. SOMERVILLE

Divine incarnation, or the "descent" *(avatara)* of the Absolute into human form, is a central theme in more than one religious tradition. However, there are somewhat different ways of approaching it.

In Christianity the appearance in time and in finite form of the eternal Word of God, the Second Person of the Trinity, is called a "mystery" because, among other things, the human mind finds it difficult to conceive how the infinite can become limited to the finite. The assumption is that there is a great gulf between the infinite Creator and the finite creation. But mystery or not, once it is clear that the Absolute can manifest itself in time, we have no reason to suppose that this could not happen more than once. What God has done once, God can do again. If God has appeared in masculine form, why not also in feminine?

The Hindu tradition, beginning with a different set of premises, offers a different picture. The Absolute has two aspects: as infinite, it is formless, without the strands *(gunas)* of which all finite things are woven. This is *Nirguna Brahman.* But as finite, the same ultimate Reality manifests itself in space, time, and myriad forms; that is, with the *gunas,* and it is called *Saguna Brahman.* What appears in the world is still the One Absolute, but the word is its self-manifestation. Thus, the pious Hindu sees God in all things but still reserves a special reverence for the fuller expressions of divinity when they appear in certain special persons called *avatars.*

From such distinctions we may append two remarks and a suggestion. First, the Christian God is conceived as Father, and is therefore thought of as male, while Hindus are equally at home imaging God as female, that is, as Mother. Second, unlike in the West where divine incarnation historically has been limited to the masculine form, Hindu incarnations have been in the form of male and female pairs. The suggestion that follows will be to the effect that a double incarnation has been present in Christianity secretly from the beginning, a notion that will be developed below.

The Gender of God

Of course, God is neither male nor female, but this has not prevented those in the East from singing ''her'' praises nor those in the West from appealing to ''him'' for forgiveness and rescue. There were historical reasons in the West for thinking of God as male. The Hebrew God, Yahweh, could scarcely be conceived initially as possessing feminine qualities. He was a warrior God, the Lord of military hosts who crushed his enemies—those of his chosen people—with his almighty power. In return he expected fidelity and obedience to his commandments from his people. His social relations with the nation were like those of a paterfamilias with his extended household. And the later conceptualization of creation sustained this sense of God as Father: through his creative Word, God gives to creation its form, especially to humans, who are made in his image. This is the contribution of a father, whose sperm in the development process of his offspring provides, not food and substance, but simply information.

The Mother Goddess, in India, could also act to protect her children by destroying (even when all the male gods failed to do so), but in all other respects she is peaceable. She generates her children as a mother does, contributing both information and substance. Thus, she is both Nirguna Brahman, the Formless One, and Saguna Brahman, manifesting as all the forms. She sustains her offspring throughout their lives and, like the earth, receives them back into herself at death. She is unfailingly accepting of all her children and makes no conditions or exactions.

In the late Jewish and Christian dispensation, the masculine warrior God was softened to become a loving Father rather than a God of vengeance, but still male. He was now more forgiving and his fidelity was secure even if his people were unfaithful. He was even willing to make great personal sacrifices for the sake of his disobedient people. Although outwardly masculine, these (usually) feminine qualities surfaced, so that psychologically at least the Christian God became almost androgynous.

Hindu representations of God were sometimes explicitly androgynous. A figure would be male on one side and female on the other. Or it would have three faces, one male, one female, one neutral. Or the Deity would be represented as two figures in marriage embrace, male and female, yet united. Particularized or personalized, deities came in pairs, such as Vishnu and Lakshmi or Shiva and Parvati.

Curiously enough, there is a fresco in a medieval church in Urschalling, Bavaria, where the three Persons of the Trinity are represented as three heads attached to a single body. The Father and the Son are bearded and are clearly male, but the Holy Spirit is beardless and, according to Jesuit scripture scholar Kevin O'Connell, appears to be female.

When it is a question of the Deity making a special appearance in human form—an incarnation or avatar—the Christian male God can appear only in the guise of a male, but the Hindu androgynous God comes as both: Rama and Sita, Krishna and Radha, Ramakrishna and Sarada Devi. This follows as the natural outcome of their respective ways of conceiving the divine.

Mary, the Hidden Incarnation?

The Roman Catholic Church has always encouraged a tender devotion to the Virgin Mary, a devotion often vested with such emotional vigor that she all but outshone her divine Son. The glorious cathedrals of Europe, dedicated to "Notre Dame," bear ample witness to the intensity of this devotion. During the 1920s and 1930s there was a movement among some Catholic enthusiasts to have the Church declare Mary Co-Redemptrix and Mediatrix of All Graces.

The Holy See has discreetly discouraged all such attempts, and the present Pope, John Paul II, though devoted to Mary himself, has reiterated the traditional view. Mary, though worthy of a special kind of devotion, is not to be accorded anything like divine honors.

All this the Church does officially and, as it were, *in abstracto,* with its right hand. But on the other hand, left-handedly, the message is mixed. In 1950 Pope Pius XII, having consulted Roman Catholic bishops and theologians and having received a response that was better than ninety percent in favor, declared that Mary, the Mother of Jesus, was assumed, body and soul, into heaven. Her Assumption, celebrated on the 15th of August, thus parallels the Ascension of Jesus, who was taken up, body and soul, into heaven after the Resurrection. And this dogma of the Assumption of Mary was promulgated just ninety-six years after an earlier Pope, Pius IX, had promulgated the dogma of the Immaculate Conception, according to which Mary was conceived in her mother's womb free from the stain of original sin, a privilege she alone shares with her divine Son.

It thus turns out that Mary, like Jesus, was sinless from the first moment of her earthly existence in her mother's womb, and that Mary, like Jesus, was assumed into heaven, body and soul. It begins to look as though the female figure of Mary has a symbolic role to play alongside the male figure of Jesus.

God's Image

In the book of Genesis it is said that God created humankind, ''male and female,'' in his own image (1:27). Is the text telling us that God, if imaged as human, must be thought of as both male and female? Or, put the other way around, would the likeness of God be adequately expressed in time and in human form if God became incarnate solely in the masculine form? The original pair, Adam and Eve, imaged God together. And it is significant that the early Fathers of the Christian Church made much of the parallel between the disobedience of the original pair and the sinlessness and fidelity of Jesus, the new Adam, and of Mary, the new Eve. The second pair seem to stand together in the work of reversing the sin and disobedience of the original pair. The first Man and Woman disobeyed God's command and ate the lethal fruit of the forbidden tree of the knowledge of good and evil. The second Adam and the paradigmatic "Woman" (*gyne*, as Mary is called in the Fourth Gospel—cf. 2:4; 19:26) obeyed the will of God and were brought together as the Tree of Life, the cross of Calvary, whose fruit is eternal life.

There is a remarkable engraving, dated A.D. 1512, which portrays the cross of the crucified Christ as a tree whose branches are heavy with fruit that is being eaten by those who stand beneath the cross. They are being nourished, not only by the words of Christ, but by his very lifeblood and substance. But where did his lifeblood and bodily substance come from? Was it not from Mary that he took the very body and blood with which he now feeds his disciples and makes them members of his (her) Body?

The Man and the Woman have been together in this story all along. In the Garden of Eden they both sinned and were accomplices in the origin of evil. But the Lord promised to provide the human race with another gyne, or woman, who would collaborate with her son in crushing the head of the serpent of evil beneath his heel (Gen. 3:15). The Gospel according to John leaves little room for doubt about the relation between Jesus and Mary as the new Adam and the new Eve, the new *anthropos* and the new gyne. When Pontius Pilate brings forth the scourge and thorn-crowned Jesus and presents him to the multitudes, he exclaims: "Behold, the *anthropos*, the Man!" And when Jesus is dying on the cross, he presents Mary to the beloved disciple with the words: "Behold the gyne, the Woman!" Together, Jesus and Mary are humanity recreated.

Mary here becomes the great archetype of the feminine, the pure and sinless Woman, the heroine of a thousand faces, womankind in its perfection.

Hindus have little difficulty in seeing Mary as the divine consort of Jesus, as an incarnation of the feminine aspect of God, paired with Jesus in the work of salvation. To varying degrees Christians resist this notion. The Protestant tradition rejects any attempt to exalt Mary to a position in any degree parallel or equal to that of Jesus. There is but one universal Mediator, "even Jesus Christ, the only Son of God." Catholics, on the other hand, while remaining doctrinally consistent, are often psychologically ambivalent, as noted above.

The Everlasting Woman

It is because of our constitution that an incarnation of God in both male and female form is important to us. Children do need pictures in their storybooks to stimulate their imaginations, and even adults with some degree of sophistication find it hard to relate to a God without form. Moreover, people want to relate to God in a personal way. Most of us are reluctant to think of our Source as an "it," since the neuter pronoun connotes an impersonal force with no concern for each one of us. We need something more nearly like ourselves, something tangible, someone with an earthly history, who can act as a mediator between the absolutely transcendent Source and our own finite condition.

Christianity has provided such a mediator, albeit in the male form alone. This is understandable. In the male-dominated society, such as existed in the Near East at the time of Jesus, it was unthinkable to represent women as in any sense equal to men. In such an environment were God to appear in human guise, it would hardly be in female form. But cultural formations and attitudes do change. Looking forward to the centuries ahead, it remains to be seen whether, as women achieve greater economic and political status in national and ecclesiastical affairs, the Virgin Mary may not emerge as the companionate divine image. Where he is proclaimed as the paradigmatic and everlasting Man, may she not also be acknowledged as the parallel everlasting Woman?

If the image of God on earth is best represented by both sexes, would it not be appropriate that the redemption of the human race would turn out to be the work of both sexes? Traditionalists might argue that Mary was only instrumental in the work of redemption, since she was merely the mother according the flesh of the one who was divine by nature. But this leaves the gyne, the Woman, in an inferior position. How would a conclave of male theologians and ecclesiastics react if it were divinely revealed that the *only* Mediator between God and humans was a woman? Would they not feel that their version of human nature and their dignity as persons had been slighted and intrinsically undermined? Or suppose a power elite of ecclesiastical women declared that men were unfit to function liturgically because they could not properly image the divine Mediatrix. . . .

The fact is that the human psyche, for whose sake incarnations descend from the heaven of the Spirit, cannot remain humane and healthy without fully recognizing and integrating both the feminine and the masculine archetypes into its sense of the real and the divine. Men are born of women; they are reared by women, and they cannot generate progeny without women. Men need women far more than women need men. To pretend that the true image of our divine Source is the human male exclusively is to turn our backs on the plain facts of both human nature and natural theology.

The Evolution of Insight

Taking a hint from another culture (e.g., India) and other philosophical systems is not unknown in the history of Christianity. Building on a Judaic base, the Church Fathers first adopted Platonism and later Aristotelianism, modifying them to suit their own particular theological needs. Organizationally, Christianity modeled itself on the institutions of the Roman Empire. Liturgically, it borrowed to some extent from most of the religions it displaced, from the Hellenistic mysteries to the pagan rites of northwest Europe and the native traditions of the Americas and Africa.

In the midst of this accommodation and absorption, Christianity continued to reflect on its own special material, its "deposit of faith." Out of this continued reflection, its views of what that deposit of faith really meant grew and developed. Sometimes things that seemed quite new emerged, but they could always be traced back to the original source, even if only in hidden ways. John Henry (Cardinal) Newman called this process ''the development of doctrine.''

What is being proposed here is a continuation of this time-honored process. It need not be specifically the Hindu approach that is adopted; that was only an example. It is much more important that attention be directed to human nature itself and the relation between nature and the concept of God. In order to have a further ''development of doctrine'' in the direction of gender equality, we need to have an evolution of insight. Meditation on God and on human nature, on one hand, and reflection on the deposit of faith, on the other, will surely permit the emergence from that faith itself the realization that humanity, in its imaging and mediatorial role between the Absolute and the finite world, must be expressed completely, that is, as male and female.

As that realization begins to shape itself concretely, why should it not avail itself of the figure most natural to it as emblem and paradigm? Mary aside, where else are we apt to find another feminine figure as an *avatara* within the Christian tradition? There is already preparation for such a descent and appearance in female human form in both doctrine and practice, in scripture itself and in the devotion of the people. The collective psyche of humanity is in urgent need of such an image and such a presence. In our era of either mutually assured destruction through atomic war or of environmental devastation through industrial expansion without restraint, the time has surely arrived for the more obvious feminine values to come to the fore to defeat the despoilers of our earth.

The memory of the species is long. The great archetypes are deeply rooted in it. Like long-submerged volcanic fires under the seas *(maria)*, when their time comes they erupt from the unconscious and create new land for human habitation in the midst of the sea. She, the everlasting Woman, has been there from the beginning as the feminine image of God. Perhaps the time has come to give her a name. In the West, she is called Maria, the one who emerges out of the waters of the unconscious to become a divine presence, Maria Avatara. The development of this insight will probably have to be left to future generations.

15

The Beguines in Medieval Europe: An Expression of Feminine Spirituality

ELIZABETH A. PETROFF

If we were to chart the history and geography of women's spirituality, looking for times and places in which women were particularly empowered to develop spiritual gifts, we'd need to return to the early thirteenth century and focus on the Beguines in the parish of Liege (medieval Lotharingia, modern Belgium), and the nearby Low Countries, Flanders, Antwerp. On the peripheries of urban centers, we'd see self-supporting communities of women who lived by the work of their hands, cared for the sick and the poor, experimented with new devotional practices that increased their compassion and wisdom, and wrote devotional and mystical treatises, works which scholars are just now appreciating and studying as remarkable explorations of human, feminine psychology. Here,

> as nowhere else in Europe, the newly emancipated women religions were able to evolve a way of life hitherto unknown in the West, free from monastic enclosure, observing the rules which they themselves devised to meet the needs of individual communities, following lives of intense activity which might be devoted to prayer, to teaching and study, to charitable works, or to all three.[1]

The end of the twelfth century and the beginning of the thirteenth was an unusual and creative time for women, unlike earlier centuries and far different from what was to come. For reasons still not entirely understood, a "Women's Movement" developed all over western Europe, a movement of women with religious vocations who were unwilling—or simply too poor—to fit into the earlier models of female monasticism or of marriage and childbearing. In great numbers, women were seeking an unstructured, nonhierarchical spiritual life that was both active (in the sense of ministering to the needs of others) and contemplative (in the sense that meditation and visionary experience were highly valued and developed).[2] The communities that evolved were radical in medieval terms, and would still be radical today.

In northern Europe, the women's movement was identified with the Beguines; in southern Europe, the same kinds of impulses and social arrangements were to be found among the Umiliati and the early followers of St. Francis and St. Clare. Lay men were also involved in this movement, and so were a few churchmen, but the majority of those involved were women, women who could not, or did not wish to, become either wives or nuns. They sought a life of evangelical poverty, so they could live as Christ and his mother had lived; they wanted the opportunity to work, wanted a self-sufficiency based not on income from property but on the work of their hands. They wanted a daily religious practice and the education to pursue that practice intelligently and the opportunity to discuss spiritual ideas among themselves. They desired flexibility of commitment and of life-style, so that there would be room for active charity in the world as well as for a solitary contemplative existence when the need arose. They were happy to live chaste lives in completely female communities, but they preferred not to take permanent vows of chastity, and they resisted strict enclosure.[3]

There is much we still have to learn about the Beguines, but we have an invaluable introduction in the *Life of Marie d'Oignies* written by her confessor and disciple, Cardinal Jacques de Vitry. Here we see the beliefs that guided a new generation of spiritually oriented women,[4] for this *Vita* was intended to publicize the activities of Marie and her followers in Liège, and to protect this new group by establishing a pedigree for it that would be acceptable to ecclesiastical authorities suspicious both toward women and toward innovations in the spiritual life.

Marie d'Oignies is the first Beguine whose biography we know: she was born around 1177 to a wealthy and respected family of Nivelles in the diocese of Liège. She was married when she was fourteen, in 1191. That same year she and her husband, agreeing on a vow of chastity, went to work in the leper colony at Williambrouk. When she decided she wanted a more austere and more spiritual life in 1207, she went to the Augustinian community of St. Nicholas of Oignies near Namur, where Jacques de Vitry was a regular canon in 1211. The community there was a coenobium or monastic community founded by secular priests for apostolic perfection, not affiliated with any religious order and admitting lay sisters and brothers. The focus of the group was a balance of contemplation and intensive pastoral care. Other women, who seem to have been immediately attracted to this life-style and to Marie's example, lived right next to the canons of St. Nicholas. But soon, perhaps by 1210 but certainly by the death of Marie in 1213, there were too many of them, and a new beguinage had to be built. Municipal records from the 1280s indicate that women had for some time been willing their houses to other single women so that they might live in the area of the new beguinage. Each sister occupied her own cottage, but the sisters spent most of their time in common and ate meals together.[5]

The term "Beguine" probably originated as a derogatory label for a female heretic, perhaps associated with the Albigensians, perhaps referring to the color of the robes worn by beguines.[6] The movement as a whole—never codified by its members and never identified with individual leaders—lasted in northern Europe (especially in the area around Liège) until the French Revolution. It is thought to have been characterized by four stages. In the first stage, individual ecstatic women lived scattered about the city, leading strict religious lives while remaining in the world. It was a spontaneous movement with no founder and no legislator, and the women were simply called "holy women," *mulieres sanctae.* Only at the beginning of the thirteenth century did these women begin to organize themselves into congregations centered on spiritual discipline and common tasks.

> The women submitted to a grand mistress, aided by a council of other mistresses, each with a specific function. In organization and daily practices they often emulated the nunnery. They held meetings, followed common exercises, performed acts of charity, and recommended compulsory prayers. But ordinary religious practices remained parochial as before. To foster piety, practical or contemplative, to hold aloof from the dangers of the world without stopping ordinary work, such was their aim.[7]

It was at this second stage of growth that the church intervened. If the women were going to build communities, those communities ought to be under the control of one of the existing orders. But the existing orders were not interested in taking in more women, especially poor women without dowries, and they made no allowance for women supporting themselves by working. At this point Jacques de Vitry became their spokesman, and the women received papal consent to form their own self-regulated communities.[8]

The third stage was that of enclosure; communities, at first quite small, grew around infirmaries and hospices in which the "holy women" worked. But other women who identified themselves as Beguines continued to live at home or as solitaries, meeting occasionally with other like-minded women. Spiritual guidance for these communities was generally provided by the friars, Franciscan or Dominican, or by the Cistercians, who were supposed to preach and hear confession regularly. The fourth stage organized the beguine enclosure into a parish:

> The full-blown beguinage comprised a church, cemetery, hospital, public square, and streets and walks lined with convents for the younger sisters and pupils and individual houses for the older and well-to-do inhabitants. In the Great Beguinage

at Ghent, with its walls and moats, there were at the beginning of the fourteenth century two churches, eighteen convents, over a hundred houses, a brewery, and an infirmary.[9]

Male writers defended these holy women on grounds of the exemplary simplicity and purity of their life-style, the importance of their economic self-sufficiency, and the profound emotionality of their spiritual life. The emotional fulfillment that may have been lacking in the medieval notion of marriage and motherhood was found by Beguine women in their relationship with the divine and, no doubt, was reinforced by their living and working together to create a supportive environment. As R. W. Southern summarizes:

> In many ways it is an idyllic picture—women escaping from the sordid frustrations of the world into the liberty of an unpretentious spiritual life: enjoying vivid experiences of a loving God, and occupied in useful services ranging from the care of the sick to the embroidery of ecclesiastical vestments.[10]

Yet he adds, "these women and their way of life raised up enemies, all in some degree afraid and not all unreasonably."[11]

Perhaps one of the reasons the new holy women elicited such varying responses was that their lives were so various—individual women or each small cluster of women might take quite different paths to the same goal of spiritual enlightenment. Bolton, speaking of the first movement of holy women around Liège, emphasizes the multiplicity of life-styles:

> . . . their lives bring us into contact with most of the possible forms of religious life available to women at the time in this area: a beguine, Mary of Oignies, a recluse Ivetta of Huy, a Dominican tertiary Margaret of Ypres, a Cistercian nun Lutgard of Aywieres and Christina of St. Trond, called *Mirabilis*, claimed by Benedictines, Cistercians and Premonstratensians alike but who in reality was not attached to any religious order nor to a beguine group.[12]

The earliest description we have of the behavior of these loosely affiliated groups of women was written by Jacques de Vitry, in his *Life of Marie d'Oignies:*

> You...saw...some of these women dissolved with such a particular and marvelous love toward God that they languished with desire, and for years had rarely been able to rise from their cots. They had no other infirmity, save that their souls were melted with desire of Him, and sweetly resting with the Lord, as they were comforted in spirit they were weakened in body....The cheeks of one were seen to waste away, while her soul was melted with the greatness of her love. Another's flow of tears had made visible furrows down her face. Others were drawn with such intoxication of spirit that in sacred silence they would remain quiet a whole day, with no sense of feeling for things about them, so that they could not be roused by clamour or feel a blow....I saw another who sometimes was seized with ecstasy five-and-twenty times a day, in which state she was motionless, and on returning to herself she was so enraptured that she could not keep from displaying her inner joy with movements of the body, like David leaping before the ark.[13]

This is the language of *The Song of Songs* and of a certain kind of medieval love poetry, of *armour courtois* and *minnemystik,* of the great Beguine writers Hadewijch and Beatrijs of Nazareth, whose works we will see shortly. The behavior described suggests that some of the women of Liège were practicing a very physical *imitatio Christi.*[14] But de Vitry is utilizing this rhetoric for specific ends. In this passage he does not speak of the contents of the visions these women were experiencing; he is describing them as credible ecstatics, primarily on the basis of their physical behavior. He is, in fact, protecting them by making them seem harmless, that is, by making them seem traditional or by assimilating them to a medieval stereotype, the holy nun. You would not expect, reading this passage, that such women were experiencing visions of violence and dismemberment as well as of erotic love. You would not think that such women could go out and change the world, yet that is exactly what they were doing. Perhaps the greatest contribution of the women associated with the Beguine movement is to be found in their writings, for it is there that they explored the experience of human and divine love in new and unforgettable ways.

In their mystical writings, both poetry and prose, in Latin and in the vernacular languages, the Beguine writers do what women have rarely done in literature: they describe, represent, praise, worship their experience of love, desire, *jouissance,* providing modern readers with an unparalleled map to the territory. Hadewijch of Brabant[15] and Beatrijs van Tienen[16] both recognize the complexity of desire, and acknowledge its experience as disturbing, exhilarating, chaotically new, even maddening, so they are concerned with mapping out this new experience, with writing topologies and typologies of it. Desire or love is *Minne,* a feminine noun; it is both a yearning for love and the nature of love itself. Although there is obviously a painful side to love, imaged as wounding, capture, transfixion, penetration (the metaphors come equally from the language of the hunt and of the crucifixion), and indicating a dependence upon love for satisfaction, it is the joys of love, desire as pleasure in itself and as a process of transformation, which dominate in their writings.

In speaking their love, these two writers, like other medieval women writers, show us a colloquy between a woman and her God that implies, as Julia Kristeva says of Plato,[17] that "at the very base of philosophical discourse love and the soul cannot be separated." The experience of love is founded not so much on what Lacan termed "desire," which is masculine, born of separation and ever-deferring satisfaction, as it is on *jouissance,* a primal contiguous sexuality, existing outside linguistic norms in the realm of the poetic.[18] This feminine experience of love, which often purported to be an "out of body" trance state, actually inscribes the body in loving. It does this through the sensuality, the eroticism, in the description of ecstatic states, in the attention to bodily functions such as eating and not eating, and in bodily illness as a symptom of love. Love must be learned through relationship, and in the representation of such a relationship we see the discovery of the woman and the mother in God, and of the God(dess) in the woman.

This loving/knowing seems prophetic of what Hélène Cixous hopes for in the future:

> I look...for a kind of desire that wouldn't be in collusion with the old story of death...[where] there would have to be a rec-

193

ognition of each other. . . thanks to the intense and passionate work of knowing. . . [where] each would take the risk of *other*, of difference, without feeling threatened by the existence of an otherness, rather, delighting to increase through the unknown that is there to discover, to respect, to favor, to cherish.[19]

It is well known that much of the literature of the Middle Ages, beginning with the twelfth century, speaks of love in the form of personal lyrics as well as in popular romances. While the vocabulary of secular love clearly influenced women's language, more directly influential are scripture (notably the Song of Songs) and scriptural commentaries, particularly the Bernardine and Cistercian commentaries on the Song of Songs, along with meditative texts on the life and crucifixion of Christ, such as the pseudo-Bonaventure *Meditations on the Life of Christ*.[20] Investigation of what devotional books Beguines owned, commissioned, composed or illuminated is just beginning, and it may be that we will find that in their private devotions female figures, such as St. Catherine of Alexandria[21] or the Virgin Mary, were just as significant as the male figure of Christ. Current philosophical ideas on the nature of love emanating from the School of Chartres may have had some influence on Hadewijch's language for love, but for the most part the women mystics are independent thinkers, using scripture to validate their experience and utilizing the vocabulary of secular poetry to describe some aspects of desire, while inventing their own terminology for experiential states not spoken of in secular love lyric. The desire they speak of is the highest good, equated with God in some way, and in other respects larger than God.

To illustrate Beguine ideas on human and divine love, I will discuss the writings of two women associated with Beguine groups: Beatrijs van Tienen and Hadewijch of Brabant. Beatrijs van Tienen was a Netherlands mystic, born about 1200 into a family that was wealthy, pious, and well educated. She was taught to read by her mother, then sent to Cistercian schools. Upon the death of her mother, her father endowed several Cistercian monasteries, and Beatrijs' brothers and sisters, as she did, took religious vows or lived in religious communities. She wrote a vernacular treatise (perhaps a section of her autobiography) called *Seven manieren van Minne* or *Seven Manners of Loving*. Minne, love, is an evolutionary process, a maturation, in which Beatrijs distinguishes seven phases or styles. Although typically these ways or manners would proceed in succession, it seems likely that one might "revert" to earlier phases from time to time.

Love, says Beatrijs, begins with a choice, a self-conscious "active longing" based on the desire for perfection and the awareness of a lack; it is a gaining of self, not a loss: "The soul striving with whole attention and great longing to preserve itself." Activity is stressed; the soul is seeking, entreating, learning, gaining love, whose nature is purity, exaltation, supreme excellence. "It is this striving which love teaches to those who love love."[22]

Beatrijs' second manner of loving is compared to a "maiden who serves her master only for her great love of him...to serve love with love, without measure, beyond measure, and beyond human sense and reason."[23] The key concepts are the boundlessness and unconditionality of love, as the soul actively serves love, limitlessly offering herself, without asking anything in return. Again, the soul *is* love, as serves her.

The third manner combines these first two; "desire grows violent" in the soul, wanting to make all its works "perfect in love, withholding nothing and counting nothing." Excess, violence, torment are words repeated here, for what the soul "longs to do is impossible and unnatural to created beings, but it cannot moderate or restrain or calm itself."[24] The lover finds she has made an absolute and active commitment of all her nature to desire, and to the pain of being unable to live out that absolute.

The fourth manner of loving brings sweetness to desire; God or love begins to work within the soul, and a new being is coming into existence. The eroticism here is delicate, unlike the violence of the previous stage. As the soul is "powerfully assailed" and "altogether conquered by love," the heart is "tenderly touched," "wholly encompassed," "lovingly embraced." The subjective experience is of "great closeness to God," "spiritual brightness," "wonderful richness," a "noble freedom" in the "great compulsion of violent love" and "overflowing fullness of great delight." This detailed analysis speaks of what happens to the body too. "The spirit sinks down into Love, the body seems to pass away, the heart to melt, every faculty to fail...the limbs and senses lose their powers."[25]

One might expect that the experience of desire could go no further, but we are only at the midpoint of Beatrijs' scheme. In the fifth manner, the soul is again very active; the eroticism and the violence are intensified, as love is "powerfully strengthened" and "rises violently up," seeming to "break the heart with its assault." Simultaneously, the soul is characterized by a seemingly limitless energy and potency, so that even when it is "resting in the sweet embrace of love," it feels "there is nothing it cannot do and perform." The soul suffers from dependence, impatience, deep dissatisfaction, but it can go no further, so the heart is wounded again and again; it seems the "veins are bursting, the marrow withering, the bones softening, the heart burning, the throat parching...in the fever of love." The soul is being transformed in the crucible of desire, and love is a "devouring fire," relentless, uncontrollable, trying to force the soul beyond what it would have believed possible. Reason has no place here; the soul is "so conquered by the boundlessness of love that it cannot rule itself by reason," for it loves through a contradiction: "What most afflicts and torments the soul is that which most heals and assuages it."[26]

The sixth manner of loving is stable and confident; the soul's transformation is complete, and desire has become, not the object of knowing, but a way of knowing. Beatrijs uses three metaphors for this state of desire. The soul is like a housewife "who has put all her household in good order and prudently arranged it and well disposed it," and she always "knows how everything should be." The soul is exploring a new world, "like the fish, swimming in the vast sea and resting in its deeps, and like the bird, boldly mounting high in the sky, so the soul feels its spirit freely moving through the vastness and the depths and the unutterable richnesses of Love.''²⁷ The following of desire has brought the soul to order and freedom.

What the soul does not yet know (for love still keeps something hidden) is that it is "master of itself...living the life of the angels here in the flesh.'' This is the seventh and final stage, in which the soul is drawn "above humanity, into love, and above human sense and reason and above all the works of the heart...with love into eternity and incomprehensibility...and into the limitless abyss of Divinity.'' But it suffers at remaining in estrangement on earth, and longs to go home, "where already it has established its dwelling.''²⁸

Hadewijch of Brabant is another Netherlands mystic contemporary with Beatrijs. She was a prolific writer, and while she reveals a great deal about her inner life, hardly anything is known of her outer life.²⁹ She seems to have edited her own works, balancing the forty-five poems in stanzas in the troubadour tradition with a group of forty-five other compositions, thirty-one letters and fourteen visions. She also wrote a number of aphoristic poems in couplets. Her theory of Minne or love is too complex to try to summarize here, and my intention in quoting from her works is to give the flavor of her personal experience of desire, in its most difficult as well as its most fulfilling moments.

Hadewijch's collection of *Letters to a Young Beguine* is intended to guide young women through *orewoet* or "stormy longing" to fruition, and she is very forthright about the frustration and suffering involved in the pursuit of Minne. In the opening letter she says: "Though I talk of an unbearable sweetness I have never, never known it, except only in the wish of my heart.''³⁰ But she clearly has experienced and feels entitled to some kind of fruition or *jouissance*, for further on in the same letter she says:

> But it is He who has taken himself away from me. What He is, that He consumes in the sweetness of his joy, and leaves me to lament thus, deprived of that delight...burdened down

> with my fruitless longings... joyless of all the joys that should replenish me.[31]

Love is playing a game with her: "Now it is as if someone were making sport of me, offering me something and then, as I stretch out my hand, knocking it away and saying, 'Wouldn't you like it?' and taking it away again."[32]

In Letter Eight, she addresses the process of the transformation of the soul into love that Beatrijs described as the fifth manner of loving; Hadewijch's representation of the experience is more brutal, more violent. She begins with observing that there are two kinds of "dread" in love. The first is that ennobling type her readers must have been familiar with from secular love poetry. The lover, afraid he is not worthy of his love, improves himself morally, grows in humility, and generally behaves himself more wisely and charitably than he had done earlier. It is the second type of dread that interests Hadewijch—the fear that love does not love one enough. "This noble mistrust," this dread, she says,

> breaks the conscience wide open. Even if a man loves until he fears that he is going mad, till his heart grows sick, till the blood chills in his veins and his soul perishes, if it is true Love which he loves, this noble mistrust prevents him from feeling or trusting Love... mistrust renews longing, for he can never be sure.... One fears that he does not love enough and that he is not loved enough.[33]

He must learn "to accept all sufferings, not justify himself with ready answers," and he must make a place in his heart "for the peace of the true love, even if this meant loving the devil himself."[34] Desire leads you straight out of society, she seems to say, into a place in the mind where there are no guidelines from past experience, no rules, just a continuing deep openness of longing.

In Letter Nine Hadewijch speaks of the mutual indwelling of love in both lovers, uniting them yet leaving them in possession of individual selves.

> Love so dwells in all the beloved that neither can perceive difference between them. But they possess one another in mutual

possession, their mouths one mouth, their hearts one heart, their bodies one body, their souls one soul, and sometimes one sweet divine nature transfuses them both, and they are one, each wholly in the other, and yet each one remains and will always remain himself.[35]

This exalted love is like that between all lovers—literally consuming: "Concealing little, giving much, finding most in their close communion with one another, each one as it were tasting all, eating all, drinking all, consuming all the other."[36]

Hadewijch sees love as her highest good, an abstract principle which yet has physical, bisexual, attributes:

In this joy no one can have a part who is without Love....but only that soul which is suckled at the breast of the boundless joy of our great Love, which is chastised by Love's fatherly rod, which cleaves inseparably to him, which reads its sentence in His countenance, and then remains in peace.[37]

"True love," she says, "is no material thing; true Love is beyond matter, immeasurable in God's great freedom, giving always from its superabundance, working always in its ability, always growing in its nobility."[38] Endlessly giving, endlessly potent, endlessly noble—this is the nature of desire. Is love more than God? In another letter she observes: "Love holds God's divinity captive within its nature."

Much common ground is apparent in these texts. The paradoxical nature of desire, a fact that yearning is both painful and satisfying in itself, and that "satisfaction," "fulfillment," (whatever those terms mean) itself encloses and releases desire suggests to me that Beguine writers envisioned love as what contemporary theorists are calling *jouissance*, a kind of boundaryless sexuality in which desire and satisfaction cannot be distinguished, just as masculine and feminine cannot be distinguished. This indistinguishability of masculine and feminine, the inherent bisexuality of loving, seems to be another common element in their representations of desire.

There are also common traits in the representation of the ideal object of desire, the ideal lover, who in turn cannot be separated from the ideal, the desired, relationship. The beloved depicted by medieval Beguines emphasizes equality—in fact, male and female in the relationship are almost interchangeable. Hadewijch speaks of the two lovers merging, becoming indistinguishable. Since one of the lovers is God, such merging implies that desire is Godlike, that God's desire is human. It is the mutuality of desire, in fact, that creates the two lovers as equals. The ideal love relationship is based on communion, communication, support; God speaks with the women he loves, tells them how wonderful they are, rewards them publicly for their actions on his behalf. Ultimately, the most important characteristic of desire for these women is that it is empowering; without love, without feeling desire, the women are alone, isolated, abandoned; once they surrender to desire and follow its lead, they are capable of anything and all things.

Notes

1. Eric Colledge, *Mediaeval Netherlands Religious Literature* (New York, 1965) p. 8.
2. On Beguines in general, see Ernest W. McDonnell, *The Beguines and Beghards in Medieval Culture* (New York: Octagon, 1969; reprint of 1953 ed.) and R. W. Southern, *Western Society and the Church in the Middle Ages* (Baltimore, Md: Penguin, 1970), esp. pp. 309-31. On the Beguines as a women's movement and its economic goals, see Elise Boulding, *The Underside of History* (Boulder: Westview Press, 1976) pp. 415 ff; Carolly Erickson, *The Medieval Vision* (Oxford: Oxford UP, 1976) pp. 210 ff; JoAnn McNamara and Suzanne Wemple, "Sanctity and Power," in *Becoming Visible: Women in European History,* ed. Renate Bridenthal and Claudia Koonz (Boston: Houghton Mifflin, 1977). On women's desires for a new spiritual life as a problem, see John B. Freed, "Urban Development and the 'Cura Monialium' in Thirteenth Century Germany," in *Viator* 3 (1972), pp. 311-27; Brenda Boulton, "Mulieres Sanctae," in *Women in Medieval Society,* ed. Susan M. Stuard (Philadelphia: Univ. of Penn. Press, 1976) and "Vitae Matrum," in *Medieval Women,* ed. Derek Baker (Oxford: Basil Blackwell, 1978) pp. 253-73. On feminine piety in the diocese of Liège in Belgium, see Simone Roisin, *L'Hagiographie cistercienne dans la diocèse de Liège au xiiie siècle* (Louvain: Bibliothèque de l'université, 1947) and "L'efflorescence cister-

cienne et le courant féminin de piété au xiiie siècle," in *Revue d'histoire ecclésiastique* 39 (1945) pp. 458-86.

3. For information on specific communities, see Roisin, *L'Hagiographie cistercienne;* Benjamin de Trouyer, "Beguines et Tertiares en Belgique et aux Pays-Bas aux XII-XIVe siècles," in *I Frati Penitenti de S. Francesco...* ed. Mariano d'Alatri (Rome: Istituto Storico dei Capuccini, 1977), pp. 133-38; and in the same volume, Peirre Peanò, "Les Béguines du Languedoc ou la crise du T.O.F. dans la France méridionale..." pp. 139-58; Joseph M. H. Albanes, *La vie de Sainte Douceline, fondatrice des béguines de Marseille* (Marseille: E. Camoin, 1879); Brenda Bolton, "Some Thirteenth Century Women in the Low Countries: A Special Case?" in *Nederlands Archief voor Kerkgeschiedenis* 61 (1981), pp. 7-29; Charles McCurry, "Religious Careers and Religious Devotion in 13th Century Metz," *Viator* 9 (1978), pp. 325-33; Dayton Phillips, *The Beguines in Medieval Strasburg* (Ann Arbor, Mich.: Univ. of Mich. Press, 1941).

4. On the importance of this *Life,* see Bolton, "Vitae Matrum," in Baker, *Medieval Women,* pp. 253-73.

5. McDonnell, *Beguines,* p. 71 ff.

6. Herbert Grundmann, *Movimenti religiosi nel Medioevo* (Bologna: il Mulino, 1974), pp. 175. This is the Italian translation of *Religiöse Bewegungen im Mittelalter,* Berlin, 1935.

7. Ernest W. McDonnell, *The Beguines and Beghards in Medieval Culture* (New York: Octagon, 1969; reprint of 1953 ed.), p. 5.

8. See Brenda Boulton, "Vitae Matrum," in *Medieval Women,* ed. Derek Baker (Oxford: Basil Blackwell, 1978) pp. 253-273, esp. p. 256.

9. McDonnell, *Beguines,* p. 479.

10. R. W. Southern, *Western Society and the Church in the Middle Ages* (Baltimore, Md: Penguin, 1970) p. 32.

11. Southern, p. 32.

12. Bolton, "Vitae Matrum," p. 260.

13. Julia O'Faolain and Lauro Martines, eds., *Not in God's Image* (New York: Harper and Row, 1973), pp. 140-41. This is De Vitry's preface to his *Life of Marie d'Oignies.*

14. This is the thesis of Walter Simons and Joanna E. Ziegler, speaking of another beguine from the diocese of Liège, Elisabeth of Spalbeek: "Elisabeth was consulted as a prophetess by various important religious and secular figures because of the fame of her revelations. But, the primary basis on which her fame rested seems to have derived from her extreme physical manifestations of religion—manifestations which she enacted routinely for audiences. Her hagiographer, Abbot Phillip, describes her enactment of the stigmata and of the Passion,

including her own crucifixion and deposition as well as the performance of the roles of Mary and John. Phillip interprets this as an example of women's function in the popularization of *imitatio Christi* in which words and writing (male) are replaced by bodily expression (female)." Abstract "Act, Word, and Image: Elisabeth of Spalbeek and Eucharistic Devotion in the Thirteenth and Fourteenth Centuries," 9/15/88.

15. The English translation of the works of Hadewijch is by Mother Columba Hart, *Hadewijch: The Complete Works* (New York, Paulist Press, 1980).

16. Beatrijs van Tienen or Beatrice of Nazareth wrote an autobiography which has yet to be translated into English (*De autobiographie van de Z. Beatrijs van Tienen*, ed. L. Reypens, Antwerp, 1964); a section of this longer work, known as "The Seven Manners of Loving,"is found in Eric Colledge, *Medieval Netherlands Religious Literature*, New York, 1965.

17. Julia Kristeva, *Tales of Love*, trans. Leon S. Roudiez (New York: Columbia UP, 1987) p. 63. In French, *Histoires d'amour* (Paris: Editions Denoël, 1983).

18. Elissa Gelfand and Virginia Hules, *French Feminist Criticism: Women, Language and Literature* (New York: Garland, 1984) p. xxii.

19. Hélène Cixous and Catherine Clément, *The Newly Born Woman*, trans. Betsy Wing, (Theory and History of Literature, vol. 24) Minneapolis: Univ. of Minn. Press, p. 78. French text *La Jeune née*, 1975.

20. Green and Ragusa, ed. and trans., *Meditations on the Life of Christ: An illustrated manuscript of the fourteenth century*, Princeton, Princeton University Press, 1961. Some editors have suggested that the original creator of these meditations was a woman, an unknown mystic, who dictated them to her Franciscan spiritual director.

21. Judith Oliver has reconstructed and studied a beguine devotional book illustrating the Life of St. Catherine of Alexandria: "Medieval Alphabet Soup," in *Gesta* XXIV/2 (1985), pp. 129-140.

22. Quotations from Beatrijs are from the translation by Erick Colledge, in my *Medieval Women's Visionary Literature* (New York: Oxford UP, 1986), pp. 200-206. The passages quoted in this paragraph are found on pages 200-201.

23. "Seven Manners of Loving," p. 201.

24. "Seven Manners of Loving," pp. 201-202.

25. "Seven Manners of Loving," p. 202.

26. "Seven Manners of Loving," pp. 202-203.

27. "Seven Manners of Loving," pp. 203-204.
28. "Seven Manners of Loving," pp. 204-206.
29. Quotations found here are from Mother Columba Hart's translation of Hadewijch's "Visions," found in *Medieval Women's Visionary Literature,* pp. 189-200, and Eric Colledge's translation of "Letters to a Young Beguine" in his *Mediaeval Netherlands Religious Literature* (New York: London House & Maxwell, 1965) pp. 33-87. For the complete works of Hadewijch, see Mother Columba Hart, *Hadewijch: The Complete Works* (New York: Paulist Press, 1980). There are evidently two different poets named Hadewijch whose works have been collected together; recent scholarship identifies a Hadewijch II. According to Paul A. Dietrich, "Included in the *Mengeldichten* of Hadewijch are thirteen poems written by a later poet, Hadewijch II or pseudo-Hadewijch, which differ in style, vocabulary, and theme from the authentic poems. In contrast to the works of Hadewijch the later poems are spare and speculative, reflecting an apophatic moment in Flemish Beguine spirituality at the end of the thirteenth century." Abstract," 'Enecheit sonder differentie': Hadewijch II and Ruusbroec on Union with God," 9/15/88.
30. "Letters to a Young Beguine," in *Mediaeval Netherlands Religious Literature,* translated by Eric Colledge (New York: London House & Maxwell, 1965), p. 34.
31. "Letter One," p. 34.
32. "Letter One," pp. 34-35.
33. "Letter Eight," p. 55.
34. "Letter Eight," p. 55.
35. "Letter Nine," p. 56.
36. "Letter Eleven," p. 59.
37. "Letter Eighteen," p. 80.
38. "Letter Nineteen," p. 83.

16
Encountering the Shechinah, The Jewish Goddess

RABBI LÉAH NOVICK

*She so pervades this lower world . . . that if you search
in deed, thought and speculation, you will find
Shechinah, for there is no beginning or end to her.*
Rabbi Joseph
13th-century mystic

Introduction

Traditional Jewish scholars have always insisted that the
Shechinah is not a separate presence from the one God
whom Jews worship. At the same time, they have given us
a Shechinah literature replete with images, descriptions, and
qualities of the most detailed and often anthropomorphic
nature. This body of commentary, poetry, and prayer provides, in my view, a filtered but consistent memory of "God
the Mother," and is the basis for the "Jewish Goddess."
I say "Jewish Goddess" pointedly to distinguish her from
the "Hebrew Goddess" that Professor Raphael Patai has
documented so well—namely the Canaanite Mother Goddess Asherah. The Bible itself tells us that the ancient He-
brews honored her until about 800 B.C.E. when King Josiah
removed the Asherah from the Jerusalem temple and destroyed the outlying shrines. While her worship had been
denounced repeatedly by the Prophets, they themselves
chronicled consistent Jewish homage to Asherah or Astarte,
Queen of Heaven. While the development of the Shechinah
may indeed be an outgrowth of earlier Middle Eastern God-

dess worship, that is not the subject of this paper. The Shechinah is a distinctly Jewish conception and contains theosophical elements which evolved after the destruction of the great temples in Jerusalem. So long as the Jews lived an agrarian life, there was less need to define the Shechinah as the source of all things in nature. The process of spelling out her attributes—like the development of the synagogue and the prayerbook—came with the exile of the Jews from their own land.

The Shechinah is defined, in traditional Jewish writings, as the "female aspect of God" or the "presence" of the infinite God in the world. She is introduced in the early rabbinical commentaries as the "immanence" or "indwelling" of the living God, whose role as the animating life force of the earth is to balance the transcendent deity. While she does not appear by name in the five books of Moses, the explicators of the Old Testament refer to her in interpreting the text. For example, when Moses encounters the burning bush, he is told to remove his shoes and prepare himself to receive the Shechinah. According to the rabbis, the choice of the simple thorn bush as the vehicle for the revelation was to emphasize the Shechinah's presence, since nothing in nature can exist without her.

In Proverbs, we are introduced to the Divine Mother as Chochmah (Wisdom), who was present from the time of creation as the loving consort and coarchitect with the YHVH. In this Solomonic portrayal, she delights in humanity and provides us with her wise direction towards the path of truth and justice. (In this form, she is related to the Sophia of the Gnostics, who were influenced by Jewish thinking, and also included Hellenized Jews in their numbers.)

This association with humanity was emphasized by the Talmudists who saw her as suffering when human beings erred: "Acts of bloodshed, incest, perversion of justice and falsification of measures cause her to depart." They tell us: "Whoever is humble will ultimately cause the Shechinah to dwell upon earth. Whoever is haughty brings about the defilement of the Earth and the departure of the Shechinah."

In the Talmudic view, actions harmful to other human beings or the earth cause the Shechinah to flee, and she rises upward to the Seven Heavens.[1] On the other side of the scale are the positive actions of humanity which attract her presence downward to the earth. Specifically, in Jewish tradition, we are told that the goodness of our patriarchs, Abraham, Isaac, and Jacob, merited her presence, although even they "lost" her at times when their behavior was amiss. (Of course I am sure she spoke to the matriarchs as well; unfortunately they didn't publish.)

The other way that the Shechinah is drawn downward is when people are in need of her as a comforting presence. The rabbis tell us she hovers at the bed of all sick individuals and is seen by the dying as they exit the world into the great light. According to tradition, the Shechinah comes to the good and true at death, giving them the opportunity to go straight up the center of the heavenly ladder in a moment of pure consciousness, into the merger with the Divine.

The Shechinah is intimately connected with expressions of human love, particularly romantic and marital bliss. It is she who blesses the happy couple; the glow of lovers is considered to be the reflection of her presence. The rabbis say: "When man and wife are worthy, the Shechinah abides in their midst. If they are unworthy, fire consumes them." Here they allude to her role as destroyer; sometimes she is presented as the punisher of mankind. While reference is made to the bank of fire that accompanies her, along with two angels, the concept is not stressed as much as her other qualities.[2]

Early Jewish mystics emphasized the splendor of the Shechinah, often envisioning her as God's glory. In their conception, she is the jewel or precious stone represented by the Torah, as the crowned bride of God. She is the luminous presence of the Divine, the great light who shines on all creatures. Similar concepts are expressed in later Jewish writings, reflecting the continuity of the received oral teachings back to the early centuries of the common era. This received knowledge or "Kabbalah" was further developed by the twelfth- and thirteenth-century German "Pietists" (also called Hasidists) and reached its zenith with the later Spanish and Safed Kabbalists.

It was the latter group, living in a spiritual enclave in Northern Israel in the sixteenth and seventeenth centuries, who articulated the qualities of the divine female in considerable detail. Within the Kabbalistic system of "sephiroth" or emanations of divine energy (known to the readers as the "tree of life" or "cosmic tree"), the ten sephiroth are equally balanced with one side of the tree representing female qualities and the other male qualities. Within this system or map of consciousness, Shechinah is most often identified with Malchuth (which translates as "sovereignty") at the base of the cosmic tree, which to me represents the energy of the earth.

In the poetry of Rabbi Isaac Luri (the Ari), leader of the Safed Kabbalistic school, there are many phrases that describe Shechinah. The Ari's liturgical poems refer to her as the "Matronit," "holy ancient one," "the old of days," "the holy old one without eyes," and the "holy apple orchard" (the latter consistent with the teaching that to experience the Shechinah one needs only to enter an apple orchard in bloom).

While the outdoor rituals and breathing practices used to induce visions of the Shechinah declined with the sacred community of Safed, the images of Shechinah as Shabbos Queen were passed on in the prayers for receiving the Sabbath, which are still used each week by Jews around the world. Because the Kabbalists were devoted to the reunification of the dyadic Godhead, all of their prayers began with blessings that invited both the YHVH and the Shechinah. This form, too, has been preserved and continues to be used.

The scholars of the Spanish and Safed schools also understood that the Shechinah could "appear" to inspired individuals (or "Prophets"), and that the form adopted would be a reflection of the divine purpose.[3] For example, Rabbi Joseph Caro—a great seventeenth-century scholar and mystic known for his compilation of the Shulchan Aruch (code of Jewish laws)—"channeled" the voice of the

Shechinah, especially on Friday nights. His guide sometimes announced, ''The Shechinah speaks to you,'' or, ''I am the Mother Who Chastises.''

Yet another contribution of the Safed school was its emphasis on spiritualized sexuality as a part of sacred practice (of course, within Jewish marital guidelines and family purity laws). Unfortunately, we lack descriptions of home life at that time and have little knowledge of women's views within that community, since there is no women's literature per se, or none that has been preserved. Despite the fact that this was an all-male esoteric movement, the writings acknowledge female orgasm and recognize the persona of wife and mother as earthly representatives of Shechinah.[4]

This view of Shechinah—resting on or being reflected in the human female form—would be further developed in Eastern European Hasidism.[5] The Baal Shem—master-teacher of the seventeenth-century movement—believed that the prayers of women ascended directly to God. He also acknowledged women's capacity for prophecy, and he attracted many female followers. In the early years when the movement was still quite radical, the openness to women's spiritual charisma resulted in the emergence of women ''rebbes,'' mostly daughters and wives of the great masters.[6] Charisma is one of the blessings of Shechinah, according to the Talmud.

Taking the teachings of Kabbalah and adapting them to community life in a more egalitarian way, Hasiduth restored the belief in each individual's ability to access the Shechinah and bring her back to earth through personal actions. The key elements in the practice were meditation and prayer with *Kavannah* (deep faith and intentionality), *devekuth* (clinging to God) accompanied by a sharing lifestyle, in which justice, mercy, and charity prevailed.[7] Added to this mixture was the inspired persona of the *Tsaddik* (saint) who provided the inspiration for devotees, facilitating and affirming personal experiences of the divine.[8]

Hasidic teachers saw the Shechinah as Goddess in exile and associated her with the redemption of the Jews.[9] Some of the early masters—like Dov Baer, the Maggid of Mezerich—emulated her wandering by serving as itinerant preachers who taught in the villages and rural areas. The great maggid, like the Kabbalists he studied, was a philosopher of elegance and depth who emphasized the importance of meditation. Meditation practice—using the traditional Hebrew prayers in a mantra-like manner—was central to the teachings of the great rebbes, as it had been to the mystical predecessors. Dov Baer, the master who followed the Baal Shem, taught the need for clearing the mind and forgetting the self in prayer—in order to pray for the return of the divine presence to the earth. Connecting the Shechinah to the ensoulment of the individual, he urged: "Think of your soul as part of the Divine Presence, as the raindrop in the sea."

As the reader can discern even from this brief and limited review of traditional teachings, there are rich sources of inspired thinking about the Jewish Goddess. While the unconscious awareness of the twentieth-century seeker may be rooted in this sacred tradition, few of us have been given the benefit of a Jewish education in which the Shechinah is even mentioned.[10]

While the knowledge is rooted in the old prayer forms, Talmudic commentary, and Hebrew poetic language, the contemporary Shechinah work is coming mostly (although not exclusively) from Jewish women. Some of the articulators are individuals who have studied Hebrew sacred texts—however women who have studied mysticism tend to do so on their own or in secondary sources. A few are rabbis, scholars, and cantors who acquired traditional knowledge and skills. The majority are musicians, dancers, storytellers, and actresses, therapists and healers, who developed their insights first and then found themselves drawn towards acquiring information to match their awareness of the energy called "Shechinah," which they express through their work.

For most of the Shechinah celebrants, experience preceded study, or was interlaced with it. In this respect, we/they depart from the traditional Jewish formula (and the male model) which says that one must study the basic texts first and go to the mystical interpretations after there is a firm grounding in the biblical exegesis. For women who must overcome the misogynistic text in order to get to the poetic metaphor, interpretation must come early in the study process. This is why Jewish women are writing new *Midrash*, expositions of the significance of biblical texts, to restore the Torah to both sexes as a meaningful source of sacred knowledge.

Contemporary Jewish feminists have had to confront sexism in religious life and language including the exclusion of women from the sacred professions. As a result of our activism, some important doors have opened in the last decade. Increasingly, we are now working on bringing forth our own images of the Divine and turning to the creation of new forms to nourish those who are ready for change. In this process, the Shechinah that is emerging—especially in North America—is a varied Goddess, indeed a Goddess with a thousand faces.[11] For what is apparent in the workshops and conferences on Jewish feminism and in the New Moon groups (which are springing up spontaneously in many places) is that Jewish women carry the imprint and the images of the Goddess within them; both the traditional Shechinah and the earlier Canaanite and Middle Eastern forms.

Because this generation is serving as the midwife for the rebirth of the Shechinah, we will have to be familiar with the ancient knowledge and traditional prayers which invoke her, at the same time that we are creating new forms. In this ancient/future subculture we will need poets and prophets, rebels and rabbis, musicians and mothers. What is clear is that we have the beginnings of a movement without a hierarchy, a central leader, or a single organization. This Goddess who shines on us as we study sacred texts is found in redwood groves and apple orchards. She is coming to us in the wind and the water, in the ocean and the mountains. Like the underground Goddess herself, this movement comes from the subterranean parts of the human psyche. It emerges from a place of discovery and awe, from a place of wonder and worship.

Lest this sound too simplistic, let me remind the reader that receiving the "inner voice" usually comes after periods of silent meditation which go along with disciplined spiritual practice. When the illumination does arrive, not all of us are ready to receive it, and for many there are years of confusion and ambivalence over what spiritual path to take.

The recognition of the Goddess for Jewish women brings us face-to-face with the traditional taboo on worshipping "other gods," on creating images of God, and the centuries-old question of whether the Shechinah is indeed a separate entity from the genderless infinite God.[12]

In workshops on Shechinah that I have conducted during the last few years, I find that men and women, Jews and non-Jews, carry concepts, feelings, and images of the Shechinah within them. Again, in most people experience precedes naming the energy or having a knowledge of her characteristics as presented or expressed in the Jewish sacred literature. Interestingly enough, when we share these experiences, we find that individuals "know" or uncover most of the traditional characteristics of Shechinah on their own. The most common experiences are of light and radiance, which is consistent with the writings of many Jewish scholars who described her as a great light which shines upon all God's creatures. Many writers considered her the light of creation itself or the place of the primordial light.

Some people's experience of Shechinah involves hearing a voice or feeling a great warmth. For myself she is most present on Friday nights after I light the Shabbat candles; that is when I hear her speaking to me. At other times I feel she is present when I begin composing songs with words that address issues or people I care about. During these times, usually in the forest or at the ocean, a great sense of joy overcomes me, and all ordinary problems fade alongside the bliss I feel. On other occasions I have experienced myself falling into a great soft whiteness that is her embrace, as if all the down feathers in the world were in a single pile waiting for me to fall into them. My favorite image came on a Friday night when I saw her "dressed" in stars and the planets. Her size was beyond imagination, and her celestial "diadem" was made up of the heavens. I was over-whelmed.

While there is clearly a rebirth of Shechinah conscious-ness, concepts of a Jewish Goddess have not yet influenced mainstream Judaism or even the larger New Age movement which tends to regard Jewish feminism as a paradox. Serious scholars, including non-Jews, have tended to regard the Shechinah as an abstraction, or a way of writing about the attributes of God rather than an energetic form to be expe-rienced. At this point, it is too early to know how this con-temporary Shechinah-consciousness will be absorbed into Judaism—and into the growing Goddess movement. What is hopeful is that more scholars are studying and researching the old material to find these connections, and increasing numbers of Jewish women and men are finding the face of God in the Shechinah. I believe that her form resonates for more of us now because there is a literature and poetry about her that are part of our usable past, which our female ancestors also used in calling on her. While she needs to be reinvented or remembered, at least our reconstruction of Shechinah fits with the sacred tradition and the inner music of our people. Their basic philosophy—that her pres-ence is needed in order to bring wholeness back to the planet—still provides a living philosophy for our own times.

Notes

1. In the literature there is a litany of how first she goes from the interior of the temple to the wall, and then from the wall to the Mount of Olives. From the Mount of Olives, she watches and waits for human beings to repent. When she loses patience in our ability to redirect our ways, she lifts off, removing herself from the planet, going up to the celestial levels.
2. In later medieval mystical thinking, this separation of female destructive power was attributed to the dark forces of Lilith. As such, it reflects the typical fear of the power of the female, and is one of the shortcomings of any philosophy that lacks female participation.

3. Maimonides spoke of Shechinah as a "created light that God causes to descend...in order to confer honor on a particular place, in a miraculous way."

4. Extremely devoted and disciplined in carrying out the Mitzvoth (the precepts or religious duties), Caro believed that his personal actions could damage the "body" of the Shechinah.

5. Also, since they believed in reincarnation, they may have envisioned themselves as female, or their wives as male, in other lives.

6. For example, devotees of the Baal Shem referred to his daughter Eidele, saying, "The Shechinah rests on her face."

7. As Hasiduth became more structured, the all-male code prevailed. The women rebbes are recalled primarily through their most visible and unusual representative "The Maid of Ludomir," Hannah Rachel Werbemacher, a Kabbalist who achieved master-teacher status without benefit of a rabbinical family.

8. These are the qualities highly valued by the Shechinah; which the earlier rabbis also emphasized in their teaching. "If a person gives one coin to a poor friend, he becomes worthy to receive the face of the Shechinah."

9. In early Hasiduth, the sharing of food and other resources (with the Rebbes court as distribution agent) was developed into a kind of tribal socialism that resembles the values of matriarchal groups.

10. In the fairy tales of Rebbe Nachman of Bratslav, she is portrayed as a wounded Goddess, the broken heart of the world, weeping for the desecration of the earth and the suffering of her children, the Jews.

11. On a personal note, although I was tutored in the Scriptures from age five and attended a prestigious Hebrew high school and teacher training academy, these concepts were never presented or taught. Likewise, in my study of Hebrew literature at the university level, few references to the female deity ever arose. In this area, until I found a friendly Kabbalah teacher, I was essentially self-taught.

12. Sadly enough, not one of them was known to Joseph Campbell, the great mythologist whose brilliant commentaries in a recent PBS special perpetuated ignorance of the Jewish female tradition. Likewise, Elaine Pagel's research did not provide her with any awareness of female God-imagery in Judaism.

13. For artists the visual images that are emerging may also challenge the ban on reproductive art shared by Judaism and Islam. Third-century Hellenized Jews overcame that obstacle as evi-

denced by the painting of the nude Shechinah holding the baby
Moses in the Dura-Europus Synagogue in northern Syria.
Nevertheless, the ban on images of God is a serious issue, so
the artist who chooses to paint the Shechinah as anything more
than a mandala or as an elegant abstraction is walking the high
wire.

Sources in English

Abelson, Joshua (1873-1940). *The Immanence of God in Rabbinic
Literature.* New York: Mount Hermon Press, 1969 (reprint of 1912
edition). Chapters IV, V, VI, VII, VIII, IX and X.

Idel, Moshe (1947-   ). *Kabbalah, New Perspectives.* New Haven
and London: Yale University Press, 1988. Chapter 5: pp. 80-87;
Chapter 7: pp. 166-70.

Ponce, Charles. *Kabbalah.* Wheaton, IL: Quest: Theosophical Publishing House, 1978. Part II, Chapter 3, pp. 216-222; Part III, pp.
253-257.

Scholem, Gershom (1897-   ). *Major Trends in Jewish Mysticism.*
New York: Schocken Books, 1946. pp. 229-233.

Scholem, Gershom. *On the Kaballah and its Symbolism.* New York:
Schocken Books, 1965 (original German edition, Zurich, 1960).
Chapter II, pp. 104-109; Chapter III, pp. 138-155.

Scholem, Gershom. *Origins of the Kabbalah.* Jewish Publication Society: Princeton University Press, 1987 (original in German, Berlin, 1962). Chapter II, Section 8, pp. 162-180.

Urbach, Efraim Elimelech (1912-   ). *The Sages, their Concepts and
Beliefs.* Jerusalem: Magnes Press, Hebrew University, 1975. Chapter
III, IV, pp. 37-79.

17

The Way of the
Uncarved Block

SHIRLEY NICHOLSON

To reveal Simplicity and to hold to the Uncarved Block...
Lao Tzu

We in the West live in a world that is primarily masculine
in a symbolic sense. Our way of life is definite, decisive, active, aggressive, assertive. Women today are striving for
freedom to compete with men on an equal footing; that is,
to take on these masculine qualities more and more. Assertiveness training, so popular today, symbolizes the spirit of
this trend. The ideal in such training is a person who can
speak up for himself and his rights, at the same time considering the rights of others.

This may be very useful for people who have been held
down and have not been able to express their wants and
views. It no doubt helps many people adapt to the competitive, aggressive society we live in. An active mode of life
has achieved great things in a material and technological
way. But there are people such as Jung and van der Post
who feel we have gone too far in the active, masculine, competitive role and need to return to a quieter, more inward,
feminine mode from which unity can emerge. Perhaps in
a world full of clashes between interests of different groups,
and ever on the brink of war, we need to search out a way
of unity and interfusion rather than assertiveness and competition.

Centuries ago, Lao Tzu gave a poetic teaching that pointed to an inward way of unity. The quiet beauty of his verses is still an inspiration to another way of life which leads not to self-fulfillment in a limited, selfish sense, but to the infinite joy of merging with all. This way rests upon the *Tao*, a word rich in connotations concerning both the way and the goal. Lao Tzu says of it:

> There was something complete and nebulous
> > Which existed before Heaven and Earth,
> > Silent, invisible,
> > Unchanging, standing as One,
> > Unceasing, ever-revolving,
> > Able to be the Mother of the World.
> I do not know its name and I call it *Tao*.
> > *Tao te Ching*
> > Chapter XXV

This Mother of the World, the Tao, is the elusive, invisible, inaudible, unfathomable ground which embraces both forms and the formless. It is all-pervading, all-embracing, everywhere, and all things. Itself indivisible, it is the source or Mother of the manifold world. In birth all things emerge from it. In death they return to it. The Tao itself is not limited to time and space but is infinite.

In the Taoist view, this infinite background is the metaphysical basis for the Great Sympathy. This is not love in an individualized, personal sense, but the secret root of all love and compassion. In the Great Sympathy the self is lost and there is interfusion and mingling with all selves. There is expansion from ego-centered consciousness to consciousness of others. This is not based on rational discrimination and evaluation, but is intuitive and unconscious. The Great Sympathy does not distinguish between good and evil, approving or disapproving, but penetrates to the inner nature of all alike. In this experience subject and object are interfused and there is identification with the other. Thus the Great Sympathy holds together man and man with all things. In the unity of the Great Sympathy "everything breaks through the shell of itself and interfuses with every other thing. The one is many and the many is one. In this realm all selves dissolve into one, and all our selves are selves only to the extent that they disappear into all other selves."[1]

In order to participate in the Great Sympathy, it is necessary to transform oneself by eliminating ego-consciousness. This is symbolized in Taoism by the Uncarved Block. A person who achieves this returns to his own simple, basic nature, and is spontaneous, unassuming, humble, and close to the world of nature. In Lao Tzu's words:

> Knowing of the Male,
>> But staying with the Female,
>> One becomes the humble Valley
>> of the World.
> Being the Valley of the World
>> He never deviates from his real nature
>> And thus returns to the innocence of
>> the infant.
>
> *Tao te Ching*
> Chapter XXVIII

Such a person is spontaneously moral and good, not through any self-conscious, artificial effort, but because his self has merged with all other selves. He is free from the conflicts of the intellect, right and wrong, the pull of the opposites. His knowledge comes from the world of no-knowledge. He may appear a simpleton to the intellectual, sophisticated man of the world. As Lao Tzu says:

> The people are gay as if enjoying a ban-
> quet and mounting a tower in spring.
> I alone, quiet and unmoved, as a babe
> unable yet to smile, am unattached,
> depending on nothing.
> People all have more than enough;
> I alone seem to have nothing left.
> So ignorant! My mind must be that of a dolt.
> People are bright and shine;
> I alone am dark and dull.
> People are clever and distinctive;
> I alone am obscure and blunt.
> Desolate, as if in the dark,
> Quiet as if concentrating on nothing.

> People all have purpose and usefulness;
> But I alone am ignorant and uncouth.
> I am different from all the others, but I draw
> nourishment from the Mother.
>
> *Tao te Ching*
> Chapter XIX, XX

Such a man of the Uncarved Block is described in the *Analects of Confucius.* One day some pupils were telling Confucius of their ambitions. One wanted to be a minister of finance, another a minister of war, etc. One pupil ignored the interchange and quietly strummed his lute. Confucius asked him to speak. He said he would like to bathe in the river in the spring with his friends and enjoy the breezes and walk home singing.

This man was free from the drive to be somebody, to achieve in the eyes of the world to increase his ego, based on "purpose and usefulness." He had no desire to be "bright and shine." He did not identify with any particular role or goal which would define his self, but felt at one with natural forces such as the wind and water. His mind was simple, yet great and free. Such a man is not self-assertive but disappears in the selves of others. The Great Sympathy is manifest in him, as it is imminent in the Uncarved Block.

A state such as this cannot be transmitted to another. It comes from the cultivation of quietude. According to Chuang Tzu:

> Tao may be known by no thoughts, no reflections. It may be approached by resting in nothingness, by following nothing, pursuing nothing."
>
> *The Works of Chuang Tzu,*
> Chapter XX-II

By quietude the man of Tao strives to return to the deep, silent roots of his being.

> Devote yourself to the utmost Void;
> Contemplate earnestly in Quiescence.
> All things are together in action,
> But I look into their nonaction.
> For things are continuously moving, restless,

Yet each is proceeding back to its origin.
Proceeding back to the origin means
Quiescence.
To be in Quiescence is to see ''being—for
itself.''

Tao te Ching
Chapter XVI

In such a state all thought has ceased, and a heavenly radiance dawns within. Lao Tzu says that one who emits this radiance sees his Real Self, and the one who cultivates his Real Self achieves the Absolute. This is the way of the Uncarved Block, the way to peace, unity and joy.

We in the West cannot completely relinquish our active roles and responsibilities in order to pursue the Great Sympathy. The pace of modern life will go on with its unremitting demands. But we can at least try to balance the aggressive mode with periods of quiescence, pursuing nothingness, breaking our identification with the active outer self and seeking the Mother, the source of unity in stillness. Perhaps such a quiet way, by binding us all together, will contribute to peace and progress more than the active, purposeful, Western way.

Reference

1. Chang Chung-yuan, *Creativity and Taoism;* New York, Julian Press, 1963.

18

The Wisewoman in the Western Tradition

PATRICIA HUNT-PERRY

The World Turned Outside In

There once was a man in search of a spiritual master who had spent many years in the quest to no avail. After many decades he was told that in a certain cave in the ancient mountains he would find his master. It was an arduous journey. He labored across rocky hillsides and climbed sheer cliffs. After pulling himself over one more ice-slick ledge he saw what he hoped was his destination. Physically exhausted but hopeful, he entered a dark crevice. At the very end of the dim cave sat a figure hidden by a hooded garment.

The seeker approached expectantly. A few feet from the figure he stopped, gasped, and stepped backward with surprise.

"Why, why, you're a woman," he said.

"Yes" came the quiet, strong reply.

"Well, I didn't know that women could be, be masters, could be realized beings."

"Oh, my son," came the reply, "that just shows you how unenlightened you are."

The man in our story is, unfortunately, not rare in his failure to recognize women as spiritual masters. While many women have been leaders and spokespersons in spiritual and esoteric traditions, they are generally less well known than the men. Yet, the tradition of the wisewoman is a strong and deep one in Western thought.

What exactly *is* a wisewoman? A popular dictionary lists "wisewoman" but not "wiseman." The nearest thing to a wiseman in that volume is "wiseguy," a term certainly not noted for its sagacity. The *Oxford-English Dictionary* (OED), on the other hand, lists both "wisewoman" and "wiseman," although the latter term receives about three times as much space as the former. There is, however, a significant distinction; "wise" takes on different meanings according to its gender relationship. The wiseman is defined first and foremost in terms of the intellect or scholarship. The first two meanings of wiseman in the *OED* are (1) a man who has good judgment, discernment and who is prudent and discreet, as well as (2) a man who is a learned person, a scholar, philosopher or a man deeply versed in "some subject of study, or in studies generally."

A wisewoman, on the other hand, in the Western tradition has been almost universally defined as one who is skilled in the hidden arts, the esoteric. Usually associated with beneficence, especially as one who helps in charms against disease or misfortune, the wisewoman is a positive figure. Moreover, in the English language there is not a female equivalent to the derogatory terms used for men, such as wiseguy, or wiseacre (a pretender to wisdom or a foolish person). Although there are certainly many women who were wise in the intellectual sense throughout history, such as Socrates' teacher, Diotima,[1] the term "wisewoman" has come, connotatively and denotatively, to be associated with the hidden arts and, secondarily, in some places, with midwifery.

So clearly a discussion of wisewomen must center itself squarely on those women who have parlance with the hidden arts.

The Western tradition abounds with such wisewomen. Well-known figures such as Madame Blavatsky and Annie Besant, the Mother (associated with Sri Aurobindo), Alice

Bailey, and native American Indian women come readily to mind. Others, less well known, have yet to receive the attention they deserve, Sojourner Truth, Mother Anne Lee, Dora Kunz, Flora Courtois, and Alexandra David-Neel are just a few examples of such women.

One key question to ask about wisewomen is whether their training and experience differs from that of wisemen. In our time some male Westerners became spokespersons for the ancient wisdom. People such as Alan Watts and Ram Dass were ''transformers'' of arcane teachings into the Western idiom. Such individuals often left their ordinary lives and spent extended periods of training with a teacher or alone in isolated surroundings.

There are, also, many role models of men who have had mystical revelations by first intensively developing the mind and/or going into religious studies and intensive retreats. While this is a legitimate avenue for some men and women, it is not the only available avenue and, indeed, it is not the avenue that has been most accessible to Western women. Because of a variety of complex social conditions and conditioning, the spiritual path—the search for knowledge of the hidden arts, a vision, enlightenment, or mystical experience—is more apt to open up to women while they are involved in quite ordinary daily activities. Women, whose own lives may be changed by revelatory experiences, are less likely to be known than their male counterparts.

The picture of a woman engaged in household activities or participating in common daily activities is culturally less spectacular than that of a man who has tramped over India and found his guru in the high Himalayas. Yet many such women, in ordinary circumstances have been wisewomen in the hidden arts. If not much is known about them and their roles in spiritual and esoteric work, it is not because such women do not exist. Clearly they did and do, and the failure to know about them is a failure of communication and scholarship, not a failure of women or a dearth of women in this tradition.

To gain perspective on how women become involved in the hidden arts and mystical experience while living quite plain lives, let us consider two women divided by historical time and life circumstances. Both Sojourner Truth and Flora Courtois had mystical experiences which cut through into their everyday lives.

Sojourner Truth

Sojourner Truth, known early in her life as Isabella, is a good example of a woman to whom revelations came in the most ordinary circumstances of life. The secular feminist movement of the 1960s and 1970s rediscovered Sojourner Truth, an outspoken nineteenth-century abolitionist and feminist. Her "ain't I a woman" speech became well known and oft quoted. Her courageous stands and outspoken comments helped to sustain generations of feminists.

What is less well known is that the basis—the foundation—of Sojourner Truth's work was spiritual and mystical. It was out of a deep spiritual foundation that all of her work arose. Indeed, without that base we probably never would have heard of Sojourner Truth—she would have remained just "Isabella."

Born a slave about 1797 in the Catskills near Hurley, in Ulster County, New York, she was known as Isabella Van Wagener. Of African origin, Isabella was the mother of five children and a slave until she "emancipated" herself by running away from her owner in the mid-1820s. Thereafter she worked as a maid.[2]

In the early 1800s she had revelations which were to change her life and have an impact on the American nation, for it was these experiences and her relationship with the mystical which gave her the strength to carry out her secular political activities.

Sojourner Truth, recognizing the strength of a natural setting as a foundation for spiritual communication, created a rural sanctuary under the "open canopy of heaven."[3] On a small island in the little stream near where she lived, she wove the branches of shrubs together, forming a wall that protected her from the outside. Here she entered daily into her "circular arched alcove, made entirely of the graceful willow.''[4] In this setting she escaped from the harsh treatment that was her lot in life and talked directly with the divine. As one commentator has observed, ''It would be an error to say that she was praying. [She] addressed God as one human being addresses another.''[5]

One day she had a ''knowing,'' today we might call it clairvoyance, that her former owner would arrive that very day and that she would return to his house with him. Arrive he did, and she was about to enter his vehicle with her son:

> But, ere she reached the vehicle, God revealed himself to her, with all the suddenness of a flash of lightening, showing her, in the twinkling of an eye, that he was all over—that he pervaded the universe—and that there was no place that God was not.[6]

When she again returned to everyday reality from this vision, she saw that her former slave master had left, and she exclaimed aloud: ''Oh, God, I did not know you were so big.'' Then, by her own account, she walked into the house to resume her daily chores! While trying to attend to her housework, however, ''a space seemed opening'' between her and the divine and she longed for someone ''worthy in the sight of heaven'' who would intervene and plead with the divine for her.

> At length a friend appeared. . . . ''Who are you?'' she exclaimed, as the vision brightened into a form distinct beaming with beauty and radiant with love.[7]

Standing there, with a ''new power of sight'' Truth said, ''I know you and I don't know you.'' When she said, ''I know you'' the visionary figure remained distinct and quiet. But it ''moved restlessly about, like agitated waters'' when she said, ''I don't know you.''[8] '' 'Who are you?' was the cry of her heart,'' Truth later reported, and her whole being yearned to have this visionary individual reveal itself to her.

> At length, after bending both soul and body with the intensity of [the desire to know who this vision was], till breath and

.

strength seemed failing, and she could maintain her position no longer, an answer came to her, saying distinctly, "It is Jesus."[9]

In subsequent years, it was this realization of her connection with the infinite and her visionary experiences that allowed the slave woman Isabella to take on the work directed by the visionary experience and become Sojourner Truth, a woman who traveled the land speaking and working for social justice. She had no doubt that it was divine intervention that interceded for her many times and made the political and social system responsive to her demands.[10]

During her own times she became a leading spokesperson for the abolitionist and women's rights movements and even won legal cases against whites, an unusual occurrence for a Black woman of her day. In the twentieth century she became a role model and oft-quoted figure for the second women's rights movement of the 1960s and 1970s. Her "ain't I a woman" political speech still rings across the land in the literature, speeches and hearts of modern-day feminists.

Flora Courtois

In our time another remarkable women, Flora Courtois, now in her sixties, had an enlightenment experience that came into her ordinary daily life. She had no models for mystical or enlightenment experiences until many years after they occurred to her directly.

From childhood Flora Courtois seemed to have a "magic communion" (as she called it) with all living things—trees, animals, people. When Flora was sixteen years old, she had minor surgery. As the ether cone was placed over her face "a great whirling spiral of light approached from an enormous distance and at great speed. At the same time a voice of unmistakable authority" seemed to say that when the center of the spiral reached her that she would "understand all things." As Flora said, "Just as the center reached me, I blacked out, but after recovering there remained an unforgettable conviction that what I had heard and seen was in some inexplicable way that deepest truth."[11]

The following year Flora found herself questioning everything she had been taught—everything that she knew. She combed through books to find the answers, but answers were not to be found there. As she said:

> I began to think it strange that with all the books of advice in the world, all the laws and admonitions from parents, teachers, priests and other elders, there was still nothing to assure me of living fully in any given moment, since every moment was unique....
>
> [At one point] I ceased to search for an answer in reading and became intensely interested in exploring everyday experience....I became increasingly aware of sights, sounds, touch and smell impressions...and the more observant I became, the more endless the vistas which seemed to open.[12]

Courtois went off to study at the University of Michigan in Ann Arbor, a decision which required her, in her second year, to borrow the money to pay her tuition and take a job as a mother's helper, doing housework and caring for the children in return for her room and board. Although she read Western philosophy, the works of Plato, Spinoza, Kant, Hegel, and others, she found such knowledge "partial and one-sided." It was not in the philosophical depths nor in the physical heights of the great Himalayas that she found the hidden world. Rather it was while standing by the kitchen window looking out at an ordinary scene that her perception changed:

> I suddenly saw the scene with a freshness and clarity that I'd never seen before. Simultaneously, as though for the first time, I fully realized I was not only on earth but of it, an intimate part and product of it. It was as if a door had opened briefly....It was as if for a long time I had been reading books on how to swim; now, for a moment, I had plunged into real water.[13]

Increasingly, Courtois found herself pulled away from the routine surface of life towards an inner quest.[14] She made futile attempts to find someone in church or the university who would understand her quest. One professor suggested that she see the university psychiatrist, while another recommended that if she wanted to discover the nature of reality, she should take his epistemology course the next semester.[15] After the latter encounter, Courtois felt quite forsaken, thinking, ''I don't want another course; what I want is the thing itself.''[16]

At about the same time, Courtois began to have occasional visions. These would occur when she was in her room alone.

> They were astoundingly clear. In one of them a scene appeared as from an incalculably remote and primitive time. I seemed to be a member of a small family of cave dwellers. There was a darkness, a gloomy darkness about our lives and surroundings. In our cave we had found a place of security and protection from what I sensed to be a hostile outside world. Gradually, however, we found within ourselves the courage as a family to venture forth together to seek a brighter, more open place. Now we found ourselves on a great, open, light plain which stretched in all directions and where the horizons seem to beckon to us with untold possibilities. To my surprise and horror, the others in my family found this threatening and decided to retreat to life in the cave again. I felt profoundly convinced that this represented a critical decision, a fork in the life of the family and indeed of the whole human race. The challenge was of the next important step upward. I now knew that the choice I had to make was whether to remain within the safe fold of the group or to continue on, leaving mankind behind. If I went on, henceforth I would go alone.[17]

Easter vacation arrived and Courtois went home to visit her parents in Detroit. There, in that midwestern city, in her parents' home, sitting quietly in her bedroom, the universe changed for Courtois. While she was

> sitting quietly on the edge of my bed and gazing at a small desk, not thinking of anything at all, in a moment too short to measure, the universe changed on its axis and my search was over.
>
> The small, pale green desk at which I'd been so thoughtlessly gazing had totally and radically changed. It appeared now with a clarity, a depth of three-dimensionality, a freshness I had never imagined possible. At the same time, in a way that is utterly indescribable, all my questions and doubts were gone as effortlessly as chaff in the wind. I knew everything and all

at once. Yet not in the sense that I had ever known anything before.[18]

Everything, she says, was still the same in her little bedroom, but paradoxically everything had changed as well. In a state of wonder, she sat on her little bed and looked with new perception.

> . . .one of the first things I realized was that the focus of my sight seemed to have changed; it had sharpened to an infinitely small point which moved ceaselessly in paths totally free of the old accustomed ones, as if flowing from a new source.

> What on earth had happened to me? So released from all tension, so ecstatically light did I feel, I seemed to float down the hall to the bathroom to look at my face in the mottled mirror over the sink. The pupils of my eyes were dark, dilated and brimming over with mirth. With a wondrous relief, I began to laugh as I'd never laughed before right from the soles of my feet up.[19]

One wonders what a man in her position might have done. It is possible that, because of the socialization process men and women undergo in Western culture, males are more likely to write and speak publically about their experiences (Huxley, Watts and others come to mind). Certainly most (although by no means all) of the leaders and founders of religions and religious sects were and are men.

Courtois, however, like Sojourner Truth, returned to her established life pattern; unlike Truth, she never spoke publically about her experiences until many decades later after finishing college and raising a family. Within a few days after this experience, she returned to Ann Arbor and lived with her newfound revelation: "There over a period of many months took place a ripening, a deepening and unfolding of this experience which filled me with wonder and gratitude at every moment." Courtois felt that "The foundation had fallen from my world." Although her inner world had changed, she returned to live a life which would be defined as "normal" by Western cultural standards. Her inner life was much different:

> I had plunged into a luminous openness which had obliterated all fixed distinctions including that of "within" and "without."

A Presence had absorbed the universe and to this I gave myself up in absolute confidence. Often, without any particular direction in mind, I found myself outside running along the street in joyous abandon. Sometimes when alone I simply danced as freely as I did as a child. The whole world seemed to have reversed itself, to have turned outside in.[20]

This is what the wisewoman in the West discovers, a world turned outside in. While some women, such as the gallant Alexandra David-Neel, seek such experiences and make long and arduous pilgrimages to holy places in Asia or elsewhere (David-Neel's lasted fourteen years), revelations and mystical experiences have come to many women while they are leading quite traditional lives. Moreover, after becoming engaged in the hidden arts or revelatory experiences, many do not break from their life circumstances but continue their work and family ties. One does not generally find women leaving kith and kin, as the Buddha did, to follow the spiritual path. Instead, womens' paths are often hewn out of lives that remain within the family or other traditional framework. When they are not, it is often after a life crisis. For example, Mother Ann Lee's four children died before she led her followers across the ocean and established herself as head of the new Shaker community in America. Although outwardly less spectacular than climbing the high Himalayas, experiences arising in the ordinary life circumstances of women can have the equal depth of mystical or revelatory power sought in some faraway place. Women who approach the mystical in this way have brought a new dimension to an understanding of spiritual life. Ordinary lives can be a fertile ground for revelatory experience, spiritual opening and acquaintance with the world of the hidden arts, as the lives of Truth and Courtois demonstrate. Women and men alike can know that the world turned outside in is the world that is here and now.

Notes

1. Plato, Symposium. *In Collected Dialogues.* New York, Pantheon, 1961, pp. 553-560.
2. Lerner, G. *Black Women in White America.* New York, Pantheon, 1972, pp. 370-371.

3. Gilbert, O., and Sojourner Truth. *The Narrative of Sojourner Truth*. New York, Arno Press and *New York Times*, 1968, p. 60. (Hereafter *Narrative*).
4. Narrative, pp. 60-71.
5. Bennett, L. *Pioneers in Protest*. Chicago, Johnson Publishing Company, 1968, p. 115. Also see Bennett, L. *Before the Mayflower: A History of the Negro in America*. 1619-1964. Baltimore, Penguin Books, 1962.
6. *Narrative*, p. 65.
7. *Narrative*, pp. 65-67.
8. *Narrative*, p. 67.
9. *Narrative*, p. 67.
10. *Narrative*, p. 70. Also see Woodson, C. G. *The Negro In Our History*. 10th ed. Washington, 1962.
11. Courtois, F. *An American Woman's Experience of Enlightenment*. Tokyo, Zen Center, 1970, p. 14. Also Quest Books, Wheaton, Ill., 1986, under the title *An Experience of Enlightenment*.
12. Ibid., p. 15.
13. Ibid., p. 18.
14. Ibid., p. 14.
15. Ibid., p. 26.
16. Ibid., p. 22.
17. Ibid., pp. 22-23.
18. Ibid., pp. 29-30.
19. Ibid., pp. 30-31.
20. Ibid., pp. 30-31.

Bibliography

Bennett, L. *Before the Mayflower: A History of the Negro in America, 1619-1964*. Baltimore, Penguin Books, 1962.

Bennett, L. *Pioneers In Protest*. Chicago, Johnson Publishing Company, 1968.

Bernard, J. *Journey Toward Freedom: The Story of Sojourner Truth*. New York, W. W. Norton, 1967.

Courtois, F. *An American Woman's Experience of Enlightenment*. Tokyo, Zen Center, 1970. Also Theosophical Publishing House, Wheaton, Ill., 1986, under the title *An Experience of Enlightenment*.

Gilbert, O., and Truth, Sojourner, *The Narrative of Sojourner Truth*. New York, Arno Press and New York Times, 1968.

Lerner, G. *Black Women In White America*. New York, Pantheon, 1972.

Ortiz, V. *Sojourner Truth, A Self-Made Woman.* New York, Lippincott, 1974.

Pauli, H. *Her Name Was Sojourner Truth.* New York, Appleton-Century-Crofts, 1962.

Plato, *The Collected Dialogues of Plato.* Edith Hamilton, ed. New York, Pantheon, 1961.

Schneir, M. *Feminism: The Essential Historical Writings.* New York, Random House, 1972.

Stanton, E. C., S. B. Anthony, and M. Gage. *History of Woman Suffrage.* New York, Fowler and Wells, 1881-1922.

Woodson, C. G., C. H. Wesley. *The Negro in Our History.* 10th ed. Washington, 1962.

19

Sacred and Legendary Women of Native North America

NANCY C. ZAK

Women of Native North America have played and do play significant roles in the lives of the people they represent. For instance, Thought Woman of the Keres conceived the earth and the original plan of creation. Women form the backbone of many a given tradition. Some, such as White Buffalo Calf Woman of the Sioux, serve as cultural heroines. Certain figures are identified with Mother Earth, others with Father Sky. Some are timeless, sacred figures (legendary) who are ever present, while others are mortal beings who, when appropriate, take on sacred functions. In this paper I will delineate a few of the many sacred and legendary women of Native North America. I will outline some of the functions they exercise within their respective cultural settings. In this way I hope to honor these women and the cultures they represent. These figures are interesting in and of themselves. In addition, some of them may perhaps serve as role models, sources of strength to enrich our lives today.[1]

Thought Woman

The first figure I will introduce is Thought Woman or *Tse che nako*, the creator goddess of the Keres.[2] The Keresan-speaking people have lived in New Mexico since pre-Columbian times; at present they constitute the pueblos of Acoma, Laguna, Zia, Santa Ana, San Felipe, Santo Domingo, and Cochiti. Theirs is a traditional agricultural society. The Keres are known for their jewelry as well as their varied and distinctive styles of pottery. Acoma is one of the oldest continuously inhabited settlements in North America.

Tse che nako, an extraordinary being, conceived the original plan of creation. She created the world by her thought. Since thought precedes action as well as creation, she can cause things to happen merely by thinking of them. She created other sacred figures to help her with creation; they coexist eternally with her, but are subservient to her, as she is the creator, the supreme being. The traditional Keres origin story states:

> In the beginning Tse che nako, Thought Woman, finished everything, thoughts, and the names of all things. She finished also all the languages. And then our mothers, Uretsete and Naotsete said they would make names and they would make thoughts. Thus they said. Thus they did. . . . A long time ago at Shipopu in the north place, underneath there, our Great Mother, Tse che nako, worked miracles. Everything that has been named developed. The sun and the moon, and the stars, and shi wana, and spirits, and Ka'-tsina, and the Cha-yah-ni, and game, and the people were completed.

Thought Woman possesses both feminine and masculine traits. According to Anthony Purley of Laguna Pueblo, "The Keres people believe that Tse che nako has more female than male attributes; therefore she is referred to and approached as if she is female."

This belief in Tse che nako being female is wholly within the Keres theological structure. Tse che nako is the all-fertile being, able to produce human beings and all other creatures: "She is the mother of us all, after Her, mother earth follows, in fertility, in holding, and taking us again back to her breast."

Purley writes, "Creation. . . includes all creation, including individual thought—which is lesser than original thought, which only Tse che nako has the power to create." Keres Indian thought maintains that Tse che nako created human beings not only for procreation, but to create as well. She did not restrict the process of creation to herself alone. Tse che nako included the power to create individual thought in all human beings and all living creatures. In other words, all living beings can create, although in different degrees. If you reflect upon this, you will realize that this is true. Even a single cell has a certain amount of decision-making power: it can decide whether to live or die; whether to divide in two; whether to accept or reject life-giving or death-dealing substances.

Thought Woman is a powerful, dynamic entity who contains all life possibilities within herself, including male and female. Her secular aspect is named Spider Woman, a largely benevolent figure who helps people in need. Tse che nako perfectly illustrates the universal metaphysical law that "thoughts are things": thought participates in creation. Creation includes the activities of reason, the mind, and its realization in matter, as well as pure biological generation, which we term procreation. Thought Woman was the first to work with creative visualization. She is ever spinning her web, developing the possibilities of life. She is far away, but ever near.

Clay Lady

The next figure I will delineate is the Clay Lady as described by the well-known potter Grace Medicine Flower, who lives at Santa Clara Pueblo near Los Alamos. Santa Clara Pueblo, one of the six Tewa-speaking pueblos in New Mexico, was built before the Conquest; it is especially known for its black pottery.[3]

Grace Medicine Flower comes from a family of potters that includes her mother Yellow Flower, now deceased, her father Camilio Tafoya or Camilio Sunflower, as he is known professionally, and her brother Joseph Lonewolf. Grace Medicine Flower meticulously shapes her delicate, finely polished red and black pottery bowls. She etches traditional designs and her own interpretation of traditional motifs on the surface of the pottery. With her father and her brother, she has developed a two-color firing method done in one firing.

As I learned in a conversation with the Santa Clara artist, Grace Medicine Flower is a very happy person. She has been creating pottery for twenty-three years, and it never ceases to delight her in spite of the fact that there are over twenty individual steps to making a single bowl. It is a long and involved process which demands patience and acceptance because a pot can be ruined at any moment along the way. However, Mrs. Medicine Flower is happy to be doing what she is doing because she feels she is being helped by and is in turn working with and for the Clay Lady.

The Clay Lady is an aspect of Mother Earth. The Santa Clara potter believes that "It's up to us to make her beautiful." She prays to the Clay Lady at every step in fashioning a bowl, from choosing the clay and digging it out of the tough New Mexico soil, to mixing it with her feet, designing it freehand, and then firing it.

At this point I would like to cite another interview the artist had, one with Jane Katz, in which she spoke at length about the Clay Lady:

> My mother taught me how to work the clay. She said, "Here's a piece of clay. Make it beautiful." The Clay Lady, Mother told me, is in the next world; she's everybody's relative. She is the spirit of past generations that comes back in the clay. And so every day I pray to the Clay Lady before I work with the clay. I ask her to make it beautiful. I say whatever is in my heart.

Before Grace Medicine Flower starts designing, she asks the Clay Lady which design is best for a particular pot:

> I ask for her help and I do think she helps me. The firing is done in the open on the ground. It has to be a really calm day, with no wind. We fire early in the morning or late in the evening. We put wood chips on the ground. Tin cans hold a steel grate, and a wire basket containing the pots is placed on the grate...you have to watch the fire carefully. If the wind blows and soot gets on the pot, it is ruined. If there's a small crack, your work is lost. Sometimes a pot you've worked on for months breaks. You can't be angry or discouraged. My dad will say, "The old ones, the ones that went before, are putting you through a test to see if you've put your whole self into a bowl, or have done it just for commercial reasons." If

you fail, you say, ''This is the way it was meant to be,'' and
you go on working. . . .

My husband and I used to live in another town. I thought
I'd go to work in the city. But after Mother died, we came here
to be with Dad. He lives with us. Dad said, ''Certain people
are picked by the Clay Lady to work with the clay.''

I'm happy with my life. I go to the city to shop, to meet people, and to attend the opera. But this is my home, and I
wouldn't live anywhere else. People often come to our home
to buy my work. I like to know that they will love my pottery
and will care for it. They will admire the Clay Lady and give
her a good home, for she really lives on in each piece of clay.

Mrs. Medicine Flower told me that many Pueblo potters
pray to the Clay Lady for help as they go about their work.
I think that each of us can relate to the Clay Lady as an aspect
of Mother Earth, that creative presence inherent in the soil
and in the pot, that presence which is waiting for us to appreciate it, and to bring out its beauty, to touch it, and in
turn be touched by it. Just like a mortal woman, this gentle
figure longs to be touched, loved, and rendered more at-
tractive. The Clay Lady is a presence to recognize, to work
with, and to be with.

Spider Woman

Now I will turn to the important and fascinating Hopi figure of Spider Woman; she is similar to, but not identical
with, the Keresan Spider Woman. The Hopi, a Pueblo people, live in northeastern Arizona. Their name, *Hopi* has been
variously translated as ''peaceful,'' ''righteous,'' or ''vir-
tuous''; its most common translation is ''peaceful people''
or ''people of peace.''[4] This agricultural people have lived
in Arizona for untold centuries; the markings of their clans
are found throughout the Southwest.

According to the Hopi artist Otellie Loloma, Spider
Woman or *Kokyang Wuhti* is a very creative being. This
sacred entity is both one person and many. She possesses
all knowledge; she is everywhere. She can appear as a
young woman, an older woman, or as a spider. She can be

seen or can become light as air. She is considered to be the mother of all:

> According to one myth, the world was created by the command of the sun god. There was also Spider Woman, who gave life to the world, creating plants, birds, animals, and finally human beings out of the earth and out of herself.

She has divine powers and unlimited wisdom. She knows all languages. She has prophetic access to the future. Kokyang Wuhti is a guardian; she sees to the protection and welfare of people in need. She is most often thought of as a vigorous old woman and is never impersonated in Hopi ceremonies. By her association with the earth, in which she lives, she has the makings of an earth goddess. She is as old as time, and as young as eternity.

It is Kokyang Wuhti who led the first creatures from the First to the Second World and from the Second to the Third World. In the Third World Spider Grandmother taught the men to weave and the women to make pots; she is identified with the arts and crafts. It is she who helped the people get from the Third World to the Upper World. According to one account, Kokyang Wuhti and her grandsons helped make the Upper World habitable. She instructs the Hopi to be mindful of their gods. Spider Grandmother is especially associated with her two grandsons; she helps them again and again as she helps virtually all those who call on her. To give one example, she saves her grandsons' limbs and their lives when they meet with the Corn Maidens at Second Mesa.

Kokyang Wuhti has a dark as well as a bright side. She is a powerful being, in the sense of having both positive and negative aspects. A Hopi acquaintance of mine told me that her father would always caution her, as a young girl, not to play near the edge of the cliff or Spider Woman would get her. Kokyang Wuhti is also a witch. The reason she knows all languages is that every year near Black Mesa she meets with all the other witches of the world. In his autobiography entitled *Sun Chief,* Hopi Don Talayesva tells of the time Kokyang Wuhti tried to take him prisoner; he recounts how he escaped from her.

Nevertheless, Spider Woman is a largely benevolent figure; she appears in the legends of many American Indian cultures, including those of the Navajo and Pueblo peoples. Joe Sando of Jemez Pueblo tells me that Spider Woman is believed to protect people with her web. Because of the Native American reverence for all forms of life, and because of the widespread occurrence of this archetypal figure, most Indians are brought up to respect spiders, not to kill them. This is certainly true of the Pueblo people. If a traditional Pueblo Indian kills a spider, for whatever reason, according to Joe Sando, he immediately says, "A blind man kills," in order to rid himself of responsibility for the spider's death. Kokyang Wuhti simultaneously represents the feminine as ever-present guide, helper, protector, and companion, and the danger inherent in this ever-presence.

Changing Woman

The next figure we will meet is the Navajo goddess, Changing Woman.[5] The Navajo have lived for centuries in the Four Corners area, in the states of Arizona, Utah, New Mexico, and Colorado. These people, who call themselves the *Dine*, are known for their beautiful rugs, their exquisite sand paintings, their powerful ceremonials, their dramatic jewelry, and their ability to incorporate the old with the new.

Changing Woman is her people's most blessed, revered, and benevolent of holy persons. She appeared in the present world supernaturally. The mother and grandmother of all, according to one version of her legend, she is the daughter of Long Life Boy and Happiness Girl, the inner forms of the earth. This holy person's benevolence "provides immunity from various evil beings." She brought with her the Blessing Way, the most beloved of Navajo ceremonials. It is used in numerous ways, including the following: as a house blessing, as a wedding rite, as a childbirth rite, for protection against illness and accident. It is especially known as the young woman's puberty rite, the *kinaalda*. It was Changing Woman who had the first kinaalda: in fact, unlike traditional young Navajo women of today, she had two of them.

Changing Woman is in charge of continuous growth and of all things on the earth's surface. According to one version of her legend, this holy person created corn, game, and animals, including horses and sheep; she is associated with seeds. Changing Woman created the ancestors of the Navajo people from the rubbings of her skin—her back, her breasts, her shoulders. After being magically impregnated by sunlight and dripping water, she became the mother of twins—Monster Slayer and Born for Water. Her sons, especially her first-born, rid the world of monsters; her second son is the parent of all the waters of the world.

This holy person, by her actions both direct and indirect, makes the earth safe for humans. She brings order to this world. This is very significant, as before her arrival on the scene, the world was in a state of chaos and disorder. Changing Woman stands for peace, and she lives forever. Her decrees are loving; she and her edicts are immortal.

Identified as she is with the kinetic life process, Changing Woman takes her name from her miraculous distinguishing ability to grow older through time, and upon reaching old age, to repeat the cycle of life again and again. Thus, she is associated with the mysterious ongoing process of life itself. One translation of her name is "the woman who is transformed time and again." The traditional Navajo year begins in October and consists of two seasons—winter and summer. Restoration unto youth is the pattern of the earth; this is the pattern of Changing Woman. According to Lucille Stillwell, this holy person, who is identified with dynamic beauty, figures as an eternal symbol of hope to the Navajo people.

White Buffalo Calf Woman

Now we will turn to three figures of importance to the Sioux.[6] The name *Sioux* is a French corruption of an Algonquian term of reproach, meaning "snake" or "enemy." The Sioux are identified with the prairies and the plains; in 1600 they lived at the headwaters of the Mississippi River; prior to 1700 they began migrating to the prairies and plains from the Woodlands area of the Midwest. This people is famous for its vision quests, its sundance, and its holy men.

White Buffalo Calf Woman comes first. She is a culture heroine. It is she who brought the Sioux the sacred pipe. A source of profound spiritual knowledge, White Buffalo Calf Woman is a powerful messenger from *Wakan-Tanka*, the Great Spirit. She herself is called *wakan*, which can mean "sacred" and "powerful," as well as "ancient," "old," and "enduring." This legendary personage has the beauty of youth and the wisdom of eternity.

Black Elk says:

> A very long time ago, they say, two scouts were out looking for bison; and when they came to the top of a high hill and looked north, they saw something coming a long way off, and when it came closer they cried out, "It is a woman!," and it was. Then one of the scouts, being foolish, had bad thoughts and spoke them; but the other said: "That is a sacred woman; throw all bad thoughts away." When she came still closer, they saw that she wore a fine white buckskin dress, that her hair was very long and that she was young and very beautiful. And she knew their thoughts and said in a voice that was like singing: "You do not know me, but if you want to do as you think, you may come." And the foolish one went; but just as he stood before her, there was a white cloud that came and covered them. And the beautiful young woman came out of the cloud, and when it blew away the foolish man was a skeleton covered with worms.
>
> Then the woman spoke to the one who was not foolish: "You shall go home and tell your people that I am coming and that a big tepee shall be built for me in the center of the nation." And the young man, who was very much afraid, went quickly and told the people, who did at once as they were told; and there around the big tepee they waited for the sacred woman. And after a while she came, very beautiful and singing, and ...she went into the tepee....And as she sang, there came from her mouth a white cloud that was good to smell. Then she gave something to the chief, and it was a pipe...."Behold!" she said. "With this you shall multiply and be a good nation. Nothing but good shall come from it. Only the hands of the good shall take care of it and the bad shall not even see it."

I would like to emphasize that smoking the pipe is a means of uniting oneself with the earth and all its creatures: it is a way to send one's voice to the Great Spirit. When you pray with the pipe, you pray for and with everything, and you bind yourself with all living creatures: each and every one of them is your relative.

While she was within the tepee, White Buffalo Calf Woman revealed to the people that:

> Every dawn as it comes is a holy event, and every day is holy, for the light comes from your Father *Wakan-Tanka;* and also you must always remember that the two-leggeds and all the other peoples who stand upon this earth are sacred and should be treated as such.

As she left the people, she said:

> Behold this pipe! Always remember how sacred it is and treat it as such, for it will take you to the end. Remember, in me there are four ages. I am leaving now, but I shall look back upon your people in every age, and at the end I shall return.

As she left the lodge, she went a short distance, sat down, and rose as a young red and brown buffalo calf. She walked on, lay down again, and rose as a white buffalo. She went further, lay down once more, and rose as a black buffalo. As such she walked further away from the people. Then she bowed to each of the four quarters of the universe and disappeared over the hill.

You might ask yourself why this woman is called "White Buffalo Calf Woman." As we have seen, this holy woman is a life-giving figure to her people. She is identified with the buffalo because she represents all of creation, as does the buffalo for the Sioux. In this respect, I cite Joseph Epes Brown:

> The buffalo was to the Sioux the most important of all four-legged animals, for it supplied their food, their clothing, and even their houses, which were made from the tanned hides. Because the buffalo contained all these things within himself, and for many other reasons, he was a natural symbol of the universe, the totality of all manifested forms. Everything is symbolically contained within this animal: the earth and all

241

that grows from her, all animals, and even the two-legged peoples; and each specific part of the beast represents for the Indian, one of these "parts" of creation. Also the buffalo has four legs, and these represent the four ages which are an integral condition of creation.

We have seen that White Buffalo Calf Woman represents cosmic knowledge and energy; like the bison, she represents totality as the universe; and also totality as the four ages. In a sense, we can see White Buffalo Calf Woman as that wise yet hidden part of ourselves which always has access to sacred, transcendent knowledge, knowledge which paradoxically relates to our lives in the everyday world.

The Badlands Woman

The Badlands Woman is one of two very powerful older women figures among the Sioux. Both of these figures exercise great authority: the first over the earth and its people, the second over the souls of the dead. I suppose we can view the Badlands Woman as the judgmental aspect of the Earth Mother, whereas the second older woman is a celestial judge more closely connected to Wakan-Tanka, the Great Spirit.

Here I will cite a personal communication from a former student, George Ghost Dog, who is Sioux. This writing concerns the Badlands Woman:

> The Sioux once were the landlords of the Plains and [as a result] many myths and legends came about. The Sioux are good people and have respect for the earth life and all living creatures. The Sioux developed a way of life in this world that would have lasted thousands of years. One day a tragic, but surprising thing happened. White people everywhere and Sioux began to diminish, and soon...the earth [will be] no more.
>
> It is said that in the Badlands of South Dakota an old woman lives by herself, and only a dog is there to keep her company. The dog is there for a reason—that can be to our advantage, or our destruction. But one day it (meaning our destruction] will come to pass.
>
> The woman is very old, and her days are spent quilling a buffalo robe. A few feet away from her is a fire, with soup slowly cooking. Each time the woman goes to stir the soup, the

dog unravels...[the] work which has been done on her buffalo robe. Again each time the woman goes back and reworks
what the dog has unraveled. It is said that...once the work
is done, it will be the end of all living creatures....So respect
...for all living creatures and for Mother Earth can save us
some time with the Great Spirit. This is a Sioux legend and
is passed from generation to generation.

George Ghost Dog implies that respect for the earth and
all living creatures will ensure our own survival and prevent the destruction of the planet. The implicit relationship
here is reciprocal, that is, if we destroy the earth, then the
earth in turn will destroy us. In other words, as you will
do unto others, then so it will be done unto you. The Badlands Woman is related to Mother Earth: her ever-watchful
presence—she is ever awake—represents the judgmental
aspect of this archetype.

She Who Pushes Them over the Bank

As I mentioned earlier, the Sioux have another powerful
older woman figure. She resides in the Milky Way, which,
according to oral tradition, is in the southern part of the sky.
For the Sioux, going south is a metaphor of death. The
South is also the source of life. This is because in the Sioux
world view, the universe is spherical: if you go far enough
in one direction, you break through to the other side. According to Joseph Brown:

> It is held by the Sioux that the released soul travels southward
> along the "Spirit Path" [the Milky Way] until it comes to a
> place where this way divides. Here an old woman called *Maya
> Owichapaha* sits...[her name means] "She Who Pushes Them
> Over the Bank"...[This woman] judges souls [that is, she
> assesses their deeds on earth]; the worthy ones she allows to
> travel on the path which goes to the right, but the unworthy
> she "pushes over the bank," to the left. Those who go to the
> right, attain union with *Wakan-Tanka* [the Great Spirit] but the
> ones who go to the left must remain in a conditioned state un-
> til they become sufficiently purified.

She Who Pushes Them Over the Bank is a powerful
woman figure who represents the soul in its faculty as judge.

One could call her an aspect of Father Sky because of her celestial position and role. Here is an entity who sees beyond and through this reality. She goes to the heart, the very soul of being, to judge distilled essence, that is, the spiritual achievement of a given human being.

Our brief tour is at an end. We have met with some of the many sacred and legendary women of Native North America. I hope in this short space to have kindled an interest in the sacred and the feminine, and a fascination with the rich and varied cultures indigenous to our soil. I feel that Western society has, to its detriment, devalued the feminine, the sacred, and much that relates to Native America. The time has come for a rediscovery and a reevaluation of these lost realms of our soul.

Notes

1. An earlier version of this paper was read for the Indian Table at St. John's College, Santa Fe, on April 12, 1983; it appeared in *WILDFIRE*, 1, No. 1 (Winter Solstice, 1984), and *WILDFIRE*, 2, Nos. 1 and 2, (September 1986). I would like to thank all who helped me put together this paper, with special mention to Professor Barre Toelken and Dave Warren.

2. The sources for this section are Anthony F. Purley, "Keres Pueblo Concepts of Deity," *American Indian Culture and Research Journal*, I, 1 (1974), 29-32, and Leslie A. White, "The World of the Keresan Pueblo Indians," in *Primitive Views of the World*, ed. Stanley Diamond (New York and London: Columbia University Press, 1964), pp. 83-94.

3. The material in this section originates from a telephone interview with Grace Medicine Flower on March 24, 1983, and the following works: Tom Bahti, *Southwestern Indian Tribes* (Las Vegas, Nevada: KC Publications, 1968); Ruth Benedict, *Tales of the Cochiti Indians* (1931; rpt. Albuquerque: University of New Mexico Press, 1981), and Jane B. Katz, ed., *This Song Remembers, Self-Portraits of Native Americans in the Arts* (Boston: Houghton Mifflin Company, 1980). According to the people of Cochiti Pueblo, Clay Old Woman with her husband Clay Old Man was created at the place of emergence underneath the earth. She came and gave the clay to the people and taught them how to make pottery.

4. The sources for this section are Linda Lomhaftewa, Otellie

Loloma, and Joe Sando, whom I interviewed personally on April 1, 1983, and the following works: Susanne and Jake Page, *Hopi* (New York: Abrams, 1982, pp. 152ff.); Ekkehart Malotki, *Hopitutuwutsi, Hopi Tales, A Bilingual Collection of Hopi Indian Stories* (Flagstaff: Museum of Northern Arizona Press, 1978); Walter O'Kane, *Sun in the Sky* (Norman: University of Oklahoma Press, 1950); Marta Weigle, *Spiders and Spinsters, Women and Mythology* (Albuquerque: University of New Mexico Press, 1982); Harold S. Colton, *Hopi Kachina Dolls, with a Key to their Identification* (Albuquerque: University of New Mexico Press, 1959); *Stories from the Land, Plateau*, 53, No. 1 (1981); Don Taleyesva, *Sun Chief, the Autobiography of a Hopi Indian*, ed. Leo W. Simmons (New Haven and London: Yale University Press, 1941); and Elsie Clews Parsons, *Pueblo Indian Religion*, 2 vols. (Chicago: University of Chicago Press, 1939).

5. Gary Witherspoon, *Language and Art in the Navajo Universe* (Ann Arbor: University of Michigan Press, 1977), p. 94. The material in this section stems from Witherspoon; Leland C. Wyman, *Blessingway* (Tucson: University of Arizona Press, 1970); Sam D. Gill, *Sacred Words, A Study of Navajo Religion and Prayer* (Westport and London: Greenwood Press, 1981). Contributions in Intercultural and Comparative Studies, no. 4; Gladys A. Reichard, *Navajo Religion: A Study of Symbolism* (New York: Princeton University Press, 1950); Aileen O'Bryan, *The Dine: Origin Myths of the Navajo Indians*, Bureau of American Ethnology, Bulletin 163 (Washington: U.S. Government Printing Office, 1956); Sheila Moon, *Changing Woman and Her Sisters* (San Francisco: Guild for Psychological Studies, 1984); a personal interview with Lucille Stillwell, spring 1985; and a telephone interview with Luci Tapahonso, April 18, 1988.

6. The material in this article derives from a telephone interview with Professor William K. Powers on April 12, 1983; from George Ghost Dog's written communication of November 1982; and from the following works: William K. Powers, *Oglala Religion* (Lincoln: University of Nebraska Press, 1977); *The Sacred Pipe, Black Elk's Account of the Seven Rites of the Oglala Sioux*, recorded and edited by Joseph Epes Brown (New York: Penguin Books, 1980); and *Black Elk Speaks, Being the Life Story of a Holy Man of the Oglala Sioux*, as told through John G. Nelhardt *(Flaming Rainbow)*, illustrated by Standing Bear (New York: Washington Square Press, 1959). The long quote by Black Elk gives the "modern traditional" version of White Buffalo Calf Woman's legend. For the older version see Marla N. Powers, *Oglala Women, Myth, Ritual, and Reality* (Chicago and London: The University of Chicago Press, 1986), pp. 43ff.

IV

Socio-Political Concerns

*Since the focus of this book is on the spiritual and psychological side of the feminine principle, it is not appropriate to dwell on the more activist issues that concern feminists. There is ample material of that kind published elsewhere. The articles in this section are just two among any number of writings by women who have lectured, demonstrated, lobbied, and upheld women's concerns in all possible ways. The pieces were chosen to indicate that the concepts in this book have practical applications that can be "grounded" in the social and political worlds.—*ED.

20
Feminism: A Vision of Love

CHAR McKEE

In my vision of the emerging Age of Aquarius, women will unfold our deepest spiritual potential and create egalitarian systems of political, economic, and social well being for all citizens of the world.

How will this ideal manifest? Why is it that we do not now live in this way?

The answer to this lies in the proper understanding of our creative power. Eighty billion times our species has replicated itself, spirals of DNA uniting, dividing, multiplying into cells and tissues and bones. Yet only now are we beginning to comprehend the power of the creative imagination, the force of nature deep within our souls from which are born our beliefs about ourselves and the world around us.

Author's note: Throughout the article I consciously chose not to use the terms "humanity," "human," "mankind," "man," when referring to our world society, because I think these words need re-visioning. I chose instead to speak of "woman, "women," and "womankind." While these terms also should be included in our revisioning process, they at least help us to shift our way of thinking. That seems an appropriate thing to do in this issue on envisioning.

I would also like to point out that the vision of feminism I have described here is my own personal vision, shaped from my experience as a white Western 34-year-old woman living in this decade. And because much of my experience has been influenced by feminist spirituality, many of my thoughts and feelings necessarily reflect this.

Char McKee

Only now are we recognizing that except for the power of nature's own miracles, her cycles of life, growth, death, and decay, everything which exists here on this planet is the result of the creative imagination. Our personal lives, our values, our political and economic systems, our work, language, and spirituality, our ways of knowing ourselves and the universe, as well as most of the suffering experienced by women and the earth, are all products of the imagination.

The Patriarchal Imagination

During the last 5,000 years most of woman's experience has been dominated by the belief system of partriarchy.[1] It has been the master thought-form which has molded us, shaped us, and formed the larger context in which we have lived and thought and dreamt our dreams. It is the thought-form which has organized our attention, and formed the framework upon which we have defined our every life experience. As children we entered a mass-produced physical and psychic reality based upon the consensual beliefs of the patriarchal culture, and throughout our lives witnessed this reality continually reinforced by conscious and unconscious assumptions, attitudes, stereotypes, customs, language, and powerful educational and political institutions. Womankind has had our personal and collective lives built upon these beliefs, and we now live out their consequences in our daily lives. [Many of the fundamental beliefs about reality stemming from the patriarchal imagination, as well as the feminist imagination,[2] are explored in the chart on pp. 254-7.[3])

A Native American shamaness recently stated ''We live in a way most unnatural to our true selves, and our true selves know this.'' This remark clearly illustrates life in our dominant patriarchal culture. In this world, where half of all the deaths of our species are due to the starvation of newborn children, where the dominant mode of being emerges from psychic imagery of violence, and where the soul is divided from matter, body, and earth, our daily experience is clearly most unnatural to our true selves.[4]

The central belief at the core of the patriarchal imagination is that all members of creation exist separately from each other as autonomous creatures apart from nature and their environment, seeking gratification for drives of power, sex, and survival, in competition with all others. From this core belief, The Great Illusion of Separateness, has come the perspective that all else except the separate ego is "the other"—other races and nations, other forms of life and the earth, even our own "other" inner selves, are all strangers to be feared. Women have thus been kept alienated from our own true selves, the source of all our power, kept ignorant and mistrustful of our judgment to be autonomous with our own lives, to be the healers of our own bodies, to be creators of our own spiritual destiny. We have been kept alienated from other cultures and races and nations, fearing them as "strangers" and "enemies," always very different from, and in competition with, ourselves. The patriarchal imagination has kept women motivated by fear and self-loathing, and we have lived our lives in a cultural trance, divided and disempowered.

In this dream we dream and call reality, fear has manifested through all vehicles of our expression, through our bodies, minds, relations. From the myths of the fear mind have grown the inventions of patriarchy—violence, poverty, pornography, toxic waste, war, racism, genocide, cancer, plutonium, rape, the divided self, the estrangement of nation from nation. Most of womankind is kept in a struggle for survival, with no time to know or develop the inner self, no time to invent equitable systems of labor and economics and decision-making and the distribution of resources, no time to dream other dreams. The foods we have eaten, the air we have breathed, the gods we have worshipped have been killing us. And some still believe such inventions as nirvana and heaven to give hope for a better day in another time in another world.

Our lives as women have been so molded upon these illusions that we can never touch what we inwardly know. In partriarchy, the hardest thing we will ever do is remember who we really are—souls of great majesty and beauty and creative power.

The Feminist Imagination

Feminism is the politics and the vision of the new age which women are beginning to usher into being. While some women equate feminism with the advancement of our rights across the planet, the passage of time will show it to encompass far more. Feminism is ultimately the single most important movement for planetary and social change in all recorded history, calling for the radical transformation of our deepest selves and the way we live our lives. As many "big picture" feminists are now expressing, our ultimate goal is to challenge and transform the fundamental beliefs of the dominant patriarchal culture and to create a new world culture based upon different beliefs.

Just as the patriarchal culture has been created from man's experience, or more precisely, from white middle-and-upper-class man's experience, feminists are creating a new world culture based upon women's experience. Just as patriarchal culture has been built upon beliefs of separateness, hierarchy, and mechanism, feminists are building a new culture based upon beliefs of interconnections and integrity of all life forms.

Feminists have realized that in the patriarchal culture of the age now decaying, reality was divided into "feminine" and "masculine" and that all things "male" were honored. And so we are now birthing a new age by embracing in our lives and culture love for all that has been considered "the feminine"—emotion, passion, nurturance, synthesis, cooperation, wholeness, intuition, matter, relation, nature. And we are, even more significantly, revaluing and reconceptualizing such constructs as "feminine" and "masculine"—we are creating a new system of knowing which will enable us to transform, and eventually move beyond, such constructs. In this historical moment, as the patriarchal imagination is beginning to lose its hold on much of womankind, the feminist imagination is speaking through every nation and language and class and profession, in the lives of millions of women across the planet. It is urging us to take action in all areas of personal and planetary need, to work creatively and constructively in the interest of our common welfare. It is informing us that the work we do, the sensitivity we feel, is for the whole of womankind and for the integrity of life itself. The creative imagination of women's experience is the shaping force of a new reality whose message is the spiritual nourishment of all creation through the enhancement of the daily life concerns of us all.

Women are withdrawing our allegiance to patriarchal gods and governments and withdrawing our consent to patriarchal imaginings. We are transforming our imagery and language and relations and are envisioning one world civilization based upon the ideals of unity within diversity, the integrity of all life-forms, and interdependence for our mutual well-being. We are envisioning new myths of ourselves, new ways of relating, new rituals and dreams and symbols, new forms of community and ways of working together, new methods of peace-making and non-violent conflict resolution, new ways of communicating and networking, all over the earth. We are defining a new language and sense of ethics, new modes of healing and educating, a new science and spirituality. We are reclaiming our power to name our experience and are speaking our stories of affirmation, validation, process, sharing, consensus, and celebration.

The Power of Love

The new age of planetary unfoldment will see the emergence of a new sensibility about love. As the patriarchal thought-form has as its core experience the sensation of fear and expresses this fear through all its institutions, the new age, formed from the feminist imagination, will have the experience of love as its foundation.

In this new age women will unite radical politics with radical spirituality, science with mysticism, heart with mind, and will uncover new definitions and new dimensions of the power of love. These definitions and dimensions will

Beliefs about Reality in the Patriarchal Imagination

The Central Theme of Creation Is Separateness.

Our species and all life forms live separately from one another, dependent upon only themselves for their own welfare.

The Only Valid Way of Knowing Reality is With the Logical Mind.

The only sanctioned way of knowing ourselves and the world around us is through the use of logical processes. The most valued method for knowing is the scientific method, which observes reality in an objective, linear, sequential, hierarchical, impersonal manner, through such processes as investigation, analysis, comparison, and deduction.

Reality Is Mechanistic.

The dominant paradigm of reality is The Mechanistic Paradigm, which considers all matter (the body, the earth, the universe) to operate like machines, and to be governed by the known laws of physics and biochemistry. Science studies matter, space, time, and energy, and has determined a set of fundamental laws, principles, building blocks, equations, and properties which govern all behavior. A dominant theme of mechanistic thought is the theory of evolution which claims all life evolves according to the principle of "the survival of the fittest," in a sequential, linear, as well as competitive manner.

Beliefs about Reality in the Feminist Imagination

The Central Theme of Creation Is Interrelatedness.

All people and all forms of life live interconnected with each other, and are interdependent upon each other for their welfare.

There Are Many Valid Ways of Knowing Reality.

There are many ways of knowing ourselves and the world around us, and all are equally valid. Among these ways of knowing are the use of the intuition, the senses, feelings, various psychic powers, as well as logical processes. Reality is observed in a holistic, cyclic, intuitive, subjective, as well as objective manner.

Reality Is Alive.

The dominant paradigm of reality is The Paradigm of Immanence[10] which considers all matter alive and possessing consciousness. Along with matter, space, time and energy, consciousness is vital to the study of everything. Some ideas of the new physics which further describe this paradigm are:

a. *The universe is formed by the repetition of thoughts and events.* A universal learning memory and a creative imagination are at work in all species to generate inner, as well as outer, reality. It is not evolutionary forces which are the creators of reality, but rather learning and creative thought. If a thought is held long enough by enough members of a species, it will manifest on its own spontaneously.

Patriarchal

Feminist

b. *All life continuously generates all the life around it.* Each particle, atom, life form helps to generate other parts of matter which in turn re-generate it. All life unfolds, rather than evolves through linear process, through the influence of what is around it. The concepts of "evolution," "fundamental laws," "equations," and "properties" are illusions, since reality is formed from continuously interrelating thoughts.

Reality Is Hierarchical and Polarized.

Some pieces of reality are of greater value or more evolved than others, and serve as the standard for other parts of reality. Some common examples of polarity are: good/bad; spirit/matter; positive/negative; superior/inferior; self/others; friends/enemies; reason/emotion; win/lose. Two common examples of polarity within a hierarchical context are:

a. *What is masculine is superior.* Much inner and outer reality is divided into two competitive poles, some of which is "masculine" (man, objectivity, reason, spirit, aggression, analysis) and superior to what is "feminine" (woman, subjectivity, emotion, matter, intuition, nurturance, synthesis).

b. *What is white is superior.* In psychic symbolism, white is "pure," "clean," "enlightened," while blackness or darkness is "impure," "dirty," "sinful," "dangerous." The white race and its culture is superior to other races and their cultures.

Reality Is Composed of Many Systems Within Systems, Wholes Within Wholes.

Our personal lives, as well as the earth and all life forms, are whole systems interrelating within whole systems. All pieces of our inner and outer reality have significance and value within the context of the whole system. Such concepts as "superior," "inferior," "masculine," "feminine," "hierarchy" have no meaning.

Patriarchal

Our Inner Nature Is Dangerous.
Our inner selves, and those of other people, possess aggressive drives and desires and emotions which can cause great harm if expressed.

The Rest of Nature Was Made for Our Species to Dominate.
Our species is the most highly evolved, the most intelligent, and the most valued of all creation. The rest of nature exists to fulfill our needs and desires.

There Are Not Enough Resources to Meet the Needs of Everyone.
In this "scarcity consciousness," there is not sufficient water, food, land, and economic means to meet the basic needs of all members of the world community.

World Problems Can Be Solved Through Science and Technology.
Such world problems as poverty, starvation, environmental, and nuclear proliferation are all separate problems arising from separate causes. Science and technology are the most efficient, effective tools for solving such problems.

Feminist

Our Natural State Is Ecstasy.
Our inner selves are by nature programmed for great joy, as shown by our hormonal, nervous, and endorphin systems. It is not the expression of our natural state which can cause great harm, but rather the suppression of this natural state.

We Are Care-Takers of the Earth and All Life Forms.
All creatures of the earth are part of a living system in which each life-form has significance and worth.

There Are Enough Resources to Meet Everyone's Needs.
In "abundance consciousness" there are enough basic resources to meet the needs of everyone within the world community, at least at the present population. More equitable, political, economic, and social systems would make these resources more equally available.

World Problems Can Be Best Solved through the United Efforts of Members of All Nations and Disciplines.
Racism, classism, sexism, anti-Semitism, and violent imaginings of our inner nature are the fundamental causes of such world problems as poverty, starvation, environmental destruction, and nuclear proliferation. All these and similar "isms" need to be transformed before our world problems can be solved. All these conditions are interconnected, and will require united efforts among all nations and disciplines to solve them.

Patriarchal	*Feminist*
Violence Is an Acceptable Solution for Conflict, and War Is an Acceptable Solution to Conflict between Nations. Violence and war are time-tested, effective methods for resolving conflicts between people and nations.	***Peaceful Resolution Is the Only Acceptable Solution to Conflict between People and Nations.*** Violence and war are unacceptable methods for resolving conflicts. Peaceful resolution to such conflicts, mutually agreed upon by all involved, is the only acceptable solution.

move us beyond patriarchal conceptions of love, distorted as they are with violent hatred of women and fear of "the feminine." We will move beyond those imaginings of love which man's experience has characterized with pornography, possession, jealousy, sentimentality, romance, impracticality, man's self-interest, and woman's self-sacrifice.

The wisdom of women's experience is generating a reconceptualization of the meaning and power of love. More and more women are coming to recognize feminism as a powerful awakening force which opens the mind and heart, a moral force whose message is love of life, love of self and others, love of all forms of life and the earth.[5] We are rethinking and revisioning love as a powerful force[6] which knows the integrity and the interrelatedness of all life forms, and which seeks to manifest this knowing by creating those conditions which best promote the economic, social, political, and spiritual well-being of all womankind, and the abundant welfare of all creation.

Emerging from the wisdom of feminist spirituality is the mystical vision of love as the natural state of our true selves, the place which remains in the unconditioned space, when the thought-forms of patriarchy have been excised. It is in this unconditioned space where we know our deepest love for ourselves and our deep love for other women, and find the courageous love we need to be powerful warriors in our work of healing a troubled world.

Reeducating Unconscious Beliefs

The power of love is now manifesting through the feminist imagination in the process of reeducating our unconscious belief systems.[7] Women are deepening our understanding of unconscious conditioning, and learning that unconscious and often even conscious patriarchal beliefs shared collectively are the fundamental causes of most, if not all, planetary problems.

The work of the feminist imagination is the reeducation of the unconscious belief systems and the transforming of them beyond patriarchal conceptions of separateness and polarity and scarcity. It is creating a new sensibility to move us beyond the world-view of competition and duality and hierarchy which has kept all oppression intact, and into a consciousness of inclusiveness, interrelation, diversity, celebration, and abundance.

One of the inventions generated by the patriarchal imagination which has had great influence on world society is "the enemy," a construct born of the ignorance and fear of personal power, and a belief in separateness from all creation. Feminists have come to the crucial understanding that the patriarchal imagination has caused the dominant portion of world society to project onto other cultures and nations their own unclaimed fears, desires, angers, their own "darkness." Feminists are communicating that "enemy-making" is a habit of the mind, and that it is this habit, born of the fear of "the other," which has generated the racism, classism, and countless other "ism's" which separate women from each other and which underlie all critical problems now facing our earth and society.

The power of love is enabling feminists to revision all that has been considered "the dark," considered somehow "negative" or "evil"—death, passion, emotion, sexuality, the unconscious, the female. Feminists are reclaiming "the dark" as part of the natural world and natural cycle of life, and transforming our fears into celebrations of our bodies, our earth, our psyches, our hearts. A new sense of love as the great transformer is giving us the courage we need to reclaim "the enemy" and "the dark" within ourselves.

As the new physics tells us, reality is the results of thoughts and actions repeated often enough by a critical number of people.[8] If objective reality is indeed the result of habit, then feminists need only to think repeatedly new thoughts, and to act off the impulses which arise from these new thoughts. As we do this, we find that the achievement of world peace and social justice will not require a change in, but rather a rethinking of, our inner natures. As we recognize that we are not enemies of each other and that our inner natures are not "dark" or "evil," we will recognize that such conceptions are inventions of the dominant patriarchal imagination which we have all internalized. We will also find that the first step toward the realization of our highest ideals is the transformation of our collectively-held unconscious conditioned beliefs. Women everywhere are discovering that as we remove our conditioning, we discover deep communion with other women and all creation, and remove barriers to our creativity and intuition and other powers of the soul. As our unconscious beliefs change, values and behaviors change, and our world transforms.

Planetary Consciousness

As womankind responds to new patterns of thought inspired by embracing these new beliefs about reality, the feminist imagination will further manifest through many developmental patterns throughout the world. These new beliefs are becoming more acceptable to more women across the planet, and the chain-reaction of feminist consciousness is fast approaching critical mass.[9] Everywhere there are signs of a transforming world.

Among the developmental patterns inspired by the feminist imagination is planetary consciousness. For the first time in recorded history, womankind is developing an awareness of herself as a whole being. Although we have been separated into thousands of languages and hundreds of nations, we are beginning to sense our interconnections and see ourselves as one dynamically relating interwoven society.

Through the new physics we are formulating a deepened understanding of womankind and our significance in the universe. We are re-learning, as woman's wisdom has told

us throughout time, that the earth is a complex, living interconnected, finite whole, and that we are each one cell in
her being, linked through our minds and hearts and wills.
We are deepening our knowing of our interconnections, and
are collectively becoming aware of all members of womankind and all creation.

As the interests of the dominant elite, the white male cor-
porate minority, are slowly losing their hold on the fabric
of world society, the long-silent voices of ''the other'' are
now being heard. As the feminist imagination is expanding
our awareness of the liberation movements of the differ-
ently-abled, the aged, the abused, and of the 90% of the
world society who are peoples of color, we are increasing
our awareness of the one world society we all share. And
we are beginning to see that the voices of those who have
been the most silenced in the patriarchal age—radical lesbians, working class and Jewish women, women of color, and
women from third world countries—will bring the greatest
wisdom to the formation of the new age. Feminists are only
beginning to witness the international dimensions of our interconnections. As we increase our networking with women
of all nations and cultures, we will expand our developing
international feminist ethic and language and vision in preparation for the birthing of a new world.

In another aspect of planetary consciousness, the feminist
imagination is causing us to become aware of our shared
problems. We are realizing that the survival of all creation
depends on women's willingness and capacity to solve the
world's economic, social, and environmental problems, and
that this will require a consciousness of interdependence and
an equal sharing of responsibility among women of all nations. As we become more conscious of our shared problems, we learn that nuclear proliferation, ecological destruction, illiteracy, racism, poverty, sexual abuse, and the denial
of basic rights cannot be solved by any one woman or one
nation alone. Women are sharing our knowledge that all
forms of oppression—political, sexual, economic, psychic—
are only pieces of a larger structure of oppression. We are
teaching that simple solutions to world problems are coun-

terproductive, and that decisions about these problems need to be made in the larger context of our interconnections. And we are claiming that it is not an improved technology or science that will solve these problems, but rather a shift in consciousness and a sense of shared responsibility for their solution.

Suffering Becoming Visible

Another developmental pattern in which the feminist imagination is now manifesting is the suffering of all creation becoming visible. There are moments, as feminists, that we feel great pain for the world and know all suffering as our own. It is in these moments that we touch our deepest selves and feel our connection with all living things.

Although as feminists we know great joy from bonding in sisterhood and sharing our triumphs and our dreams, we know, too, another side. Opening to the feminist vision involves awakening to many kinds of pain—physical, spiritual, emotional, moral. And as feminists we know the source of this pain as the loss of the spirit, the integrity, the worth of each living being. And we are horrified, enraged, we are put in mourning by this knowing.

After this awakening, we can never not know, not feel, not see, again. We must continuously observe that there is nothing left untouched by the patriarchal imagination; the life of all we know has been harmed. In the all-pervasive thought-force of patriarchy, there is no ocean, no psyche, no growing child which has been left unharmed.

Feminists have awakened to the intolerable acts of violence toward all life and resultant suffering by women, by peoples of color, by animals and the earth. The feminist vision tells us of the integrity in all races and all bodies, yet we feel the depths of racist and pornographic imaginings, layers upon layers of unconscious conditioning. We know the abundance of resources of the earth, yet we see that the meeting of basic survival needs is the entire context of more than a billion women's lives. We know that work can be a loving service for all living things, yet we see that in the industrialized countries the masses of women are lost in "making a living," lost in the purchases they have been trained to desire. We sense the purpose of life is to integrate with all life unfolding, yet we witness that 90% of all primeval forests are gone forever, lost to acid rain and land-stripping and homes. The feminist mythos tells us the earth is alive, yet we learn that 80% of her topsoil has been destroyed, and that with each passing year hundreds of plants and animal species become extinct, never to exist on earth again. We know the richness in the diversity of women's societies, yet we see that most native cultures throughout the world have been mortally wounded, never to share the depth of their wisdom. We know our capacity to understand all life forms and that deep communication exists between species, yet each year we witness the torturous deaths of hundreds of millions of dogs, monkeys, rabbits, deer, seals, whales, and other animals in the name of science and sport and industry. We know the integrity of the hand to heal with touch, yet as children we learn thousands of methods of killing each other.

As the feminist spirituality movement expands, more and more women will be inspired to transform their pain and their rage and their mourning for the world into loving, affirming actions, into what Buddhists have called "moral action." Our knowing of love will inspire more of us to actions which serve no master but the voice of our own souls and the needs of womankind whom we serve.

In this interim time, the bridge between the old and the new, the suffering of all creation is coming more into conscious awareness so that we may know it as the consequence of patriarchal beliefs, values, and behavior. Now is the time for feminists to name the suffering and the problems of the world, to name where responsibility for them lies, and to name where our work of transformation begins.

The Transformation of Disciplines

Another developing pattern through which the feminist imagination is now manifesting is the transformation of intellectual disciplines. Feminism is challenging all the basic assumptions of the thought-forms of patriarchy and is re-conceptualizing every field of study. Women are develop-ing new ways of knowing and a new sense of what is of value to know.

In this interim stage between the old age and the new, the feminist imagination is uncovering the many mythic premises which underlie all scientific, social, and philosoph-ical beliefs of the patriarchal culture, and is transforming and moving beyond existing intellectual disciplines. What fem-inists are uncovering is that the assumptions about the nature of reality in such fields as politics, religion, history, psychology, anthropology, sociology, ethics, biology, all re-flect the mass beliefs of the patriarchal imagination isolated into separate areas of study, and all reflect the definition of man's experience and a ''masculine'' orientation to the world.

What the collective genius of the feminist imagination is developing is an intellectual revolution which will bring the full manifestation of the wisdom of women's experience to inform the new age. Foremost in the development of these new disciplines is the emergence of new images of our deep selves and new ways of living which honor our true selves. Women's wisdom is rekindling our child-like sense of wonder about the world and our sense of magic in all crea-tion. We know we are made from the stars, from the earth, from ''the dark.'' We know we have borrowed matter from the earth, cycling it through our blood and tissues and bones, and will return it to the soil and the air at our death. We know the language of our true self is creativity, and that ecstasy is the center of our being.

As we allow the voice of the true self to speak loudest in our lives, we know the miracles of the stages of the cycles of life: conscious birthing, conscious growing, conscious liv-ing, relation, friendship, sexual passion, touch, healing, decay, transformation, conscious dying. And we are build-ing a culture to celebrate these stages.

Foremost in the development of our new educational sys-tems is the evolvement of a new way of knowing ourselves

263

and the world around us, a way of knowing which will integrate the senses, the intellect, and the intuition. Our new educational systems will teach us about women's experience and the miracles of life, about the earth and all forms of life living within her, about better forms of communication between friends, lovers, nations, and species, about the healing powers of the body-mind-soul, about healing internalized racism, classism, and homophobia, and about methods of attunement with our deepest selves.

From these new images of ourselves and this new way of knowing will come the disciplines of the new age. The historical challenge for feminist intellectual activists is the invention of a comprehensive interdisciplinary psychology, philosophy, sociology, anthropology, economics, spirituality, and politics for womankind as a whole which have as their foundation the beliefs underlying the feminist imagination. Intellectual activists are now transforming, and moving beyond, existing disciplines within academic arenas, and are also creating refuges where feminists from across the world can meet to bring women's perspectives towards the solving of current world problems, and to re-invent the disciplines necessary to serve the needs of womankind.

These new disciplines will help answer such questions as: What are the optimum conditions for the cultivation of women's experience, and how can these conditions be implemented world-wide? How can the earth's resources be best preserved and most optimally distributed to meet the needs of all womankind? What are effective and equitable means for decision-making and non-violent conflict resolution among individuals and among nations? How can we best structure our society to ensure the provision of the basic life needs for all women and all life on earth?

Among the central themes in the new disciplines is the enhancement of daily living for all womankind, and all creatures of the earth, which will move us beyond the often-encountered narrow focus on intellectualism and abstractionism for their own sake. Another theme involves a solutions-oriented approach to problems faced by women and the environment, with long-range planning to consider consequences of actions for many generations to come. A third theme is the erasure of clear divisions between the areas of study and the emergence of interrelated, holistic inter-disciplines.

And above all in the new disciplines is the focus on the reality of the one life we share with all creation. It will be the power of love, as expressed through the feminist imag-ination, which will enable the political ramifications of this mystical vision to finally manifest on the earth. The wisdom of women's experience will at last generate the ideals of so-cial justice, environmental harmony, and peaceful, loving relations to inform our daily lives in the new age.

Notes

1. The term "patriarchy" is used in this article to represent the dominant mode of experience of Western Civilization, partic-ularly in the last 1000 years, which is characterized by male domination of women and of all that has been considered "fe-male." Mention should also be made that there have been numerous cultures, such as many Native American and African traditions, which may have shared some, but not all, of the patriarchal beliefs explored in this piece.
2. This article is intended to explore feminism in an historical framework, and not as it may influence any one woman's per-sonal life. The terms "the patriarchal imagination" and "the feminist imagination" are meant to represent the collective ex-perience of beliefs in their respective systems of thought.
3. I realize that I have used the patriarchal method of polarizing in my attempt to compare "the patriarchal imagination" with "the feminist imagination." I do wish I had been aware of another way to present this material.
4. I have used "true self," "inner self," and "soul" as synony-mous terms.
5. It is a good example of reversal thinking so common in patri-archy that feminism is often judged as being "man-hating," when in truth it is essentially a vision of love.
6. I am indebted for this understanding to a wise spiritual teacher. Isabel Hickey, who often stated "Love is a principle, not an emotion" and expressed that this would be a major teaching in the Aquarian Age.

7. Some techniques commonly used for reeducating unconscious beliefs are consciousness-raising groups, affirmation repetitions, guided imagery, and self-hypnosis.

8, 9. Critical number and critical mass are terms used in the new physics to designate that amount of energy (e.g., thought-force, or the number of people necessary to generate this thought-force) which is necessary for an event to occur.

Suggested Reading

The following materials are suggested as resources for further reading. This is by no means a complete listing of valuable readings on these topics; rather, it represents those sources which have been most valuable to me.

The Creative Imagination

Gawain, Shakti, *Creative Visualization*. Whatever Publishing Co., 1978.

Ross, Ruth, *Prospering Woman*. Whatever Publishing Co., 1982.

The Patriarchal Imagination

Gray, Elizabeth Dodson, *Patriarchy As A Conceptual Trap*. Round Table Press, 1982.

Griffin, Susan, *Woman and Nature: The Roaring Inside Her*. Harper Colophon Books, 1978.

Merchant, Carolyn, *Death In Nature: Women, Ecology, and The Scientific Revolution*. Harper and Row, 1983.

Reeducating Unconscious Beliefs

Daly, Mary, *Pure Lust: Elemental Feminist Philosophy*. Beacon Press, 1984.

Dworkin, Andrea, *Pornography: Men Possessing Women*. Perigee Books, 1981.

Griffin, Susan, in "Faces of the Enemy," Tarrytown Newsletter, April, 1983.

Lorde, Audre, *Sister Outsider: Essays and Speeches*, Crossing Press, 1984.

Lorde, Audre, "Uses of the Erotic: The Erotic as Power," Out and Out Pamphlet Series, Out and Out Books.

Spretnak, Charlene, *The Politics of Women's Spirituality*, Anchor Press/Doubleday, 1982.

Starhawk, *Dreaming the Dark*, Beacon Press, 1982.

Planetary Consciousness

ISIS International Women's Information and Communication Service, *Women in Development: A Guide for Organization and Action*, New Society Publishers, 1984.

Morgan, Robin, *Sisterhood is Global: The International Women's Movement Anthology*. Anchor Books, 1984.

Suffering Becoming Visible

Macy, Joanna Rogers, *Despair And Personal Power in the Nuclear Age*, New Society Publishers, 1983.

The Transformation of Disciplines

Beck, Evelyn T., editor, *Nice Jewish Girls: A Lesbian Anthology*, Crossing Press, 1984.

Bethel, Lorraine, and Smith, Barbara, editors, *Conditions Five: The Black Women's Issue*, Conditions.

Gilligan, Carol, *A Different Voice: Psychological Theory and Women's Development*, Harvard University Press, 1982.

Smith, Barbara, editor, *Home Girls: A Black Feminist Anthology*, Kitchen Table: Women of Color Press, 1983.

Walker, Alice, *In Search of Our Mother's Gardens*, Harcourt Brace Jovanovich, 1983.

The New Physics

Ferguson, Marilyn, *The Aquarian Conspiracy: Personal and Social Transformation in the 1980s*, J. P. Tarcher, 1980.

21

Nature as an Act of Imagination

ELIZABETH DODSON GRAY

The Bad Dream

All of life is an act of imagination. Women today are waking up from the dream—the act of imagination—which men have dreamt. For centuries men have found themselves born [of women's bodies] into a wondrous world of diversity. But immediately they have dreamt their dream and begun to rank that diversity into a hierarchy of prestige, power and oppression. Phyllis McGinley in her Phi Beta Kappa poem "In Praise of Diversity" chose to challenge the entire premise of such a scholastic honorary society which by its very nature ranked diversity and honored those judged to excel:

> ...*One whimsical beatitude*
> *Concocted for his gain and glory,*
> *Has man most stoutly misconstrued*
> *Of all the primal category—*
> *Counting no blessing, but a flaw,*
> *That Difference is the mortal law.*
> ...*And still the sons of Adam's clay*
> *Labor in person or by proxy*
> *At altering to a common way*
> *The planet's holy heterodoxy.*
> *Till now, so dogged is the breed,*
> *Almost it seems that they succeed.*
> ...*Yet who would dare*

Deny that nature planned it other,
When every freckled thrush can wear
A dapple various from his brother,
When each pale snowflake in the storm
Is false to some imagined norm.

McGinley ends her challenge to all such attempts at ranking by some imagined yardstick of excellence with this summation:

. . . Let us devoutly take no blame
If similar does not mean the same.
And grateful for the wit to see
Prospects through doors we cannot enter,
Ah! let us praise Diversity
Which holds the world upon its center.[1]

But despite such occasional challenges, the Western version of that bad dream of diversity ranked into a hierarchy of value (and even being) has meant that all of us have been dreamers of this dream. All of us have been socialized into this sort of "picture in our mind of the world beyond our reach," as Walter Lippmann once named it.[2] Males have imagined reality to be a profoundly "up" and "down" affair. In the Judeo-Christian version (which became the basis for this dream in Western civilization), we find God, imagined as pure spirit, at the apex of a vast cosmological pyramid. Below God are angels (like God, invisible or spiritual, but lesser). Then generic Man, then the rest of creation "underneath *his* feet." In Psalm 8:3-8* in Hebrew scriptures we find a perfect snapshot of this biblical ladder of hierarchical reality.

All of us, male and female, who have been raised in Western civilization or in these Judeo-Christian traditions have been socialized into this dream's way of perceiving the

---

*This Psalm says, in condensed form, "What is man that thou art mindful of him? . . . . For thou hast made him little lower than the angels, and has crowned him with glory and honor. Thou madest him to have dominion over the works of thy hands; thou hast put all things under his feet."

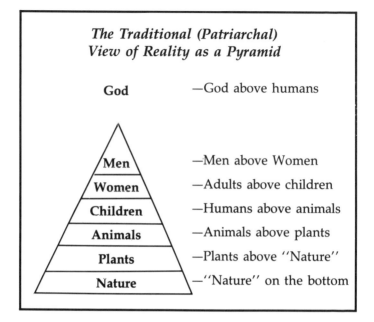

world—as a sacred order which ranks all diversity in relation to some preordained cosmic value. What is taken for granted in most of our heads can be charted, as shown.

What we are dealing with is a chain of command that runs from what is up ("higher") to what is down ("lower"). It is assumed here that those above (adults, males, and ultimately God) give orders and create order, and that which is below (women, children, the rest of nature) is to adjust and simply obey. Real "spirit"—that which has power and gives power and is valued, and is to be obeyed—dwells only in the top echelons of this pyramidal reality that characterizes dominion theology. From Augustine at the end of the Roman Empire through medieval times and the Reformation and on into the nineteenth century, this pyramidal view of reality was known as "the great chain of being."

I am certain that Darwin, in *The Origin of the Species* and more explicitly in his last book *The Descent of Man*, felt he was challenging that sacred order when he was suggesting that we humans were actually descended from monkeys (which dropped males four or so levels on the pyramid). But in a very interesting way by the time evolution was accepted a century later, Bronowski could entitle his book and PBS television series "The Ascent of Man." The hierarchical pyramid was still firmly in place in men's minds with only God removed from its apex. But humans still reign, now supreme, above nature as the most "evolved" species, and are popularly viewed as the teleological culmination of the whole process of evolution.[3]

As the world changes, so much of it also stays the same. Above all it is perceived by and within the male imagination and continues to feature the male's apparent "need" to rank diversity. This need seems to go back very early in our human history and be rooted in the male awe of women's power to bring new human life. If women could do all this, the question for men must have been "What could men do that was nearly so impressive?" What men could do—and did do in a kind of massive "reaction-formation"—was to shape a culture to reassure themselves.[4]

Culture shaped to reassure males—that act of imagination totally done from a male point of view—has been the social construction of reality into which we have all been born and socialized.[5] Only recently have we begun to realize, as the pace and intensity of our environmental disasters have increased, that this cosmic pyramid of human dominion over nature is a fiction, and that nature is *not* "below" us and will *not* adapt to whatever we do.

Today women of power are struggling to free our minds and our imaginations from that insidious need and its resulting habit of mind. Ranking diversity so that some are imputed to be of greater value, greater prestige, greater status or power simply does not do justice to the variety and complexity that exists among males and females, among whites and blacks, among straight and gay, among so-called "civilized" and "primitive." Nor does such ranking of diversity guide us in reliable ways of thinking and acting in the ecological realm. We find that again and again we are betrayed by environmental "surprises" that constitute the boomerang-effects of cultural assumptions that are deep and strong in maintaining in our imaginations that humans are of more value to the planet than trees or animals or insects or rolling hills, streams and rocks.[6]

The Power of Our Symbolic Imagination

Women today are discovering the power of our own symbolic imagination to create the world afresh in imaginings of our own. May Sarton in *Plant Dreaming Deep* writes powerfully of the role and power of positive symbolization: "I had first to dream the house alive inside myself."[7] We today have the power "to dream the house" of our life together on this planet alive in a new and different way, a just and peaceful way. What we are doing is re-mything our world and dreaming a better dream. In *Green Paradise Lost* I wrote of our coming to "see a new vision, a vision of the Garden revisited, without the old oppressive patriarchal stories. It is a vision of justice among groups, races, sexes, species. It is a vision of harmony, of wholeness. It is a vision of human life—from the cell to the household to the whole human society—caught up in a symbolic dance of cosmic energy and sensual beauty, throbbed by a rhythm that is greater than our own, which births us into being and decays us into dying, yet whose gifts of life are incredibly good though mortal and fleeting."[8]

And it is happening. Everywhere I go I hear people saying with awe in their voices, as though discovering it for the first time, "Everything is interconnected." All this is very gratifying for those of us who have been writing about that interconnection[9] and trying to live for some years in the light of such an interconnected reality. With the help of ecology we are beginning to see ourselves living within the interconnected system of natural or biological reality on this planet, in a nonverbal companionship with the sky, the sea, the trees, the birds, the animals, the insects—a companionship in which diversity is valued and appreciated and never ranked.

Women especially are being able to unfetter their deep

emotional affinity for nature. A seventy-five-year-old woman, a long-term social activist and good friend of mine, recently told me, "Whenever I get upset, I go out and hug a tree." We women no longer apologize for our high moments of mystical illumination in natural settings—in the mountains or by meadows or the sea. The sacredness of nature, indeed the sacredness of all life is being felt and given voice by women. It is being celebrated in song, in poetry, in ritual, in fiction, in thealogy. With the power of our woman's symbolic imagination, we *are* re-mything the world.

Projection Hides True Identity

But the power of our women's symbolic imagination needs to be wielded by us wisely. This is especially the case in relation to nature, lest we perpetuate old problems or create new ones. A part of the deep sickness of the male dream is its projections, which allowed the male never to encounter the true identity of either nature *or* women. In their psychological projections upon both nature and women, men have used their men's symbolic imagination to project upon women both status (inferior) and qualities (passive, emotional, sexually receptive, and so on). It was these projections of male symbolic imagination which, embodied in myth, religion and social role, kept women's true identity and power "in the closet" of oppression for millennia.

The same projecting and oppressing was done to nature. Men projected qualities of femaleness onto nature ("Mother Nature," virgin resources, the "rape" of the earth) as well as attributing to nature a status below our status as humans. Ernest Schachtel writes, "Nature is to man whatever name he wants to give her, according to the relation and perspective he chooses."[10] Modern science itself is such a naming of nature. One of the progenitors of modern science was Francis Bacon. "Knowledge itself is power," wrote Bacon.[11] Bacon's views of knowledge and power were themselves deeply embedded in an extended sexual metaphor which pervades Bacon's writings: "I am come in very truth leading to you Nature with all her children to bind her to your service and make her your slave."[12] Evelyn Fox Keller in *Reflections on Gender and Science* gives us a brilliant analysis of Bacon's continuing and complex use of the sexual metaphor for the relationship between man and nature through science. It is clear that in Francis Bacon we are dealing not with the occasional projections upon nature of an ordinary man-in-the-street but instead with the fundamental myths and metaphors contained in the mind and projected upon his world as he perceived it, of a man whose conceptionality was to be basic to the subsequent formulations of modern science itself.

The sexism of Francis Bacon's symbolic imagination was never questioned by male culture, because male culture itself was permeated with these same qualities. Because of that erroneous projection upon nature, male science and male technology always assumed that the bounty of nature was always there (like mother), was there to use and to use up (like mother), and was always going to be there to exploit (like passive women). This unfortunate projection by males of female attributes and status upon nature prevented male culture from understanding the actual place which human life has within the life-sustaining natural cycles of the biosphere. Whenever we are busy projecting inadequate or erroneous symbolic images of another, we are unable to discern the other's true character and identity.

I am disturbed that today a part of women's symbolic imagination is continuing earlier inadequate male symbolizations of nature. Some women today are still projecting female attributes upon nature. In some feminist circles "The Great Mother" and "The Goddess" are the preferred images used to describe planet Earth. Likewise many in New Age circles are uncritically adopting the Gaia hypothesis[13] even though in certain critical respects it comes from that old tired male imagination.

Now I must tell you that this gives me great cause for concern because it is the old game of projection *upon* nature *from* the human *for* human needs. Such projecting out of a self-centered and self-serving imagination will never break apart that old male dream. Such projection only continues that same sick dynamic. Just as in the past it prevented males from experiencing women and nature in their true identities, such projecting always prevents us as the ones who do the projecting from discovering the true identity of the other.

In this case the truth is that nature *is* itself. It is neither male human *nor* female human. That really should be so obvious to us. But unfortunately it is not. The ground we walk upon is not "Mother Earth"; it is living soil with a chemistry and a biology of its own which we must come both to understand and respect. We live on a fragile and lovely spaceship. This spherical spaceship has a fuzz like a tennis ball that is five miles high, and in this thin fuzz are all the biological processes of the biosphere which work like a life-support system to sustain in life everything which is alive, including us. Within that biosphere, that five-mile-thick fuzz, everything is profoundly and complexly inter-related. We live within energy cycles, water cycles, oxygen cycles, nitrogen and carbon cycles—environmental cycles in which the waste from one part of the cycle becomes the raw material for the next part of the cycle—and the waste of that second part becomes in turn raw material for the first part. So plants give off oxygen as their waste, which humans need to breathe in. And humans give off carbon dioxide, which the plants need for their photosynthesis. These environmental cycles are indefinitely sustainable, as long as the sun continues to power them. Furthermore, these environmental cycles *manage* themselves. They are self-organizing. They are not dependent upon us. Rather, we are dependent upon them. It is the reverse of the Judeo-Christian dream of man's dominion over nature.

We must struggle to tear from the eyes of our minds those old blinders of sexual projection, so that we can come to the natural world with fresh eyes, trying really to "see" and "understand" it for the first time.

Seeing the World for the First Bright Time

"To pull the blinds of habit from the eyes, to see the world without names for the first bright time, to wander through its mystery, to wonder at every age and stage, at one with it—to be alive—''[14]

Paul Shepard has written,

> The evolution of mind is not like a great river of species, emptying only into us. It is a tangle that diverges instead of coming together. It is not a single great crescendo of emergence, but a pulsing or surging, separated by still pools of time....
>
> The flowering plants and mammals which were to revolutionize that world were at first a minor part of it... ''Gradually the flowers evoked and responded in their own evolution to a growing host of insects. The insects supervised flower pollination, engaging with them in alliances that would gradually spread color and deepen the organic blanket across the earth for a hundred million years....''The plant-insect symbiosis gave birth to true humus and soil, the most complex organic system in the world. Until then, the land was only freckled with life....
>
> Because of flowers, a thin, sour, silent world was turned into a sweet nursery, and out of its microbial ferment came three-quarters of the world's million species of animals, the insects still being discovered at more than a thousand new species a year.... The diversity of flowering plants and the complexity of plant structure, especially of the flowers proper, and the vast array of insects associated with particular species, are the foundation upon which the world's ecological stability rests.[15]

Energy has powered this vast proliferation of life as well as the profusion and variety of human cultures. The giant turbines of industry, the silent decentralized exchange of energy in photosynthesis, the fusion-intensity of energy being generated by our star—the sun—and the quiet diffusion of the sun's rays upon the earth, and the awesome power in the heart of the atom—all these bear witness to the cycles of energy which cascade through the universe.

The energy of the world flows in a gigantic system. It all begins with the huge amount of energy in the sun. This comes from ninety-three million miles away into the earth's atmosphere to power the life-supporting systems of the biosphere—the weather, the water system of rain and rivers and oceans and evaporation, and the oxygen cycle, the carbon cycle, and the nitrogen cycle. Energy passes through all these natural systems in energy chains which (like food chains) capture, concentrate, store, and pass on energy. The earth's energy system in this cascade of energy, cycling and recycling with its power the atoms and molecules upon which all life depends.

The earth's energy system has come to us through centuries of geologic time. It is designed to last almost forever—to provide energy to recycle atoms and molecules until our star, the sun wears out. So the earth is full of energy, energy synchronized to a human time-scale in trees and crops which grow in a season or in the seasons of a human lifetime—trees and crops which capture energy in photosynthesis over and over again.

But there is another kind of energy—energy captured long ago, which geologic time and pressure have preserved for us. This is the energy of oil, coal, and natural gas. This energy is the legacy of the earth's geologic history, and is held in store for all the generations upon the earth. By all this our lives as humans are empowered, as is the life of all that share with us the privilege and gift of being alive upon this planet.[16]

The Power to Create a New World Which Sees Clearly

It is time for us as women to open our minds and our imaginations. It is time for us to see the reality and the true identity of our partners in this dance of energy we share with all other species on this planet. It is time to come inside this circle of creation and, with our powerful women's imagination, to open ourselves up, to attune ourselves with sensitivity and empathy to our partners in nature. Women at the core of their being understand caring attention and empathic relating, and with these capacities we can engage in a nonverbal mutuality. Warmed by the sun, caressed by the wind, shaded by the trees, refreshed by the flowers, our thirst assuaged by essential water, we receive these singular gifts of warmth, coolness, aroma, color, intricacy of blossom, and moistness itself.

We as women in our turn can give back our caregiving, a caregiving learned by us in the emotional crucible of caring for children, siblings, lovers, husbands, parents, friends, neighbors and those who are sick. For millennia birds and insects and trees and soils have "held up the sky" of ecological stability. Now all these need our most sensitive caretaking as they struggle to withstand the onslaught of a market-driven industrial technology. Acid rains from the American Midwest today are destroying the trees and streams and related ecosystems of the U.S. and Canadian northeast. Tropical rainforests that constitute one-of-a-kind ecosystems supporting unnamed and unknown treasures of plant, animal, insect and bird species, are being cut down in Central and South America as well as in Southeast Asia, because human resource needs and human habitats are encroaching upon rural habitats and wilderness habitats that are home to these species.

Responsive Caregiving

I would like to see women break the old pattern of male projection toward nature. I would like to see women discover in our own deep woman-psyche a new ethic for relating to the biological and environmental cycles which move through our bodies and the bodies of all that live, sustaining us and all in life. I want a new ethic based upon the sensitivity of attunement to the *real* identity of our natural partners. I want an ethic which would enable us as women of power to *lead* this culture into the skills of responsive caregiving.

Such caregiving is responsive in the deepest way. We give care to our natural partners because they give care to us. They hold us in life by their growing and their dying. By their pollinating and rain-making, by their transmutations of molecules as they oxidize and release their energy we are fed and warmed and maintained in being. It seems only fitting that we women who open our wombs to bring life, who bake the bread of life, who play patty-cake with the young and new to this life—we women may have the strong but

278

playful power of our symbolic imaginations to lead the way
into a new kind of responsive dialogue that enlarges the circle from the human family to include the *real* other dancers
in our dance of life on this planet.

Notes

1. Phyllis McGinley, *The Love Letters of Phyllis McGinley* (New York: Viking Press, Compass Books, 1954), page 12.
2. Walter Lippmann, *Public Opinion* (New York: Macmillan Co., 1922).
3. See *Green Paradise Lost*, by Elizabeth Dodson Gray (Wellesley, Mass.: Roundtable Press, 1979), chapter 1, "Man-Above, The Anthropocentric Illusion," for a more extended treatment of the ranking of diversity.
4. See *Patriarchy As a Conceptual Trap*, by Elizabeth Dodson Gray (Wellesley, Mass.: Roundtable Press, 1982), page 31ff. for a more extended treatment of the origins of patriarchy.
5. See *Patriarchy As a Conceptual Trap*, page 37ff. for a more extended treatment of reality as socially constructed by shared acts of human imagination.
6. See *Green Paradise Lost*, page 144ff. and *Patriarchy As a Conceptual Trap*, page 132ff.
7. May Sarton, *Plant Dreaming Deep* (New York: W.W. Norton and Co., 1968), page 31.
8. *Green Paradise Lost*, pages 157-158.
9. See *Green Paradise Lost*, chapters 7-15.
10. Ernest Schachtel, *Metamorphosis* (New York: Basic Books, 1959) page 202, cited in Evelyn Fox Keller, *Reflections on Gender and Science* (New Haven, Conn.: Yale University Press, 1985), page 17.
11. Francis Bacon, *Religious Meditations*, "Of Heresies" in *The Works of Francis Bacon*, ed. Spedding, Ellis and Heath, vol. 7, page 253, cited in *Man's Responsibility for Nature: Ecological Problems and Western Traditions*, by John Passmore (New York: Charles Scribner's Sons, 1974), page 18.
12. Benjamin Farrington, "Temporis Partus Masculus: An Untranslated Writing of Francis Bacon" (*Centaurus*, 1 [1951], page 197), cited in Keller, page 36.
13. James E. Lovelock, *Gaia: A New Look at Life on Earth* (New York: Oxford University Press, 1979).
14. *To Be Alive*, a film produced by Francis Thompson, Inc., for Johnson Wax (text and pictures published New York: Mac-

millan Co., 1966), page 1, Cited in *The Energy Oratorio*, by Elizabeth Dodson Gray (New York: National Council of Churches, Energy Study Project, 1978), section 2.

15. Paul Shepard, *Thinking Animals* (New York: Viking Press, 1978), pages 3-5. Cited in *The Energy Oratorio*, Section 1.

16. Elizabeth Dodson Gray, *The Energy Oratorio*, section 2.